CHRIST
MADE

UPDATE

Page 24 **Initial Ideas** are now at Chene Court, Poundwell Street, Modbury, Devon PL21 0QJ. Telephone and Fax numbers remain unchanged.

Page 31 **Listening Post** is no longer trading.

Page 48 **Johnny Loves Rosie** is now at 32-38 Osborn Street, London E1 6TD. Telephone 0171 247 1496.

Page 63 **Frog Hollow** is now at 91 High Street, Markyate Hertfordshire AL3 8JG. Telephone 01582 842117.

Page 84 **Shilasdair** and **Di Gilpin** now have separate catalogues:

Shilasdair is at Waternish, Isle of Skye, IV55 8GL. Telephone 01470 592297.

Di Gilpin is at Struan Craft Workshop, Struan, Isle of Skye, IV56 8FE. Telephone 01470 572284.

Page 137 **Nordic Style at Moussie** is now at 109 Lots Road, London SW10 0RN. Telephone remains unchanged.

Page 201 **WaterAid** is now at PO Box 220, 14-20 Eldon Way, Paddock Wood, Kent TN12 6BE. Telephone 01892 837800.

Page 227 **Smallwood Christmas Trees** no longer offers mail order.

Page 228 **Specialist Crafts** now have a dedicated mail-order department, Homecrafts Direct, PO Box 38, Leicester LE1 9BU. Telephone 0116 251 3139.

CHRISTMAS MADE EASY

Christmas Shopping by Mail Order

LESLIE GEDDES-BROWN

metro

First published in Great Britain in 1996
by Metro Books (an imprint of Metro Publishing Limited),
19 Gerrard Street, London W1V 7LA

British Library Cataloguing in Publication Data.
A CIP record of this book is available on request from the
British Library.

ISBN 1 90051205 X

10 9 8 7 6 5 4 3 2 1

Design and computer make-up by Penelope Mills
Printed in Great Britain by Clays Ltd, St Ives plc

Illustrations by Michael Hill

Dedicated to all my dogs

CONTENTS

PART TWO – CELEBRATING CHRISTMAS

INTRODUCTION

Mail-order shopping is booming. Whereas once the choice was limited, today you can buy anything from an old master to a go-karting trip. It has also become much easier. First credit cards, then Switch and Eurocards and now international e-mail mean that your order can be dispatched in hours – there's no need to wait for a cheque to clear before it can be sent.

There are also no barriers to buying goods from around the world – credit cards are a single currency. With *Christmas Made Easy*, UK shoppers can buy a cake from Texas, while a family in Tokyo can order chocolates from Harrogate. Indeed, in Japan there are mail-order clubs where members select from catalogues from all over the world. Many companies are only just waking up to this, but when they do, world shopping will be a reality.

One reason for the rise in mail-ordering food is the use of vacuum packing and overnight couriers. Smoked venison from the West Highlands, for example, can now be delivered to West Sussex in under twenty-four hours. This has made the sale of perishable foods possible nationwide (though not yet worldwide) and indeed one of the largest sections in this guide covers food and drink. Chocolates, fresh crayfish, wild boar and loaves of bread are just some of the pleasures on offer through the post. There are companies which will mail boxes of rare chocolates on a standing order, or which search for beers all over the world. There are farmhouses where Christmas cakes and puddings are made to secret recipes, where hams are cured and smoked or ducks and geese specially bred for the table. Many offer guarantees against additives and promise to treat their livestock humanely. Others specialise in food for people with allergies.

Most important of all is the convenience of mail-order shopping – no mile-long check-out queues in supermarkets so busy that they've run out of trolleys; no grappling with ten different toy departments to find ten stocking fillers. With mail-order shopping, you don't have to heave heavy packages for great distances or spend hours afterwards wrapping them up – the suppliers will do it for you. Firms will gift-wrap, enclose messages and then post them where you tell them. They will organise a dinner party menu and deliver it to your door. They will even organise the Christmas tree, its baubles, the streamers and crackers.

These labour-saving devices will come as a relief to many of us, particularly given the recent trend in newspapers and magazines to dole out advice that makes the holiday ever more hard work. You don't just hang the decorations but make them out of old seashells and raffia. You don't just make the chestnut stuffing, you make it to a new, complicated recipe including hard-to-find ingredients (fresh Mexican chillies and the like). You don't just fix a stocking for the children but for every family member, including the dog.

I don't believe any of this is really necessary. Christmas should be fun and, with a little organisation, it *can* run smoothly. The answer is to CHEAT. Stuff the chilli stuffing and order your bird ready-stuffed from the specialist breeder; get your decorations ready-made by someone else through the post; buy stocking fillers in one go from a catalogue which specialises in tiny gifts (such as the NSPCC's catalogue). Order all your gifts, even for the most problematic people, with a few phone calls.

Mail-order shopping is not only convenient – it is beginning to take over from the dying breed of speciality shops. Small mail-order companies can often do what large ones cannot. They will hand-knit or sew to order, they will make up collages of photographs or decorate your dog's bean bag with his name. Many such companies are run as one- or two-man bands. Such small business should be encouraged because they are offering a service which is rare and because we should help brave enterprises. These are the people who will chat over the phone and solve problems direct.

HOW TO USE THIS BOOK

In organising this book, I have found that many companies will fall into more than one category. For example, you may want to give a Christmas cake as a present as well as order your own. In such cases, I have mentioned the companies under both sections, cross-referencing the address.

Where clothes or accessories fit into a number of different sections, I have had to make a judgement of the most obvious category (umbrellas under men's clothes, for instance) and then cross-refer. Other sections, such as gifts for old people and teenagers, consist almost entirely of cross-references.

Each listing ends with a summary of key details (price, delivery times and so on). These are intended as an approximate guide only – prices inevitably change, postal rates go up, the range of goods changes. Sometimes a firm has no stated refund policy – but this may simply be because they have never been asked for a refund. I suggest ways of dealing with this at the end of the book in the chapter about the laws controlling mail order.

Mail-order firms get nowhere without the telephone and even the smallest have answer phones or faxes or both. You can therefore usually make an order at any time of day or night once you have the catalogue details. However, this only works if the firm takes credit cards. If firms do not take cards or you want to pay by cheque, you will need to order by post and leave time for the cheque to clear the bank.

Do remember that many companies will be overwhelmed by the Christmas rush, so order well in advance. If you do get going early, Christmas will be made easy. Your presents will be more thoughtful; your cards more interesting; your food of a higher quality; your house more welcoming. Most importantly, your temper will be intact.

Finally, although in putting together this guide, I have selected from a vast number of catalogues, there will inevitably be omissions. I rely on readers' comments and suggestions to improve future editions.

Eenie, Meenie   Order   queue   Satisfaction

PART ONE

PRESENTS

Chapter One

PRESENTS FOR EVERYONE

GENERAL CATALOGUES

Some of the general catalogues from places like Harrods and Fortnum's cover virtually every present you might want to give, cost being no object, of course. Others are collections put together by small companies who specialise in a particular item, such as Objets Extraordinaires and Hitchcocks' by Post.

Each catalogue offers a distinct style. If you know Harrods and the General Trading Company, you know what their catalogues are going to feature; similarly, if you like the shops from which the smaller catalogues come, you'll probably find good ideas in them.

Mail-order catalogues are very incestuous. Some are put out by craftsmen who want to tap markets other than retail shops; the same designers' work may then turn up in a catalogue devoted to new designers or in one put out by a shop which stocks their wares. Or the designer may make special, exclusive ranges for a single shop or catalogue. It's a fascinating maze.

The mail-order world is also as competitive as they come. Put forward a new idea and, within minutes, someone else picks it up. I once discovered a new square-shaped terracotta melon pot on an antique stall and featured it in the *Mail on Sunday*. A few months later new copies turned up in a gardening catalogue and then in The Conran Shop. Less than a year after that, I spotted the same melon pot in Gumps, San Francisco. So, when you plunge into these general catalogues, you are being offered ideas dreamed up by buyers and designers all over the world.

GENERAL CATALOGUES – LISTINGS

America Direct America Direct is a new company which is riding high on a wave of interest about all things American. Some of its ideas may turn up in other catalogues; others it has kept exclusive. 'American' is the chic style to adopt now and this catalogue imports its own goods from all over the States – New England, rural Appalachia, California, New Orleans. There's native American work from the South-west and, of course, Shaker-style goods. I adore the semi-precious fetish necklaces of tiny birds and animals and the spirit stones with ravens, eagles, deer and bear. The range is expanding fast.

America Direct Ltd, 85 Woodside Avenue, Muswell Hill, London N10 3HF.

Tel: 0181 365 2544. **Fax:** 0181 365 2820.

Price range: £5 to £150. Catalogue free.

Payment: cheque, Access, Visa, Mastercard, Eurocard, Switch.

Postage & packing: £2.50 for orders up to £25, £3.50 between £25 and £75, thereafter free.

Delivery: last Christmas orders 19 December.

Refunds: yes.

Specials: competitions, 1 per cent turnover to charity, £2 off next order if packing returned for environmental reasons.

Barclay & Bodie This small London firm's catalogue is highly individual and you will probably not find its goods anywhere else. They vary from the elegant little French sewing kit in silk with its own pair of stork-shaped scissors to an ironing board printed with a sexy nude chap. There's a set of tiny ornamental vegetable teapots, less than three inches high, and delightful pottery with leaves in relief or painted olives. This firm is always ahead of the pack and you can bet on finding something new and original here.

Barclay & Bodie, 7-9 Blenheim Terrace, London NW8 0EH.

Tel: 0171 372 5705. **Fax:** 0171 328 4266.

Price range: £5.95 to £145. Catalogue £2.
Payment: cheque, Access, Visa, Amex.
Postage & packing: £4.50 per address.
Delivery: allow up to 28 days.
Refunds: if returned within 14 days.
Specials: gift service.

Basket Express The constant feature of this catalogue is that – as the name suggests – all gifts arrive in a basket. These range from traditional hampers with cheese, wine and chocolates to lacy baskets with scents and pillows; from baskets with photo frames, soap and scent to baskets for babies. Men's baskets include tennis accessories, a bridge basket, and things to put on the desk and there are special Christmas baskets with seasonal food.

Basket Express, 4 Vale Close, Maida Vale, London W9 1RR.
Tel/Fax: 0171 289 2636.
Price range: £30 to £450. Catalogue free.
Payment: cheque, Mastercard, Visa, Amex.
Postage & packing: £3.50 in London, £8 nationwide, £12 next day.
Delivery: last Christmas delivery 20 December in UK, 24 December in London.
Refunds: yes, if damaged.

Beckett & Graham This catalogue includes presents which are very much 'smart London' taste – ideal for townies. Leopardskin, découpage, neat black and white striped bags and elephant bookends are featured, as is china decorated with old garden tools, glass vases and glitzy ice buckets.

Beckett & Graham, 3 Langton Street, London SW10 0JL.
Tel: 0171 376 3855. **Fax:** 0171 376 3856.
Price range: £1.30 to about £400. £1.75 to join mailing list and receive catalogue.
Payment: cheque, Visa, Access.
Postage & packing: £4.95.
Delivery: allow 21 days, but probably less.
Refunds: credit note if returned in perfect condition.

The Finishing Touch There are some things that you'd never buy yourself but which make good presents. This catalogue is full of them – tiny initialled boxes in black leather, Parisian purses and bags with little Scottie decorations, silver-plated notepads and photo frames. Stylish and universal presents, good for people you don't know well.

The Finishing Touch, 197 New King's Road, London SW6 4SR.
Tel: 0171 736 0410. **Fax:** 0171 371 9102.
Price range: £2.99 to £100. Catalogue free.
Payment: cheque, Switch, Visa, Mastercard, Access.
Postage & packing: £2.99 in UK.
Delivery: if engraved, by 10 December, otherwise last GPO posting date for Christmas.
Refunds: yes.

Flights of Fancy This catalogue seems to have an overall 'green' bias. There are plenty of 'bird' presents such as whistles which imitate bird calls, stick decoy geese and puffins which stand up in mud and move in the wind, plus parrot and owl fridge magnets. There are also twig whistles and pencils, whistling walking sticks (in case you lose each other) and scented logs.

Flights of Fancy, 15 New Street, Leamington Spa, Warwickshire CV31 1HP.
Tel: 01926 423436. **Fax:** 01926 311925.
Price range: £1.50 to £17.50. Catalogue free.
Payment: cheque, Visa, Access.
Postage & packing: £2.50, over £20 free.
Delivery: last Christmas delivery 14 December.
Refunds: never been asked.

Fortnum & Mason Though much of the catalogue is full of Fortnum's celebrated hampers, bowls of caviar (what an antidote to turkey), boxes of rare varieties of apples and their Winter Fruits selection of crystallised fruits, there's much more. It includes amber for necklaces and earrings, a huge range of French perfumes and the company's own English lavender. Children are offered old-fashioned clothes, toy chess sets and clever fluffy toys. Grannies might appreciate a silver tea-strainer. There are also excellent candles and crackers.

Fortnum & Mason, Freepost 33, London W1E 6YZ.

Tel: 0171 465 8666.

Fax: 0171 437 3278.

Price range: £7.50 to £1,500. Catalogue £3 by post in UK.

Payment: cheque, FM account, credit cards.

Postage & packing: chart in catalogue.

Delivery: last Christmas orders 8 December.

Refunds: by arrangement.

General Trading Company The shop so beloved of Sloane Rangers produces a small catalogue at Christmas which epitomises its wares. These are ideal for country folk with style and for young people setting up house. There are esoteric silver champagne stoppers (if you don't drink the whole bottle), silk ties decorated with colourful rugger shirts, stethoscopes or gavels (aimed at Henry's game or profession) and good Italian leather luggage. Also upmarket tree decorations, candles and crackers in GTC's own *fleur de lys* symbol in smart dark green and red and tartan card hangers.

General Trading Company, 144 Sloane Street, London SW1X 9BL.

Tel: 0171 730 7220. **Fax:** 0171 823 4624.

Price range: £4.50 to £500. Catalogue £1.50.

Payment: cheque, Visa, Access, Diners, Amex, JCB.

Postage & packing: £5.50 in UK.

Delivery: 48-hour datapost. Last Christmas orders around 20 December.

Refunds: yes.

Goodwood Racing Colours and Festival of Speed collections One of the best-marketed set of goods connected with this grand house and its events calendar. The Racing Colours (for Glorious Goodwood) goods are based on the Richmond scarlet and yellow colours and an old Stubbs painting in the house. There are brilliant panamas, cufflinks, umbrellas and braces, Racing Colours socks, travel rugs, bridge cards and chocolates. The Festival of Speed goods are black and white, usually incorporating the chequered finishing flag. Baseball caps, sweatshirts, children's T-shirts, bumbags and mugs are included. Extremely stylish, very dashing.

Racecourse Merchandise or Festival of Speed Merchandise, Mail Order Department, Goodwood House, Goodwood, Chichester, West Sussex PO18 0PX.
Tel: 01243 774107. **Fax:** 01243 774313.
Price range: 50p to £95. Catalogue free.
Payment: cheque, Access, Visa, Amex for Racing Colours, Switch for FOS.
Postage & packing: £2.90 per order.
Delivery: last Christmas order by 13 December.
Refunds: refund faulty goods, exchange others.

The Green Store This catalogue has an excellent range of recycled and natural goods, endorsed by Friends of the Earth. It features clothes made of organically produced cotton – mostly T-shirts and pullovers, socks and underwear in nice, soft shades like cream, olive and rose. Recycled stationery, cream, unbleached cotton bedlinen, string bags, oven gloves and aprons, and a range of hefty recycled glasses are also available. The admirable thing about the catalogue is that everything looks good, too.

The Green Store Mail-Order Catalogue, Admail 641, Bath BA1 1AD.
Tel: 01225 442288. **Fax:** 01225 469673.
Price range: £1.95 to £79.95. Catalogue free.
Payment: cheque, Visa, Access.
Postage & packing: £1.25 for orders to £5, £3.50 between £5 and £10, thereafter free.

Delivery: last Christmas orders by 2 December.
Refunds: yes, if returned in 28 days.

Harrods Each Christmas Harrods produces a glossy catalogue featuring some of the best goods it has to offer and these can be mail ordered. They range from designs by top fashion names such as Thierry Mugler and Cartier to Theo Fennell's cult jewellery, pure silk pyjamas and cashmere sweaters. There are drinks and cakes from the famous food hall and the Harrods teddy bear and watch which are regularly updated. The formal children's party clothes, in sumptuous fabrics like black velvet, are delightful.

Harrods Ltd, Knightsbridge, London SW1X 7XL.
Tel: 0171 730 1234. Tel orders: 0800 730123. Hampers and gift boxes: 0171 225 5805. **Fax:** 0171 581 0470.
Price range: £1.50 to £12,000. Catalogue free to account customers. Otherwise ring for one; there will be a charge.
Payment: cheque, Harrods card, Amex, Visa, Mastercard, Diners, JCB.
Postage & packing: will be quoted on order.
Delivery: last orders 10 December.
Refunds: 28-day returns policy on most goods.

Hitchcocks' by Post This craft gallery, which has just started a small mail-order brochure, has a good mixture of items for sale: Mary Rose Young's celebrated bright floral pottery, crystal glasses with coloured rims by Tim Casey and Ian McKay's rocking boats on chunky seas, a fine hand-framed Shetland sweater for women and a funky felted hat appliquéd with stars and circles. Prints and etchings, painted ties and cushions and a small, velvety toy mole all feature in the catalogue.

Hitchcocks' by Post, 10 Chapel Row, Queens Square, Bath BA1 1HN.
Tel/Fax: 01225 330646.
Price range: £5.95 to £150. Catalogue to be confirmed.
Payment: cheque, Visa, Access, Switch, Delta.

Postage & packing: up to £3.50 an order in UK.
Delivery: allow up to 28 days.
Refunds: yes.

H.L. Barnett Specialises in English gifts such as chocolates from Elizabeth Shaw, Thornton's and Quality Street, bouquets of carnations, daffodils and chincherinchees, Woods of Windsor soap, china from Royal Doulton and Alastor enamelled boxes. Although not very exciting for an English person, these are excellent presents for foreigners and ex-pats pining for home.

H. L. Barnett, 31 Norwich Road, Strumpshaw, Norwich NR13 4AG.
Tel: 01603 715242. **Fax:** 01603 713220.
Price range: £7.99 to £300. Catalogue free.
Payment: cheque, Access, Visa, Amex, Diners, Eurocard, Connect, Mastercard.
Postage & packing: included.
Delivery: last Christmas orders by 1 December.
Refunds: by arrangement.
Specials: catalogue quotes prices for delivery in Europe and Worldwide.

Initial Ideas Lots of present ideas from engraved gold signet rings to the famous Lazyfish corkscrew as well as toys, bookplates, braces, personalised 'Post-it' notes, shoe-cleaning kits and chopping boards. You should find a present for all the family in this one collection.

Initial Ideas, Ford House, 48 Brownston Street, Modbury, Ivybridge, Devon PL21 0RQ.
Tel: 01548 831070. **Fax:** 01548 831074.
Price range: £2.50 to £150. Catalogue free.
Payment: cheque, Visa, Access, Mastercard, Amex, Switch, Delta, JCB, Eurocard.
Postage & packing: £3.50, £8 for next day delivery.
Delivery: last Christmas orders 6 December in UK. Some goods in short supply near Christmas.
Refunds: yes, but contact office.

L.L. Bean This classic American catalogue seems to cater for your every need. It specialises in tough outdoor clothes for men and women. There are padded parkas, multi-pocketed jackets which professional photographers love, cotton sweatshirts and turtlenecks and shoes to take you from mountain to boardroom. But there's also a range of kitbags, all-cotton flannel sheets in dark blues and greens, simple ash Mission furniture (a shade like Shaker), braided rugs and hammocks. You could get presents for all the family with this catalogue, especially teenagers who will appreciate the trainers, hikers and campus hip bags.

L.L. Bean, Freeport, Maine 04033-0001, USA.

Tel: 0800 962954 (free UK order line), or 0800 891297 for queries. **Fax:** (001) 207 878 2104.

Price range: $21 to $450. Catalogue free.

Payment: in dollars only via Visa, Access, Mastercard, Amex.

Postage & packing: $9.75 for shipping.

Delivery: approx 12 working days.

Refunds: yes, any time, any reason.

Specials: monogramming service $5 a line.

Marks & Spencer Though the store will not deliver groceries to your door – more's the pity – it has a large catalogue for its home collection. Items range from double beds and wardrobes to luggage, linen and photo frames – so you can do everything from create a new bedroom for Christmas visitors to buying more towels and also choose ideal presents for friends and family. As you would expect, the range is very middle of the road. The easy chairs and sofas are excellent shapes and the china and glass good-looking and traditional. The stainless steel kitchenware is superb but the bedlinen is, in my view, over fussily designed.

Marks and Spencer Home Delivery Service, Freepost, PO Box 288, Warrington, Cheshire WA1 2BR.

Tel: 01925 858500. **Fax:** 01925 812485.

Price range: £5 to £800. Catalogue £2.

Payment: cheque, M&S card, Delta, Switch.

Postage & packing: £3.50, furniture and orders over £200 free.

Refunds: ring 0171 268 1390 to discuss.

Muji The fashionable Japanese 'no name' shop is adored by minimalists since its goods are so plain. Aluminium is a favourite for pencils, clipboards, clock frames and personal organisers; luggage is made from tent tarpaulin and the brilliant orange PVC used for basketballs. Storage boxes and systems use more aluminium, cardboard, hardboard and wood. There's plain white bedding and minimalist clothes in shades of grey, black, blue and white. This is a good catalogue for adult stocking fillers.

Muji, 26 Great Marlborough Street, London W1V 1HL.

Tel: 0171 494 1197. **Fax:** 0171 494 1193.

Price range: 75p to £475. Catalogue free.

Payment: cheque, Visa, Access, Mastercard, Switch, Amex, Diners, JCB, Liberty account card.

Postage & packing: £1.60 for up to £10 then by degrees.

Delivery: GPO last posting date for Christmas but generally 10 days.

Refunds: yes, if within a month in perfect condition with receipt and packing.

Nether Wallop Trading Company It's not clear how this company came to put its selection together – maybe they simply found each object useful. The tool gobbler certainly is. Made of heavy canvas, a bucket fits in the centre and there are twenty-three deep pockets around it – ideal for gardeners, horse folk, DIY-ers. There are also beech trivets for hot pots, carving boards for salmon, chopping boards shaped like hearts and pigs, door wedges and handles, and dibbers.

Nether Wallop Trading Company, Maltings, Nether Wallop, Hampshire SO20 8EW.

Tel/Fax: 01264 781734.

Price range: £3 to £30. Catalogue free.

Payment: cheque, Access, Visa, Mastercard, Eurocard.

Postage & packing: £1 under £10 order, £2 between £10 and £20, £3.50 thereafter.
Delivery: last Christmas orders 12 December.
Refunds: yes.

Objets Extraordinaires A very personal collection of gifts collected by Andrew Saville-Edells from cushions embroidered with jokes and messages – 'Eat, Drink and Remarry' for example – to little porcelain boxes shaped like champagne corks or pineapples and soap dishes like baths. Jokey and charming, occasionally useful, this is full of ideas for people who have everything.

Objects Extraordinaires, 79 Walton Street, London SW3 2HP.
Tel: 0171 589 8414. **Fax:** 0171 225 1935.
Price range: £6 to £140. Catalogue free.
Payment: cheque, Access, Visa, Mastercard, Amex.
Postage & packing: £3.95.
Delivery: allow 21 to 28 days. Last Christmas orders by 10 December.
Refunds: yes, if returned in good condition in 7 days.

Overseas Posting Company This is the really easy way to Christmas shop. Ask Jo Andrews and Rebecca Harris to find your present, send it abroad and deal with all the hassle. They have posted anything from a jar of Marmite (essential to some ex-pats) to a bouncy castle for a European school. At Christmas they will find Father Christmas outfits, stocking fillers, decorations, wrapping paper and ribbon for a traditional Christmas anywhere in the world. When I asked about us poor folk in Britain, Jo Andrews said she'd organise Christmas for us too.

The Overseas Posting Company, 74 Denmark Road, London SW19 4PQ.
Tel/Fax: 0181 944 7719.
Price range: not applicable. 15% service charge. Free brochure explains what they do.
Payment: cheque, Mastercard, Visa, Delta.
Postage & packing: advised.
Delivery: by arrangement.
Refunds: no.

Premier Baskets Not just food baskets but baskets of pot pourri, scented candles and soap, chef's baskets with whisks, wooden spoons and herbs and relaxation baskets with bath foam, sponges, soap dishes. The firm will make up special baskets to suit anyone so you could invent, say, a minty basket, a basket for a sportsman or one celebrating the 1940s.

Premier Baskets, phone only.
Tel: 01243 773573.
Price range: from £25. Catalogue free.
Payment: cheque and major credit cards.
Postage & packing: £5 in UK.
Delivery: last Christmas order by 20 December.
Refunds: by arrangement.
Specials: will organise gifts for all the family or from any list.

Presents for Men Exactly what it says. Not just clothes, though there are plenty of jokey boxer shorts patterned with rugger shirts or shooting dogs, red braces and ties featuring golf clubs. But if your man is a gardener, a keen shot, a rider or a computer fiend, then there's something here for him. The catalogue includes foods like Gentlemen's Relish, anchovy paste and gunpowder tea (the leaves are rolled up like shot) and a whole slew of wine accessories. There are even stocking fillers for those who still believe in Santa, and practical items such as folding scissors, an emergency blanket or screwdriver set.

Presents for Men, PO Box 16, Banbury, Oxfordshire OX17 1TF.
Tel: 01295 750100. **Fax:** 01295 750800.
Price range: 65p to £95. Send large SAE, 1st class stamp, for catalogue.
Payment: cheque, Access, Visa.
Postage & packing: £2.50 to £4.50.
Delivery: last Christmas orders 6 December.
Refunds: no.

The Spotted Duck Based on the shop of the same name, 3,000 square feet offering a huge choice of gifts for all ages, this mail-order catalogue is just a list, with no prices. The list amply justifies The Spotted Duck's claim to have one of the largest selections of gifts under a single roof. There are divining rods, potato clocks, foods and wines, silver tea caddies and peppermills, door stops, crackers and decorations.

The Spotted Duck, The Market Square, Wilton, nr Salisbury, Wiltshire SP2 0HX.
Tel: 01722 743999. **Fax:** 01722 744550.
Price range: from under £1 upwards (phone for prices). List free.
Payment: cheque, major credit cards except Amex.
Postage & packing: by arrangement.
Delivery: allow 28 days.
Refunds: by arrangement.
Specials: gift wrapping, gift vouchers.

See also: most charities do general gift catalogues (Charities).

BOOKS, CASSETTES, CDS AND VIDEOS

Some of my most treasured books have been given to me as Christmas gifts. Some I yearned for but felt I couldn't really afford. The pleasure, therefore, is slow-burning and long-lasting.

These presents are easy to choose and easy to post. Most of us can produce an instant list of videos, books and music we would like to own. The ever-growing talking book range is another excellent area – books that are difficult to read and assimilate are made easy on tape, read by actors. This applies to classics as well as language and history lessons.

I have to own up that the whole area of computer games is a mystery to me so I consulted the two young sons of a computer games publisher. They said that the whole business moves so fast I could not predict anything a few months ahead and recommended that anyone charged with buying the latest games should go to two magazines to find the mail-order firms to oblige. These are *Games Master*, filled with appalling monsters and day-glo panels, by Future Publishing, 30 Monmouth Street, Bath BA1 2DL (01225 442244) and *PC Games* from the same address.

BOOKS, CASSETTES, CDS AND VIDEOS – LISTINGS

Dillons This bookshop reckons it has five miles of bookshelves and over 250,000 titles in stock at any time. It can trace rare and out-of-print books for you, produce signed first editions or giftwrap books and send them to another address as presents. There are also gift vouchers, which may be boring to receive on Christmas day but are very useful thereafter.

Dillons Mail Order Department, 82 Gower Street, London WC1E 6EQ.

Tel: 0171 636 1577. **Fax:** 0171 580 7680.

Price range: general book prices. Catalogue free (from October).

Payment: cheque, Access, Visa, Amex, Dillons and Hatchards cards.

Postage & packing: 10% of book value on orders to £50, 5% thereafter in UK.
Delivery: next day despatch on mid-week orders.
Refunds: by arrangement.
Specials: see above. Discounted books.

Listening Post
This company deals in the growing market of audio books. These are good for learning and listening to in the car, for the blind and those who find turning pages difficult, and as a way to ease into books which are hard going on the page. The skilful actors and actresses manage to make classics easier to handle. Also recommended as gifts for travellers on long flights.

Listening Post, Greatness Lane, Sevenoaks, Kent TN14 5BQ.
Tel: 01732 743732.
Price range: £5.99 to £199 (the Bible). Catalogue free.
Payment: cheques, Access, Visa.
Postage & packing: £1.50 per order under £20, free thereafter.
Delivery: last Christmas orders by 1 December.
Refunds: yes.

The Red House
This is a children's bookclub offering a selection of over 100 books a month. Categories range from children's non-fiction/reference to children's classics and picture books/fiction selections. There is also a general family selection including quality fiction, non-fiction and reference. There is no obligation to buy but you may be tempted by the incentives! Catalogues are mailed 13 times a year and list the books according to their age grouping.

The Red House, Witney, Oxford OX8 5YF
Tel: 01993 779959.
Price range: from £1.50.
Payment: cheque, postal order, Access, Visa
Postage & packing: £1.50.
Delivery: usually within a week.
Refunds: yes.
Specials: discounts of up to 50% on books.

Sotheby's An excellent service for books on art, antiques, decor and architecture along the lines of the expanded bookshop at the Bond Street saleroom.

Sotheby's Bookshop, 34-35 New Bond Street, London W1A 2AA.
Tel: 0171 493 8080. **Fax:** 0171 409 3100.
Price range: £10 to £100. Catalogue free.
Payment: cheques, Amex, Visa, Access, Mastercard.
Postage & packing: included.
Delivery: last Christmas orders by end November.
Refunds: yes, if undamaged and valid.

Tadpole Lane Videos celebrating Britain: great houses like Chatsworth and Chartwell, gardens (known and secret), the Chelsea Flower Show and a drive in search of the best English villages. The sort of thing to give at Christmas to remind us of spring and summer.

Tadpole Lane, Unit 13, Winnall Valley Road, Winchester, Hampshire SO23 8LU.
Tel: 01962 841100. **Fax:** 01962 840004.
Price range: £9.95 to £12.95. Catalogue free.
Payment: cheque, Visa, Connect, Mastercard, Access.
Postage & packing: £2 per video but free in UK for 3 or more.
Delivery: last orders by GPO Christmas deadline.
Refunds: yes, if damaged or poor quality.

Video Plus Direct and Talking Tapes Direct Whenever I'm faced with a catalogue which claims to be comprehensive – as this does – I test it by asking for something obscure. The catalogue won. It seems to have everything the video enthusiast would want from old films to tourist guides and teach yourself balti cooking. The Talking Tapes catalogue is equally good.

Video Plus Direct and Talking Tapes Direct, 19-24 Manasty Road, Orton Southgate, Peterborough PE2 6UP.
Tel: 01733 2328000. **Fax:** 01733 238966.
Price range: £6 to £30. Catalogue £2.99, redeemable against purchase.
Payment: cheque, Mastercard, Visa, Amex, Diners.

Postage & packing: £1.75 per video.
Delivery: allow 14 days.
Refunds: if faulty.

Waterstone's Dedicated to good books, the firm puts out a catalogue at Christmas detailing new books available but in fact they will post to you any book in print as long as they can get it from the publisher (not always as easy as it should be). Take the trouble to find out what friends and relatives want and order well in advance.

Waterstone's Mailing Service, 4/5 Milsom Street, Bath BA1 1DA.
Tel: 01225 448595. **Fax:** 01225 444732/420575.
Price range: general book prices. Catalogue free.
Payment: cheque, Visa, Mastercard, Diners, Amex, Switch.
Postage & packing: £3, orders over £45 free.
Delivery: last Christmas orders from catalogue 18 December; non-catalogue orders add a month.
Refunds: by arrangement.

WCP Video This is an independent company with a strangely mixed selection of instructional videos but all are good entertainment too. There is Beth Chatto talking about gardening, Jane Packer on flower arranging, Carolyn Warrender explaining stencils and – this is the surprise – bird of prey expert Jemima Parry-Jones on owls and falconry. Especially useful at this time is Jane Packer's video on flowers for Christmas.

WCP Video, Stone House, Main Street, Seaton, Rutland LE15 9HU.
Tel: 01572 747692. **Fax:** 01572 747693.
Price range: £10.99 to £19.99. Catalogue free.
Payment: cheque, money orders, Eurocheques for overseas.
Postage & packing: £2.
Delivery: within 24 hours, 2nd class post (for Christmas, 1st class post as a present).
Refunds: only if there are technical problems. Exchanges possible.

See also: Squires Kitchen for cakemaking videos (Bread, Puddings and Cakes), National Trust for video of its first 100 years (Art and Replicas), Arty-Zan and Jayem Videos who make videos from family films (Personalised Presents), Salmon & Trout Association for fishing videos, Explore Trader for adventure holiday videos (Sports), Culpeper for herbal books (Luxuries), Periwinkle Productions for garden tips on video (Gardening).

CHILDREN

Buying presents for children can be great fun but it is also a minefield. The fluffy rabbit you found so adorable may be rejected as 'babyish' by a self-sufficient four-year-old; and the latest computer game you felt so proud of (yes, you were being up to date) spurned by a child wedded to outdoor activities. Adults need to use their imagination when choosing toys, as children appreciate fantasies (clear proof is that Roald Dahl is their favourite author). Many of the toys listed here encourage children to create their own fantasy worlds. The little cottages, rocking sheep and glove puppets can be used in all sorts of ways and adapt as children grow older. And even if young children initially show a disconcerting fondness for the box rather than its contents, over the months they will usually learn to love carefully thought-out gifts.

The right toys can be invaluable in helping children develop skills and use their imagination. Children need games to become dextrous while other toys extend memory and knowledge. But don't let your ulterior motive be too obvious. If children realise that a plaything is really intended for education, they will feel cheated and rapidly lose interest.

Parents are equally hard to please. While some parents may not mind a plethora of brightly coloured plastic crocodiles and dragons with goggling eyes, others may prefer the discreet charm of pale wooden toys which don't clash with the living room and which may become heirlooms for the next generation. An inappropriate present – I know someone who offended sensibilities by giving a nine-year-old a football rattle – can end friendships.

Finally, keeping up to date with trends is an art in itself. If, like me, you find it hard to keep abreast of what is suitable for various ages of children – the goalposts keep changing – have a quiet word with the parents or pick the brains of the toy companies. Many are run by young parents who have gone into the business to provide toys which their children lacked. Their knowledge is often enormous.

Above all, avoid buying last year's fashionable toy. Every autumn a new craze appears, spreading from school to school like wildfire. The previous year's 'must-have' is dropped ruthlessly to be replaced by the latest trend. Either choose a classic toy or otherwise make sure you get your facts right. It is pointless to try to speculate what this year's trend might be because no one will know till it happens.

CHILDREN – LISTINGS

Children's Cottage Company A little house for your children is a lovely idea – if you can afford it. These tiny cottages come thatched with reed or tiled with cedar, all have a stable door, windows at each side and, if you like, window boxes. Each one is made to order and styles can be varied, though the most popular size is 6 x 4 feet. Curtains, wallpaper and tiny furniture are optional extras. Outside can be painted pale blue, terracotta or a pale pink, among other shades.

The Children's Cottage Company, The Sanctuary, Shobrooke, Crediton, Devon EX17 1BG.
Tel: 01363 772061. **Fax:** 01363 777868.

Price range: £550 to £1,899. Catalogue free.

Payment: cheque, 50% with order, 50% on completion.

Postage & packing: delivery at cost.

Delivery: last order for Christmas 7 November.

Refunds: no, made to order.

Special: show cottage in London, tel 0171 720 3912.

Direct to your Door A real boon – a toy-seller who has gone mail order. The ranges stocked include Playmobil, with 257 products, wooden railways from Brio and Thomas the Tank Engine, last year's craze, K'nex, and the full range of Lego and Duplo. Others may be added later.

Direct to your Door Ltd, PO Box 40, Middlesbrough, Cleveland TS8 9YG.

Tel: 01642 324544. **Fax:** 01642 324545. Freephone 0800 137880.

Price range: £1.99 to £200. Catalogue free.

Payment: cheque, Switch, Delta, Visa, Access, Mastercard.

Postage & packing: phone for quotation.

Delivery: within 3 working days. Christmas orders despatched 24-hour delivery but supplies might be limited.

Refunds: yes.

The Dolls' House Catalogue Dolls' houses have been fascinating children – not just girls – since medieval times. This firm sells anything from a kit of a half-timbered Tudor village dolls' house to a Palladian mansion. Then there's the furniture and accessories – tiny bureau bookcases and Davenport desks, a double bass, a grandfather clock or a set of miniature blue and white china, a chess set and patchwork quilt. You can find high-level flush WCs, medieval cots, boar's head for supper and dinky Agas, deck chairs and mangles. Add people and pets of your choice. Completely addictive, I'd say.

The Dolls' House Catalogue, Market Place, Northleach, near Cheltenham, Gloucestershire GL54 3EJ.

Tel/Fax: 01451 860431.

Price range: £1.50 to £800. Catalogue £3.50.

Payment: cheque, Barclaycard, Mastercard, Amex.

Postage & packing: from £1 to £5.

Delivery: allow 2 weeks before Christmas though many items limited.

Refunds: yes, if properly returned.

The Green Board Game Co

Green, that is, as in environment. I'm a great believer in teaching young children through play, and here there are games about food chains, trick questions about whether a tomato is a fruit or vegetable and a Saxon Fox and Goose chase game. Others pose questions on geography, the classics and the animal kingdom.

The Green Board Game Company Ltd, 34 Amersham Hill Drive, High Wycombe, Buckinghamshire HP13 6QY.

Tel: 01494 538999. **Fax:** 01494 538646.

Price range: £1 to £30. Catalogue free.

Payment: cheque.

Postage & packing: I game £3.50, 2 £4.50, 3 or more £5.50.

Delivery: last Christmas orders 5 postal days before Christmas.

Refunds: yes.

Grove

This firm supplies playgroups and nurseries with toys which are both fun and educational. Some are like 3-D jigsaws which fit together to make boxes, aircraft or animals. Others stick to walls to make names or street scenes. There are giant games like Big Foot (children have to move the giant feet around) and outsize building blocks. Some games are suitable for toddlers, others for older children.

Grove Leisure and Marketing Services Ltd, The Barn, Crowsheath Farm, Hawkswood Road, Downham, Essex CM11 1JT.

Tel: 01268 711619. **Fax:** 01268 711620.

Price range: £4.99 to £22.50. Catalogue free.

Payment: cheque, Access, Visa.

Postage & packing: included.

Delivery: last Christmas orders by 15 December.

Refunds: yes, if returned in 14 days.

Haddon Rocking Horses Victorian rocking horses were made with strong pillar stands; 18th-century ones have bow rockers which are better looking but harder to ride. This firm makes four ranges of horse: the Traditional, Relko and Heritage range which have stand rockers; the Thoroughbred which has a bow. Some are dappled, some laminated ply, others mahogany or walnut. The manes and tails are horsehair.

ANTIQUE ROCKING HORSE
PLEASE KEEP OFF !!

Haddon Traditional Toy Craft, 5 Telford Road, Clacton-on-Sea, Essex CO15 4LP.

Tel: 01255 424745. **Fax:** 01255 475505.

Price range: £500 upwards. Catalogue free.

Payment: cheque, Access, Visa.

Postage & packing: £12 to £40.

Delivery: 4 weeks; Christmas orders by 30 November.

Refunds: by arrangement.

The Hill Toy Company Hosts of good ideas, including lots of dressing-up clothes such as dalmatian and witch outfits, little drummer boys and fairies. Also monster masks of paper. Charming dressed mice like Nanny Cheshire and Baby Stilton, shops and puppet theatres for older children. Both stocking fillers and big, expensive gifts.

The Hill Toy Company, PO Box 100, Ripon, North Yorkshire HG4 4XZ.

Tel: 01765 689955. **Fax:** 01765 689111.

Price range: 99p to £160. Catalogue £1

Payment: cheque, Access, Mastercard, Visa.

Postage & packing: £2 on orders to £20, £3.50 up to £40, £5.50 to £125, free thereafter.

Delivery: allow 28 days, next day delivery for £3 extra.

Refunds: yes, if told in 7 days.

Specials: gift wrapping.

Infant Isle Innovative toys for young children. There are bugs on wheels, scorpions, stag beetles, spiders which pull along; quicksand which can be sculpted when mixed with water and wizbits which slot together like games of Consequences. Because the firm tries to get ahead of the pack, children probably won't have seen these toys before.

> **Infant Isle**, The Frank Whittle Business Centre, Great Central Way, Rugby, CV21 3XH.
> **Tel:** 01788 537893. **Fax:** 01788 576017.
> **Price range:** £3 to £15. Catalogue free.
> **Payment:** cheque, Access, Visa.
> **Postage & packing:** see catalogue.
> **Delivery:** last Christmas orders 1 day before final GPO date.
> **Refunds:** yes, if returned in 7 days.

Jigroll If jigsaws are a feature of Christmas, try giving this present which solves the problem of unfinished business lying in a major gangway or on the dining-room table. Jigroll, in four sizes and taking anything up to a 5,000 piece puzzle, is a felt sheet marked with a working area. It arrives in a tube with four straps. A jigsaw in progress can be rolled up on the felt and popped into the tube. You can even travel with it.

> **Jigroll**, Freepost, Barton, Cambridge CB3 7BR.
> **Tel/Fax:** 01223 262592.
> **Price range:** £25 to £50. Catalogue free.
> **Payment:** cheque.
> **Postage & packing:** included.
> **Delivery:** allow 3 weeks from order.
> **Refunds:** yes, if returned unused.

Kiddie Wise This company sells garden playthings which can be mixed and matched to create great playgrounds. Starting with sandboxes for toddlers, the range takes in swings, see-saws, slides and marvellous treehouses, playhouses and miniature garden furniture for play. What is extra special about this range is that much is made from natural wood rather than bright coloured plastic and will therefore look good in the garden and weather well.

> **Kiddie Wise,** Katella Ltd, PO Box 433, Leek, Staffordshire ST13 7TZ.
> **Tel:** 01538 304235. **Fax:** 01538 304575.
> **Price range:** £14.20 to £1,352. Catalogue free.
> **Payment:** cheque, Visa, Access, Mastercard.
> **Postage & packing:** included.
> **Delivery:** last orders for Christmas 30 November.
> **Refunds:** yes, if notified in 14 days.

Layden Designs Sellers of Takeradi, a compulsive African game which involves each player stacking wooden bricks with one hand only, each trying to build as high as possible before it collapses. It's thought that the idea originated with RAF flyers based at Takoradi station during the war. There is more to it, however, in that each of the forty-eight wooden bricks is made of a different timber, from English oak to Lebanon cedar, jarrah from Australia to afromosia found in central Africa. It teaches children about woods and looks most handsome. The blocks are packed in a wooden presentation box.

> **Layden Designs,** Arbour Hill, Patrick Brompton, Bedale, North Yorkshire DL8 1JX.
> **Tel:** 01677 450642. **Fax:** 01677 450766.
> **Price:** £45. Details of game free on request.
> **Payment:** cheque, postal order.
> **Postage & packing:** £3.50 for 1 set, £4.75 for 2, £5.50 for 3; free thereafter.
> **Delivery:** about a week but allow 10 days over Christmas; next day delivery for extra cost. Large orders of over 30 may take time.
> **Refunds:** by arrangement.
> **Special:** a royalty is paid to a disabled charity.

Letterbox When you buy toys as presents it's worth thinking of the parents as well as the children – and Letterbox's catalogue is in impeccable good taste. There are plenty of toys in hand-painted wood such as pullalong daisy cow and a steam train with a letter on each carriage so you can make a name. There's a little painted hand mirror for vain little girls, plus easy jigsaws. Older children can have small gardeners' tools and plants, a mini guitar and binoculars for trekking. There's also a good stocking-filler collection with red velvet rabbits, green sponge frogs and a tin kazoo, all under £5. A few ideas – a Harley Davidson pen, cassette, CD and video boxes – are good for teenagers.

Letterbox, PO Box 114, Truro, Cornwall TR1 1FZ.
Tel: 01872 580885. **Fax:** 01872 580866.
Price range: £1.50 to £150. Catalogue free.
Payment: cheque, Visa, Access, Mastercard, Eurocard, Switch.
Postage & packing: £2 for orders to £19.99, £20 to £99.99 £3.50, free thereafter.
Delivery: for Christmas, last orders 13 December; personalised gifts, 25 November.
Refunds: yes, if notified in 7 days and returned in resaleable condition.

Mrs J. Pickering's Doll's Clothes Mrs Pickering runs a genuine cottage industry – a dressmaker for dolls rather than humans. She will make clothes to order for favourite Barbie and Sindy dolls, for Tiny Tears and for well-loved teddies and large dolls. There are ball gowns, wedding dresses, anoraks and nurse's uniforms for little girl dolls – even copies of a child's own school uniform. Accessories include hairbands, satchels, scarves and T-shirts. Teddies are more difficult to cater for (being all shapes) but there again, a favourite toy can have a child's own school tie or, rather unlikely, a teddy wedding dress.

Mrs Pickering's Doll's Clothes, Dept C, The Pines, Decoy Road, Potter Heigham, Great Yarmouth, Norfolk NR29 5LX.
Tel: 01692 670407.
Price range: 20p to £10. Send 9″ x 4″ SAE for catalogue.
Payment: cheque or postal order with order.
Postage & packing: 50p, free with 7 plus items. (All 2nd class post).

Delivery: allow 28 days. Order in November for Christmas.
Refunds: yes, if resaleable.

Orchard Toys Really splendid jigsaws – such as a red London bus full of people and a big yellow cement mixer – are made of thick board and intended to be laid on the floor. There's a smashing tractor, a female foreman working on a crane and lots of action in a crowded swimming pool. They vary from three to 100 pieces and are variously intended for two- to nine-year-olds. Most have a cartoon jokiness and ask questions of the children.

Orchard Toys, Debdale Lane, Keyworth, Nottingham NG12 5HN.
Tel: 0115 937 3547. **Fax:** 0115 937 6575.
Price range: £1.99 to £8.95. Catalogue free.
Payment: cheque.
Post & packing: £3.50 up to £20, £5 on £20 to £70 orders, free thereafter.
Delivery: last Christmas order 14 December.
Refunds: by arrangement.

Robert Mullis At one point rocking horses almost disappeared from nurseries, but now craftsmen have revived the breed. Robert Mullis makes to order with a series of traditional 18th- and 19th-century horses and the Moonraker collection, little rockers featuring friendly animals like ducks and tortoises which come dressed. The body/seat is squashily upholstered in comfy corduroy. Mrs Duck has a blue bonnet and body and a little basket of dried flowers; Nessie the Loch Ness monster wears a red tam o' shanter and sports a sporran.

Robert Mullis, 55 Berkeley Road, Wroughton, Swindon, Wiltshire SN4 9BN.
Tel: 01793 813583.
Price range: £350 to £1,575. Catalogue free.
Payment: 10% deposit with order (all made to order). Balance by cheque, Access or Visa.
Postage & packing: at cost.
Delivery: each takes 6-8 weeks to make. Order asap.
Refunds: by arrangement.

The Rocking Sheep Centre Real sheepskin from special breeds of sheep is used to make these charming rocking sheep and rams which are gentler and more unusual than rocking horses – children love them. There is a blackface ram with curly horns, a piebald black, brown and white Jacob ram, a black Welsh ram, a flop-eared blackface lamb seat (no rockers) and an extremely fluffy white blackface ewe in the range.

> **The Rocking Sheep Centre**, Penllyn Workshops, Plasey Street, Bala, Gwynedd LL23 7SW.
> **Tel:** 01678 521232. **Fax:** 01678 521111.
> **Price range:** £190 to £380. Catalogue free.
> **Payment:** cheque, Visa, Mastercard, Amex, JCB.
> **Post & packing:** included in EU.
> **Delivery:** allow 28 days in UK.
> **Refunds:** if returned in 28 days.

Skipper Yachts The appeal of old-fashioned pond yachts for children (and their fathers) never goes out of fashion, and this is one of the few places you can still buy them. They are wooden, and guaranteed to sail, with varnished decks and genuine sailcloth sails. The smallest, at six inches, are a tartan barge and Thames barge in bright yellow with blue sails, and the largest, the 32" Ocean Racer, a smart red job with white sails.

> **Skipper Yachts Ltd**, Granary Yacht Harbour, Dock Lane, Melton, Suffolk IP12 1PE.
> **Tel:** 01394 380703. **Fax:** 01394 380936.
> **Price range:** £2.99 to £154.80. Send large SAE for catalogue.
> **Payment:** cheque, prepaid.
> **Postage & packing:** from £1.50 to £5.
> **Delivery:** allow 14 days.
> **Refunds:** will be replaced if faulty.

Spottiswoode Trading Primary coloured cotton toys, pram strings, mobiles, wall-hangings and bags which are particularly attractive to young children. The cat, duck, hen and rabbit pram strings, each with five animals to entertain the baby, are an especially good idea, as is a basket full of eight different fluffy animals. They are machine washable too.

> **Spottiswoode Trading**, PO Box 3009, Littlehampton, West Sussex BN17 5SJ.
>
> **Tel:** 01903 733123. **Fax:** 01903 713777.
>
> **Price range:** £10 to £30. Catalogue free.
>
> **Payment:** cheque, Switch, Visa, Mastercard.
>
> **Postage & packing:** about £1.50 per item.
>
> **Delivery:** Christmas orders by 15 December; later orders may pay extra to ensure delivery.
>
> **Refunds:** if returned in 7 days, unused.

Stevenson Brothers The Stevensons produce fine, handsome rocking horses which have a touch of fairground galloper about their lively faces. Available as either a traditional dapple grey, often with a suede saddle and red velvet saddle blanket, or a copy of the French velocipede which has a tricycle instead of rocker. They also do other toys including teddies and rocking ducks.

> **Stevenson Brothers**, The Workshop, Ashford Road, Bethersden, Ashford, Kent TN26 3AP.
>
> **Tel:** 01233 820363/820772. **Fax:** 01233 820580.
>
> **Price range:** £175 to £11,000. Catalogue free.
>
> **Payment:** £235 deposit on rocking horses, rest by cheque or major cards.
>
> **Postage & packing:** around £40.
>
> **Delivery:** each takes 6 weeks to carve. Telephone for details.
>
> **Refunds:** yes, if returned in 7 days. All guaranteed against bad workmanship.
>
> **Specials:** the body cavity can be made as a time capsule, for mementoes for future generations.

Super Tramp Trampolines are marvellous fun and this firm makes them for people of all ages, from twelve-year-olds to their fourteen-stone fathers. They also sell the Wobbler, a new craze where you use your feet and balance to persuade balls through a maze into holes.

Super Tramp, Langlands, Uffculme, Cullompton, Devon EX15 3DA.
Tel: 01884 841305. **Fax:** 01884 841319.
Price range: £34 to £1,349. Catalogue free.
Payment: cheque, Visa, Mastercard, Delta, Switch, Amex.
Postage & packing: included.
Delivery: 24-hour carrier. Last orders for Christmas by 20 December.
Refunds: yes, within 10 days.

Teddy Bears of Witney We know that teddy bears are not just for children and some of these are clearly meant for adults dotty about bears. But teddy-love is engendered young and should be encouraged. The catalogue includes the fabulous Steiff bears (antiques fetch thousands at auction) and a miniature of Alfonzo, the red bear owned by Princess Xenia of Russia. There are also Paddington bears, Pooh bears and Rupert bears. The catalogue is a joy and full of bear history.

Teddy Bears of Witney, 99 High Street, Witney, Oxfordshire OX8 6LY.
Tel: 01993 702616/706616. **Fax:** 01993 702344.
Price range: £35 to £425. Catalogue £5.
Payment: cheque, Visa, Mastercard, Eurocard.
Postage & packing: £3 per bear, mainland UK.
Delivery: within 2 working days on request.
Refunds: please discuss your order before buying.

Tous Mes Amis Learn to love France by loving the country's toys. This new firm homes in on classic French children's characters – Babar, Asterix, Madeline, Becassine and the Little Prince. They are featured in toys, books, videos and themed mugs and T-shirts. The toy Babar is a brilliant green, with black soles to his feet, tiny tusks, and he's very cuddly. I think it's a brilliant idea. Now let's export Rupert Bear, Ratty and Pooh to the French.

Tous Mes Amis, PO Box 154, Farnham, Surrey GU9 8YD.
Tel: 01252 733188. **Fax:** 01252 733533.
Price range: about £5 to £50. Catalogue £2, refundable against order.

Payment: cheque, Visa, Access, Mastercard, Switch.
Postage & packing: £1.95 for orders to £20, £3.95 over £20.
Delivery: last Christmas order 16 December.
Refunds: yes, if returned in 14 days.

Tridias! Good-looking toys for pre-teen children with an educational element – the sort that parents welcome. I love the furry bee glove puppet with black fingers and yellow and black body, the wooden country farm with cowshed, pens and stables, and English hardwood wild animals like badgers, deer and foxes. There are also science games such as a clock run by potatoes and a shrimp hatchery.

Tridias! Toys, 124 Walcot Street, Bath BA1 5BG.
Tel: 01225 469455. Fax 01225 448592.
Price range: 25p to £585. Catalogue free.
Payment: cheques, Visa, Access.
Postage & packing: £2.95 standard.
Delivery: within 14 days; express service in 3 days at £4 extra. Christmas orders by 20 December.
Refunds: yes.

Windmill Antiques This firm supplies genuine antique rocking horses and faithful copies made to order. The antiques are restored by craftsmen used to dealing with antiques. All date from about 1880 to 1925, were carved in pine and covered in plaster before being painted.

Windmill Antiques, 4 Montpellier Mews, Harrogate, North Yorkshire HG1 2TJ.
Tel: 01423 530502.
Price range: new from £1,100; antique from £1,700. Catalogue free.
Payment: 25% deposit, balance 2 weeks before delivery if cheque. Or Visa, Mastercard, JCB.
Postage & packing: £60 on UK mainland.
Delivery: 6 weeks' notice for new, one week before Christmas for antiques, if available.
Refunds: by arrangement.

See also: L'Artisan Parfumeur for baby cologne (Luxuries), Anta for delightful children's pottery, Annie Cole Traditional Knitting and Melin Tregwynt for cot blankets and shawls (Home Interest), Obelisk Collection for initialled child's hairbrush and comb (Art and Replicas), English Stamp Company for decorative children's room stamps, Panduro for toys and dolls, Specialist Crafts for painting and modelling equipment (Christmas Trees and Decorations), Faerie Shop for fairy outfits, Magic by Post for all the tricks (Enthusiasms), Billie Bond Designs for children's furniture (Personalised Presents), all entries under Stocking Fillers.

TEENAGERS

Does anyone know what a teenager wants for Christmas? Do teenagers themselves? Teenagers are by far the hardest people to buy presents for but, nevertheless, cannot be ignored. One tip from numerous parents is not to bust a gut thinking of pleasing teenagers in general but to try to find out what pleases any one in particular. It may seem hard to buy them black lipstick or skull-and-crossbones jewellery but if that's what they want, that's what you will have to do. (It's even harder to buy them train-spotter anoraks or nerd-like computer software, but that may have to be faced too.)

One possibility, because teenagers always need more money, is to buy them a subscription to one of their regular magazines (just pull out the subscription order coupon when they're not looking and send it off). Another is to listen to them whingeing about what they want and haven't got and hope they haven't changed their mind by Christmas Day. Otherwise clothes and accessories are the safest bet, especially for girls. The suppliers below include designers and buyers who are still young enough to be on the right wavelength.

TEENAGERS – LISTINGS

Johnny Loves Rosie There's some really wacky stuff here, imported from America, which is at the forefront of fashion. There's a range of hair slides made of real Liquorice Allsorts, nuts and a dog biscuit embalmed in plastic, glitter Alice bands, maribou pony-tail ties, day-glo scrunchies and fake animal fur cuff-covers. Stick pins come like silver knives and forks and there are button covers from old cola bottle lids. Flowery hair-clips and brooches and beaded hairsticks are rather prettier.

> **Johnny Loves Rosie Ltd**, 131 Greenhill, Prince Arthur Road, London NW3 5TY.
> **Tel:** 0171 435 0089. **Fax:** 0171 794 0534.
> **Price range:** £2.50 to £59. Catalogue free.
> **Payment:** cheque, Switch, Visa, Mastercard, Eurocard.
> **Postage & packing:** £1.95.
> **Delivery:** normal post. Items may be in limited supply.
> **Refunds:** if returned by recorded post.

Rosie Nieper Funky T-shirts for all the family but especially for hard-to-please teenagers. The firm uses top cartoonists to produce jokey designs and messages. There are updates on Forties strips ('If only everything in life was as reliable as a woman'), Jacky Fleming jokes on trolley rage and real chic, while Simon Drew's multi-coloured slogans show motorbiking prawns ('Prawn to be wild') and Dali Havidson bikes with melting wheels.

> **Rosie Nieper**, 12 Munster Road, Teddington, Middlesex, TW11 9LL.
> **Tel:** 0181 255 9926.
> **Price range:** £7.99 to £29.99. Catalogue free.
> **Payment:** cheque, Switch, Connect, Delta, Access, Mastercard.
> **Postage & packing:** included.
> **Delivery:** last Christmas orders 16 December.
> **Refunds:** yes.

Tyrrell Katz Top designers James Tyrrell and Julia Katz decided to leave the fashion mega businesses and set up on their own. They say it's fun and their designs prove it. Their T-shirts, bags, make-up cases and wash bags generally feature rows of cartoon people, animals and bugs. There are rugby pattern cartoons (haka and hand off), cows like Silly Moo and Jersey (wearing a sweater) and frogs (a whole slew of species plus 'Jean-Paul' frog). Get the idea?

> **Tyrrell Katz**, 14 Conlan Street, London W10 5AR.
> **Tel:** 0181 960 9934. **Fax:** 0181 964 2848.
> **Price range:** £5.95 to £18.95. Catalogue free.
> **Payment:** cheque, Access, Mastercard, Visa, Switch.
> **Postage & packing:** £1 per item to a maximum of £3.
> **Delivery:** last Christmas orders by GPO final posting date.
> **Refunds:** exchanges at £1 p&p extra.

See also: L.L. Bean (General Catalogues), Racing Green, Word Out for poetry T-shirts (Women's Clothes), The Iron Bed Company for teenage beds (Home Interest), Castle Combe Skid Pan & Kart Track for kart race vouchers, Explore Trader for rugged holiday equipment, Red Letter Days for hang-gliding and other virile sports, Drive it All for rally and other circuit driving (Sports), Letterbox for CD and Video boxes in smart checks (Children), NSPCC has a special teen stocking filler section (Charities).

OLD PEOPLE

If there are catalogues dedicated to the elderly, I have yet to find them. The closest comes from Help the Aged, which sells gadgets to help stiff old women pull up their tights or cut their toe nails. It features warm shoulder wraps, tap turners for arthritic fingers and cushions to support weak limbs. These are undoubtedly useful but don't make exciting presents.

My own feeling is that elderly people should not be patronised or treated differently from the rest of us. I know a top fashion buyer who buys Jean Muir clothes for her octogenarian mother. Muir's clothes are elegant and expensive but the styles are comfortable and ageless. The same goes for cashmere sweaters and silk shirts, soft moccasins (see Jeremy Law) and warm gloves and scarves. Gilly Forge's pull-on hats will keep old heads warm – but stylishly.

Buying for older people, especially if they are infirm, ill or forgetful, needs imagination. People who have problems reading will welcome talking books while interesting foods are always a good idea. There are fruit hampers, for instance, or foods which take you down memory lane, like Patum Peperium.

These extra special foods work well for those in residential homes, as do presents which turn up regularly. As well as subscriptions to magazines, bunches of flowers or boxes of chocolates can be delivered in this way. People tend to deluge the elderly with love and affection at Christmas time when smaller, year-round reminders might be more welcome.

In many cases, it's hard to generalise simply because a recipient is a certain age. Active older people may share the hobbies and interests covered in the relevant sections and enjoy topflight fashion and food. Those who are no longer fit may long for presents which make life more enjoyable. As with any recipient, identify their interests and you'll be able to find a present to suit.

Refer to: Imperial War Museum for packs of WWII memorabilia (Art and Replicas), Jeremy Law, Kingshill (Women's Clothes), Rachel Riley (Children's Clothes), Help the Aged for presents for old people (Charities), flowers by post from Groom and Pinks by Post (Luxuries), hampers, cakes and chocolates by post (Food for Presents), talking books, cassettes, videos of old films (Books, Cassettes, CDs and Videos).

PROBLEM PEOPLE

Problem people divide into two categories: there are those who can't help it and those who can.

Those who can't help it are people who have genuine difficulties such as allergies, illnesses or chronic conditions which mean that presents must fulfil special needs. Such conditions include diabetes, arthritis, asthma, eczema, allergies to additives and to certain foods such as gluten and sugar (see the end of this section for firms which help). If you want to buy presents for people who have these difficulties and cannot find a supplier, try talking to the appropriate charity or association. They will be able to put you in touch with relevant suppliers.

The second category of problem people are those who have everything – or who want nothing. This is not the same thing. Those who appear to have everything will have desires – but they may be too expensive for the average present giver. Those who want nothing have enough for all their needs and aren't able to think of anything else.

So it is up to us to think for them. One area to look at is perishable foods. We all run out of food or drink or might wish to try something new. Try new foods like exotic chutneys or specialised chocolates. Or drinks like teas flavoured with lemon and orange peel, spices and herbs. Introduce them to something they never knew they needed. Send them boxes of fruit and vegetables, great bunches of fresh daffodils and pinks, a pair of kippers every month.

For those who are satisfied with life, give them the chance to adopt an animal at the zoo (even if it's a gerbil) or have a star of their very own. Give them tickets to a concert and a meal afterwards, arrange a red-letter day at a posh hotel or the chance to fly an old aeroplane.

If there is nothing suitable currently on offer but you have an idea in mind, just ask! In writing this book, I have been staggered at the ingenuity shown by firms in coming up with new ideas and responding to consumers' demands. If no one has caught on to your or your relation's needs, talk to the companies operating in the relevant area and you will almost certainly find one willing to oblige.

PROBLEM PEOPLE – LISTINGS

Anything Left-Handed Just what it says and if, like me, you've struggled with a right-handed potato peeler for years, even this is a present worth having. Other implements include pens, knives, secateurs and scythes, nail scissors and tin openers. There are also books to help people cope with being sinister.

> **Anything Left-Handed Ltd**, 18 Avenue Road, Belmont, Surrey SM2 6JD.
> **Tel:** 0181 770 3722. **Fax:** 0181 715 1220.
> **Price range:** £1.15 to £56.95. Catalogues free.
> **Payment:** cheque, Mastercard, Visa.
> **Postage & packing:** 75p up to £7.50, £1.50 over £7.50.
> **Delivery:** allow 28 days.
> **Refunds:** by arrangement.

International Star Registry About 15 million stars have so far been identified and the ISR can arrange to name one of them for you. The name is entered in Britain, America and Switzerland and copyrighted in the listing of all star names, which is lodged in the British Library and the Library of Congress. You also get a certificate of registration with the star's telescopic co-ordinates. There is, too, an astronomical chart pinpointing your choice. A present for someone who has nearly everything?

International Star Registry, 24 Highbury Grove, London N5 2DQ.

Tel: 0171 226 6886. **Fax:** 0171 226 8668.
E-mail: orion@starregistry.co.uk

Price range: £55 fixed fee. Catalogue free.

Payment: cheque, Visa, Access, Amex, Diners, Switch, bank draft, transfer.

Postage & packing: included.

Delivery: last Christmas order 18 December.

Refunds: yes.

London Zoo Adopt an animal at the zoo. Horace the cross-eyed spider, for instance, or Hilary, a male giraffe. Hilary would set you back £1,500, but you can adopt part of an animal for £30 or a less-favoured beast like an ant, cockroach or piranha fish for £20. It helps the zoo's financial problems and, if you live near enough, it's nice to drop in and feel you have a stake in it. When you become a new parent, whether to a crocodile or a beetle, you get a certificate, a picture of a similar animal, a car sticker, a free ticket to the zoo and a year's subscription to its magazine. Your name will also be listed on a board in the zoo.

Adopt an Animal, London Zoo, Regent's Park, London NW1 4RY.

Tel: 0171 586 4443.

Price range: £20 for a dormouse to £6,000 for an elephant. Leaflet free.

Payment: cheque, Access, Mastercard, Visa, Amex.

Postage & packing: not applicable.

Delivery: allow a few days to process.

Refunds: no.

Theatre Tokens More than 150 theatres and concert halls all over Britain will accept these tokens, including many in the West End. The tokens are sent in a good-looking wallet and people can 'spend' them on tickets of their choice. Other ideas include vouchers for programmes and drinks during the performance, vouchers which arrive with a box of Godiva chocolates (see Food for Presents) or a bottle of champagne, and others which include vouchers for meals in restaurants such as Chez Gerard, Bertorelli's or Chutney Mary.

> **Theatre Tokens**, by telephone only. **Tel:** 0171 240 8800
> **Price range:** tokens £1, £5, £10, £20. No catalogue.
> **Payment:** cheque, Visa, Access, Diners, Connect with Mastercard or Visa logo.
> **Postage & packing:** included.
> **Delivery:** orders posted up to last GPO lst class Christmas posting date.
> **Refunds:** no, but no expiry on tokens.

See also: Farmer John Quilts duvets for asthmatics (Home Interest), Higginbotham for luxury cotton nightwear, Jeremy Law soft moccasins for foot complaints and arthritics, Cyrillus for pregnant mothers and large sizes, Kingshill for large size high fashion (Women's Clothes), The Finishing Touch and Objets Extraordinaires for presents for people who have everything, L.L. Bean for cold conditions (General Catalogues), Glenelg Candles to alleviate migraine etc (Luxuries), Meg Rivers cakes for wheat-free cakes (Food for Presents), Doves Farm Organic for gluten-free flour, Village Bakery for yeast-, wheat- and sugar-free cakes and puddings, food for vegetarians and vegans (Bread, Puddings and Cakes), Christmas, Vintage Roots for organically grown wines, spirits, beers and cider (Drink), Help the Aged for presents for old people (Charities), Cotton-on for clothes for children with eczema (Children's Clothes), Red Letter Days (Sports).

TRADITIONAL IDEAS WITH A TWIST

There are some presents whose predictability stuns recipients into astonished boredom. We can all name them – talcum powder (does anyone still use it?), a box of chocolates, a bottle of whisky, ties, socks, handkerchiefs and soap.

These presents became type-cast because everyone used them as solid standbys. The idea itself was sound but the quality control went awry. So if you're looking for presents in these categories, try a variation on the theme – soaps with sex appeal, chocs with oomph, pens and pencils with panache and socks with style. Alternatively, try to make up packs of everyday items. A new scarlet sponge bag with toothbrush, flannel, mirror and make-up all in red; a pack of paper, envelopes and scratch pad cut from old maps, a set of dazzling white handkerchiefs in an aluminium box and so on. Simple presents cleverly combined and presented will be so instantly appealing that no one will notice it's boring old ties, socks and hankies again.

Refer to: Officina Profuma Santa Maria Novella for medieval soaps and other smart toiletries at Czech & Speake and Penhaligon's (Luxuries), The Chocolate Society for chocs with oomph, Fine Cheese Co for hampers of cheese and wine like 'A Pair of Wellingtons' and a hatbox of cheese history (Food for Presents), Muji for hi-tech everyday things (General Catalogues), Higginbotham for nightwear in the finest Jermyn Street shirting (Women's Clothes), Peta Flint socks for superb old-fashioned knitted socks (Men's Clothes).

PERSONALISED PRESENTS

All sorts of new processes have made it possible to organise a present which means something special. Machines can monogram anything from shirts to sheets, printing techniques make jigsaws of family snaps possible and videos are now so easily made that a special family film costs little.

Presents which are carefully chosen to give pleasure to a specific person or family take both organisation and thought. You have to set about finding photographs for jigsaws or portraits of favourite cars months in advance, secretly. Often the firms which do personalised presents are tiny and work by hand, so they need lots of notice. But the reward is great – people really appreciate the trouble you've taken.

PERSONALISED PRESENTS – LISTINGS

Arty-Zan This company will turn your photograph – any size, black and white or colour – into a jigsaw although, if it's a bad or fuzzy photograph, the jigsaw will be the same (could make solving it even harder). They will also make jigsaws from children's drawings, postcards or any other picture you care to send them. Jigsaws come in four sizes, the cheapest a doddle of thirty pieces; the most expensive a fiend of 280.

> **Arty-Zan**, Fairholme Farm, 14 Croydon Lane, Banstead, Surrey SM7 3AN.
>
> **Tel:** 0181 740 5439.
>
> **Price range:** £9.99 to £12.99. No catalogue.
>
> **Payment:** cheque or postal order.
>
> **Postage & packing:** included in UK.
>
> **Delivery:** last Christmas order 18 December.
>
> **Refunds:** yes.

Billie Bond Designs This company produces the most delightful children's furniture, notably a paradise for young cowboys or girls – a bunk bed on top of a tiny cabin. You enter through a stable door and find desk, mirror, tiny chairs and wardrobe inside, all designed in Wild West mode. Cacti are stencilled on the outside and a ladder goes up to the bed. The same set-up also comes in American country folk style, white-washed and stencilled with figures. These, along with toy boxes featuring farm animals and safari animals, are made from reclaimed pine. All can be personalised – the little cabin chair with the owner's name, for instance. Just great.

Billie Bond Designs, 2 Warners Farm Cottage, Howe Street, Great Waltham, Essex CM3 1BL.

Tel/Fax: 01245 360164.

Price range: £7.99 to £491. Catalogue £1.50.

Payment: cheque, Visa, Mastercard.

Postage & packing: £3.50 for small gifts, from £15 for furniture and boxes.

Delivery: within 14 days. Boxes and furniture made to order 6-8 weeks.

Refunds: not when made to order.

Jayem Jigsaws Personalised jigsaws made from your photographs. They will make any size from 4-inches square to a maximum of 20 x 15 inches. They will send the jumbled puzzle with no clue to the subject, so you have to do the jigsaw to find out what it is.

Jayem Jigsaws, Fountain House, Goudhurst, Kent TN17 1AL.

Tel: 01580 211223. **Fax:** 01580 212421.

Price range: £14.95 and £19.95. No catalogue.

Payment: cheque and major credit cards.

Postage & packing: included.

Delivery: usually within 2 weeks. Last order for Christmas 17 December.

Refunds: yes.

Kingston Collection This company was founded in 1879 to make bagpipes and now uses the skills acquired to create watches, clocks, hip flasks and cases for calculators and cards in highly polished stainless steel, mostly for corporate gifts. These, however, translate well into personalised presents beautifully engraved. I particularly like the Voyager clock which is designed like an old-fashioned compass.

> **Kingston Collection**, 7 Young Street, Elgin, Morayshire IV30 1TG.
> **Tel:** 01343 540053. **Fax:** 01343 540032.
> **Price range:** £10.95 to £65. Catalogue free.
> **Payment:** cheque, Visa, Mastercard, Amex, JCB, Access, Diners.
> **Postage & packing:** £2.95 per order.
> **Delivery:** posted within 3 days, engraved may take an extra day. Last orders for Christmas, 20 December.
> **Refunds:** not when engraved.

Magic Calendar Company Want to send a distant relative a set of photos of the family or friends? Setting these out in calendar form makes a year-round present which can later be put in the archives. The firm will make up four-page calendars with four photos to twelve-page calendars with a different snap for each month.

> **Magic Calendar Company**, PO Box 6, Manchester M60 3EL.
> **Tel/Fax:** 0161 236 5404.
> **Price range:** from £8.99. Catalogue free.
> **Payment:** cheque.
> **Postage & packing:** £1 per order.
> **Delivery:** Last Christmas order 15 December.
> **Refunds:** yes.

Marie Perkins Marie will paint plates and jugs to match your wallpaper, to label your children's rooms or to celebrate events. She paints on plain white china, but the end results are not meant to fulfil their original function and are not dishwasher safe. Designs include brilliant apples and daisies, fish and flowers, and brightly coloured bears and ducks for children.

Decorative Ceramics by Marie Perkins, 13 Inwood Crescent, Brighton, East Sussex BN1 5AP.

Tel: 01273 502754.

Price range: £7 to £15. Send SAE for brochure.

Payment: cheque.

Postage & packing: from £3.50 per item.

Delivery: last Christmas orders by 25 November.

Refunds: yes, if returned in 14 days.

Memories on Video Films, slides and photographs are all copied onto video tape by this firm which has been going since 1984. They will also copy foreign videos to play in the UK and put old reel-to-reel sound recordings onto modern audio cassette. This is a marvellous opportunity to create a collage of still and moving memories into a single video – your children for grand-parents; your grandparents for your children; a video to send to relations overseas and so on. Cliff Williams, who runs the service, will also copy photographs and other visuals onto mugs and other ceramics in a way that is permanent and dishwasher proof.

Memories on Video and Cliff Williams (Ceramics), 24 York Gardens, Winterbourne, Bristol BS17 1QT.

Tel: 0117 956 2555/956 2666. **Fax:** 0117 956 2700.

Price range: £7 upwards. Brochure free.

Payment: cheque, postal order, Access, Visa.

Postage & packing: £1 for ceramics.

Delivery: within 28 days but allow longer before Christmas.

Refunds: by arrangement.

Picture This Instead of celebrating great days with a video or photo album, Caroline Plunket-Checkemian will create a collage of objects as a permanent reminder. Think of mixes of dried flow-ers, menus, drawings, musical scores, tassels, pulled crackers and wine labels and you will see the possibilities. Caroline trained at Chelsea and among her more esoteric commissions is a framed collection celebrating eighteen months' work in Bolivia by two World Service journalists. Each collection comes in a box frame.

Picture This, 10 Edenvale Street, Fulham, London SW6 2SF.

Tel: 0171 736 7065.

Price range: from £150 plus framing. Catalogue free.

Payment: cheque including deposit.

Postage & packing: carriage by arrangement.

Delivery: last Christmas orders by 31 October but her time may run out.

Refunds: no.

Remember When The company holds nearly 2 million newspapers from 1642 to 1995 and can supply an original issue to commemorate a special date. These can be sent in a postal tube or in a dark green presentation case with certificate of authenticity.

Remember When, The Tithe Barn, 520 Purley Way, Croydon, Surrey CR0 4RE.

Tel: 0181 688 6323. **Fax:** 0181 781 1227.

Price range: £17 to £32.50 for ordinary papers. Other prices on request. Brochure free.

Payment: cheque, Visa, Switch, Access, Mastercard, Amex.

Postage & packing: included.

Delivery: postal service.

Refunds: no.

Roger Alsop This watercolour painter does dashing portraits of cars to commission which make marvellous presents for people who are besotted by their old banger. The paintings are realistic but with flowing brushwork and lots of highlights, measuring about 14 x 10 inches. The car can be set against a suitable background (French café for an old Citroën) or on its own. The more characterful the car, the better it works.

Roger Alsop, 4 St John's Villas, London N19 3EG.

Tel: 0171 263 8067.

Price range: £200 a painting. No catalogue, but photos of earlier paintings sent.

Payment: cheque.

Postage & packing: included in UK.

Delivery: last order for Christmas 15 December. But not if he's already working.

Refunds: yes.

Tetbury Video Workshop Like Memories on Video, this firm will transfer a ragbag of photos, films and graphics onto a single video.

> **Tetbury Video Workshop**, Owls Nest, 2 The Cottages, Foxmoor Lane, Stroud, Gloucestershire GL5 4QD.
>
> **Tel:** 01453 823475. Fax by notice: 01453 823475. **Mobile** 0831 193091.
>
> **Price range:** £2 upwards. Catalogue free.
>
> **Payment:** cheque with order. Estimates given.
>
> **Postage & packing:** £4 for orders up to £30, £6 thereafter.
>
> **Delivery:** 5-7 days in general.
>
> **Refunds:** yes.

Wright & Logan This Portsmouth firm has been taking pictures of Royal Navy ships since 1924 and has an archive of over 50,000 different negatives. So, if you want to give a neat present to a sailor, they'll probably have a picture of his ship. Though no pictures were taken during World War II, they still reckon on a 90% success rate in matching ship to sailor. If they find your ship, a photograph will be specially printed and will come with its own frame and label.

> **Wright & Logan**, 20 Queen Street, Portsea, Portsmouth PO1 3HL.
>
> **Tel:** 01705 829555. **Fax:** 01705 824447.
>
> **Price range:** £14.95 to £29.95. Catalogue free.
>
> **Payment:** cheque or postal order.
>
> **Postage & packing:** included.
>
> **Delivery:** 7-10 days.
>
> **Refunds:** yes.

See also: Charbonnel et Walker, Godiva for personalised chocolate boxes, Meg Rivers cakes for specially iced cakes with names etc (Food for Presents), Master of Malt for special whisky labels (Drink), Friars Goose for alphabet tiles, Morgan Bellows for crested, initialled bellows etc, Silver Direct engraved to order (Home Interest), Obelisk Collection for engraved silver and faux ivory (Art and Replicas), Balloon City for named balloons

(Christmas Trees and Decorations). Planta Vera can supply violets with girl's names (Gardening). C.N.A. Ruff does signet rings and other personal jewellery (Jewellery). Brian Jarrett does personalised knot boards (Enthusiasms). Letterbox for children's bags, towels, chairs, sweatshirts etc all named (Children), Penhaligon's for engraved scent bottles, hairbrushes, dressing table mirrors (Luxuries), Rosie Nieper for personal T-shirts (Teenagers), Chuffs for initialled luggage (Men's Clothes).

STOCKING FILLERS

Whoever invented the Christmas stocking (Prince Albert at a guess) would probably be torn limb from limb by parents today. Cheap presents are just as hard to choose and as annoying to buy on the high street as expensive ones. Luckily, mail-order firms now have whole pages devoted to providing, say, ten extra presents for every child in the house.

The stocking's up-side comes on Christmas morning. However exhausted the adults are from having waited all night for Father Christmas and, in my family at least, from the nice glass of whisky left out for him, the shrieks of delight are compensation. The sight and sound of excited, thrilled children burrowing in the stocking and turning up present after present is one of the best parts of Christmas day.

Stocking presents should be cheap. Many catalogues offer

scores of presents under £1, the old-fashioned sorts of toys that everyone loves. These are kazoos, balloons, chocolate animals, cards and games. Add lots of food, a cassette or two, little fun jewels, the odd free object like a pretty stone or shell. Then wait for Santa to deliver.

STOCKING FILLERS – LISTINGS

Frog Hollow Though most toy catalogues have some cheap and cheery stocking fillers, this one has more than most – even special packs of goodies for stockings. These might include a bag of chocolate coins, jumping beans, a whoopee cushion and a croaking sponge (for any age or sex) or a little girl's pack of fan, purse, silk notebook and teddy. You can get personalised pencils and little leather boxes along with personalised stockings and a Jumbo Victorian one.

> **Frog Hollow,** 21 High Street, Pewsey, Wiltshire SN9 5AF.
> **Tel:** 01672 564222. **Fax:** 01672 562462.
> **Price range:** £5 to £50. Catalogue free.
> **Payment:** cheque, Access, Visa, Mastercard.
> **Postage & packing:** £2.99.
> **Delivery:** last Christmas orders 15 December. Some goods may be in short supply near Christmas.
> **Refunds:** yes. Notify in 5 days if damaged or missing; return in 14 if faulty. If disliked, return in 14 days.

Hawkin by Post Toys for all the family: wind-up penguins and monkeys, Edwardian mini masks, snake in the box which springs out, finger puppets, kazoos. The firm produces a large catalogue of objects which anyone from a toddler to an ancient would enjoy. There are over sixty items at less than £1 each, plus lots of old-fashioned toys like slithery snakes and tiny carved nuts with insects inside. Great for the child in all of us.

> **Hawkin & Co,** St Margaret, Harleston, Norfolk IP20 0PJ.

Tel: 01986 782536. **Fax:** 01986 782468.

Price range: 27p to £85.95. Catalogue free.

Payment; cheque, Visa, Access, Mastercard, Eurocard, Switch.

Postage & packing: £2.95; orders over £25 free.

Delivery: last Christmas orders by 3 December.

Refunds: yes.

See also: all the entries under Children and Children's Clothes, Presents for Men, The Spotted Duck (General Catalogues), Tobias and the Angel for lovely floor cloths and dusters (Home Interest), Bettys for chocolate bears etc (Food for Presents) and all charity catalogues (Charities). Most of these have stocking fillers but the NSPCC specialises in stocking fillers for all members of the family and is an excellent source.

Chapter Two

CLOTHES AND ACCESSORIES

CHILDREN'S CLOTHES

Buying clothes for children is one way of giving a present useful to both child *and* parents. And yes, there are alternatives to the ubiquitous joggers and baseball caps (whether worn forwards or backwards). In fact, it looks as if there's a return to formal children's clothes. Surprisingly, it seems that even children are going along with this – I recently went to a photo shoot with a ten-year-old boy who refused to wear anything but his navy blazer and flannels.

Many of the mail-order firms selling children's clothes have been started in response to a need which is not being met by high-street shops. At least two sell smocked party frocks and neat shirts for girls and boys in old-fashioned Viyella, which make lovely presents from doting grandparents. Other companies have taken advantage of the emergence of cotton as an all-year, easy-care fabric to create stylish ranges of mix-and-match outfits in strong primary colours teamed with the perennial denim.

One firm listed here, Cotton-on, was started by a mother who had to cope with her own child's eczema. She found it hard to buy clothes which did not exacerbate the condition and now sells outfits for other suffering children. Another mother tests every one of her designs on her own children. As all mothers know, if children feel idiotic or uncomfortable in an outfit, they cannot be forced to wear it.

Another Nineties trend is to spend a lot of money on children's clothes, despite the fact they are outgrown so quickly. Parents want their children to look good and that means buying clothes in quality fabrics. Firms are selling hand-knitted jerseys in wool and cotton (even tiny Guernseys), little jackets in proper tweed and corduroy, wool socks and leather shoes. These are generally packaged superbly and make ideal gifts.

There is now also a move towards doing seasonal collections for children. I'm not sure whether that's such a great thing for parents but, given that the life of children's clothes is barely a year, at least it means you can always make sure the clothes you buy as Christmas presents are in the latest styles.

right or wrong

CHILDREN'S CLOTHES – LISTINGS

Beetle Bug Fun cotton knitted jumpers such as a navy crew neck with an appliquéd purple hippo round the tum, moss-stitch sweater or cable sweater in denim colours along with pixie scarf hats, berets and fun rucksacks. They are for babies and children from under six months to eight years.

Beetle Bug, 28 Tooting High Street, London SW17 0RG.
Tel: 0181 672 4465. **Fax:** 0181 767 3247.

Price range: £6.50 to £30. Catalogue free.
Payment: cheque, Access, Visa.
Postage & packing: £2.
Delivery: allow 28 days.
Refunds: yes, if returned unworn in 14 days.

Cotton Moon Suzanne Youles' two children test every design that she makes before the clothes are added to her mail-order catalogue. 'As every mother knows,' she says, 'there's no sense in buying something if your child won't wear it.' Her cotton fabrics mostly come from Scandinavia and America and are sassy but pretty with stylised flowers, indigo and red stripes, and ginghams in primary colours. There are cardigans, shirts, easy trousers, hats, socks and rompers for both boys and girls. Suzanne produces winter and summer collections.

Cotton Moon, PO Box 280, London SE3 8DZ.
Tel enquiries and orders: 0181 305 0012. **Fax and brochure requests:** 0181 305 0011.
Price range: £2.25 to £26. Catalogue free.
Payment: cheque, Visa, Mastercard, Access, Switch.
Postage & packing: £2.50; free on orders over £75 in UK.
Delivery: last Christmas order 16 December. Supplies can be limited.
Refunds: yes, if returned in 21 days unworn.

Cotton-on Cotton has made huge strides in the last ten years, with warm, fluffy yet washable knits now all-season comforters. This firm swears by the fabric and makes every effort to reduce impurities and chemicals in the yarn, which makes its clothes perfect for those with eczema. The styles for babies and children are bright and modern and there are some clothes for women.

Cotton-on Ltd, Monmouth Place, Bath BA1 2NP.
Tel: 01225 461155. **Fax:** 01225 461464.
Price range: £3 to £40. Catalogue free.
Payment: cheque, Access, Visa, Eurocard, Delta, Switch, Mastercard.

Postage & packing: £2.75.

Delivery: allow 28 days.

Refunds: yes, if returned unworn in 10 days.

Giggles Girlswear Lynn Forster has been making 100% cotton pinafore dresses for little girls for five years. People find that they are both easy to wash and versatile – add a T-shirt for daytime or a smart, frilled blouse for parties. The fabrics are cerise needlecord with black spot, purple and green, navy and rose or ivory and rose floral and a red paisley; sizes from six months to eight years. She also sells matching headbands and scrunchies.

Giggles Girlswear, 98 Cedar Close, Ampthill, Bedfordshire MK45 2UD.

Tel: 01525 402532.

Price range: £1.50 to £20. Catalogue free.

Payment: cheque, Visa, Mastercard.

Postage & packing: included.

Delivery: allow 28 days but last Christmas orders 2 weeks before 25 December.

Refunds: yes, if returned in perfect condition in 14 days.

Happy Flannelies One way to make bathtime more appealing to children is to give them a towelling bath-time cuddle robe shaped like a frog, or a poncho like a rabbit, pig or bear. The company also does comfy dressing gowns and washbags in towelling plus green frog mitts with goggly eyes, pink smiling pigs and dark brown bears. Designed for children up to five, these are lovely ideas.

Happy Flannelies, The Crystal Garden Company, The White House, Dancers Hill Road, Bentley Heath, Barnet, Hertfordshire EN5 4RY.

Tel: 0181 449 0443. **Fax:** 0181 441 6201.

Price range: £6.95 to £24.95. Catalogue free.

Payment: cheque, Access, Visa.

Postage & packing: £2.50 on UK mainland.

Delivery: last Christmas orders 1 December.

Refunds: no, as made to order.

Jitterbug A range of well-designed and amusing sweaters and hats in washable wool and cotton and in updated Fair Isle patterns, using scarlet, navy, pale blues and green. The company is notable for its pixie, Noddy and elf hats, often with bells on the tips. Warm and wearable for winter.

> **Jitterbug**, Wisteria House, Mortimer Lane, Mortimer, Berkshire RG7 3AJ.
> **Tel/Fax:** 01734 331384.
> **Price range:** £7.50 to £45. Catalogue free.
> **Payment:** cheque, Access, Mastercard, Visa, Switch, Delta.
> **Postage & packing:** £2.50, orders over £75 free.
> **Delivery:** last Christmas orders 6 December.
> **Refunds:** yes, if returned undamaged and unworn in 10 days.

Little Treasures This company sells clothes like children *used* to wear – smocked dresses, skirts trimmed with ribbons and jodhpurs for little girls, long shorts with turn-ups, knicker-bockers and waistcoats for little boys in tartans, gingham and Tattersall checks, for babies to ten-year-olds. There is also some classic women's wear such as nighties, riding skirts and jodh-purs.

> **Little Treasures**, 10 Braemar Crescent, Leigh-on-Sea, Essex SS9 3RL.
> **Tel/Fax:** 01702 559005.
> **Price range:** £18 to £70. Catalogue free in UK.
> **Payment:** cheque, Visa, Access, Mastercard.
> **Postage & packing:** £3 in EU.
> **Delivery:** up to 28 days but deadlines met where possible.
> **Refunds:** yes, if unworn and undamaged in 7 days, except special orders.

Monday's Child This company has stylish clothes for chil-dren aged between two and sixteen with a few adult clothes too. Mostly cotton or Viyella, the clothes are generally in bright tartans or checks and include jogging sweatshirts and bottoms in a good range of colours, jokey socks with animal patterns, T-shirts and even baseball caps. A special Christmas catalogue includes Compagnie de Provence soaps and adult sweatshirts with horse and rider designs.

> **Monday's Child**, Sunwillow Farm, Childrey, Wantage, Oxfordshire OX12 9XQ.
> **Tel:** 01235 751527. **Fax:** 01235 751528.
> **Price range:** £7.95 to £38.50. Catalogue free.
> **Payment:** cheque, Mastercard, Visa.
> **Postage & packing:** £2.50, orders over £100 free.
> **Delivery:** last Christmas orders 15 December.
> **Refunds:** yes, if unused.

Motley Crew A range of heavyweight, unbleached cotton T-shirts which, they say, are ruthlessly tested by children. Sizes are for children aged between two and ten, plus for teenagers and adults. Designs include dog and crossbones, knights and ladies, ghosts, pirates and mermaids, but the patch-eyed dog with bones, in white on a black sweatshirt, is my favourite.

> **Motley Crew**, 9 St Johns Church Road, London E9 6EJ.
> **Tel/Fax:** 0181 985 5472.
> **Price range:** £8 to £20. Catalogue free.
> **Payment:** cheque, Visa, Mastercard, Access, Eurocard, Delta
> **Postage & packing:** £1 per UK order, 3 or more shirts free.
> **Delivery:** last Christmas orders by 16 December.
> **Refunds:** yes, if returned unworn in 14 days.

Mouse Using traditional designs, the firm hand-makes tiny sweaters and shirts. There are little Guernseys in white cotton, navy wool fisherman's jackets with brass buttons, striped crewneck cottons in dark and light blue or green, and a navy cotton sweater with a knitted American flag centre front. There's also a plain T-shirt and two bobbly hats in dark indigo and natural cottons.

> **Mouse Clothing Ltd**, 51 Black Lion Lane, London W6 9BG.
> **Tel/Fax:** 0181 563 0958.
> **Price range:** £9.50 to £49.50. Catalogue free.
> **Payment:** cheque.

Postage & packing: £3 per item.
Delivery: allow 30 days to knit them.
Refunds: by arrangement.

Rachel Riley Rachel is a former model who lives on the Loire with her French husband and three children. She specialises in old-fashioned children's clothes in the best fabrics, which include tough woollens and tweeds, Viyella and cotton. Styles for boys are shirts and long trousers with smart jackets; little girls have smocked dresses, shirts, pretty gathered skirts and the sort of taffeta party frock they can't be parted from. There are charming nighties and pyjamas, dressing gowns and slippers and old-fashioned Start-rite shoes. Everything is put together with deep nostalgia for Britain as it used to be and arrives in the prettiest boxes.

Rachel Riley, La Roche Froissard, Gennes, 49350, France.
Tel: (0033) 41 38 04 93. **Fax:** (0033) 41 38 02 20.
Price range: £7 to £98. Catalogue free. (In French and English with prices in pounds, dollars and francs.)
Payment: sterling cheques, Access, Visa, Mastercard.
Postage & packing: £6 to £10, hand-made box £6 extra.
Delivery: Christmas orders by end of November or earlier if possible.
Refunds: yes, if returned in perfect condition within 2 weeks.

Sasti Would you like your children dressed up as wild cats or dragons? This is a lovely catalogue of wild clothes from 'three young women who have a love for children but a funky outlook on life', they say. Everything is hand-made to order so you can pick from the wild colour chart and mix the motifs. The cat suit is in fake leopard with ears and tail; dragons have tails and scaly hoods.

Sasti, 23 Portobello Green, 281 Portbello Road, London W10 5TY.
Tel: 0181 960 1125.
Price range: £6 to £25. Catalogue free.
Payment: cheque, Access, Eurocard, Mastercard, Visa.

Postage & packing: from £2.99 to £3.99 depending on size of order.
Delivery: last Christmas orders by 14 December.
Refunds: yes.

Zed This company features children's clothes which deliberately ignore cuteness in favour of styles inspired by adult fashions, while managing somehow not to be precocious. There are dungarees, shorts, T-shirts and a whole load of denims. Some designs, like the pinafore and shifts, come from adult clothes which were originally inspired by younger designs – the wheel has come full circle. Colouring is bright but restrained.

Zed, PO Box 9696, London NW6 1WE.
Tel: 0171 435 5322. **Fax:** 0171 435 8208.
Price range: £3 to £20. Catalogue free.
Payment: cheque, Access, Mastercard, Visa.
Postage & packing: £2.75. Orders over £50 free.
Delivery: allow 28 days, but it will probably be less.
Refunds: yes, if returned unworn with despatch note in 10 days.

See also: Cyrillus for French children's clothes, Margaret Anne Gloves, Polo Neck Designs, PS Polos, Shetland Knitwear Associates for babies' shawls, Wealth of Nations for ethnic designs (Women's Clothes), Boden, G-D-S Shirts (Men's Clothes), Rosie Nieper and Tyrrell Katz for jokey clothes (Teenagers).

WOMEN'S CLOTHES

Every husband or boyfriend thinks it's easy to buy clothes for a woman. It isn't, as any underwhelmed recipient or assistant in a smart lingerie shop will tell you. Come late December there are queues of women exchanging naughty nighties and knickers for 'something more sensible'.

The basic rule when buying clothes for women is to buy what you think they would like – not what *you* like. Observe the colours they regularly wear. A friend of mine, who prefers dark purple, crimson and chocolate brown in winter, is regularly given powder blue cashmere woollies by her husband. She changes them every year and he still hasn't noticed. Pale colours, along with bright yellow and scarlet and all the citrus shades, are quite hard to wear, especially in winter. Stick with neutrals, dark colours and, best of all, black. There's hardly anyone it doesn't flatter.

I would also be cautious about buying high-fashion presents without careful knowledge of the recipient, although women interested in high style will probably have favourites among the designers and it should be safe to follow that. Mail-order for high fashion was once considered impossible, but Kingshill (see page 80) which launched its catalogue doing just that only a few years ago, has caught on like wildfire. With a sensible returns policy – which makes buying for others equally possible – buying clothes by post is an excellent idea.

Kingshill, and others like it, sensibly stick to the less way out designer creations, offering clothes in beautiful fabrics, carefully coloured and tailored but not too outrageous. Kingshill is already introducing accessories, shoes, jewellery and ranges for large sizes.

Other mail-order clothes firms have started up to offer specific designs and types of clothes. There are quite a few companies selling country clothes to suit the UK's winter weather – stylish versions of the basic waxed jacket or ones using their own fabrics. Coats and jackets are easier presents to buy than skirts and trousers because fit is generally less crucial, especially in countrywear which should always leave room for bulky sweaters.

Hats are another good idea. I am particularly keen on Gilly Forge, who sells in big London stores but has a small mailorder catalogue. Her hats are both stylish and practical – my own waxed cotton rain hat has a soft fake fur inner brim and brilliant yellow satin lining (it also keeps the rain out).

I have included sellers of sexy underwear. Men love buying it and, if it is well-chosen, women love wearing it. I would, however, leave red and black combinations alone. Black by itself is perfect, so is a wonderful oyster beige. In this area above all others, observe what the woman in your life really loves and buy it for her. Don't give underwear to women you hardly know, they'll be affronted or, for that matter, to those you know too well. Mothers, grannies and sisters should be ruled out.

WOMEN'S CLOTHES – LISTINGS

Lingerie

David Nieper The catalogue has sexy lingerie to give as presents as well as more prosaic knickers and tights to buy by post. Tights include the excellent Wolford brand, there are knickers in pure silk and sensible cotton, and bras by Gossard and Triumph. The nightgowns, negligees and petticoats made by Nieper are in colours such as oyster, palest pink, pale coffee and white, lavishly trimmed with lace.

> **David Nieper**, Saulgrove House, Freepost, Somercotes, Derbyshire DE55 9BR.
> **Tel:** 01773 836000. **Fax:** 01773 520246.
> **Price range:** £5.50 to £165. Catalogue free.

Payment: cheque, Amex, Visa, Access, Diners, Switch.

Postage & packing: £2.95 in UK.

Delivery: allow 28 days.

Refunds: yes.

Specials: gift wrapping, alterations. Large sizes.

Higginbotham

Pure cotton nightwear is, to me, as comfortable and luxurious as silk but a great deal easier to care for. Higginbotham uses fine poplin in shirting stripes for men's and women's pyjamas, nightshirts, piped dressing gowns and loose kimonos. All are blue and red with white, plus one red and white stripe with a touch of green. They are generously sized and extremely comfortable. Arriving tissue-wrapped in a good brown box, they make ideal presents.

Higginbotham, PO Box 121, Diss, Norfolk IP21 4JN.

Tel: 01379 668833. **Fax:** 01379 668844.

Price range: £45 to £75. Catalogue free.

Payment: cheques, Switch, Delta, Visa, Mastercard.

Postage & packing: £3 in UK.

Delivery: Christmas orders by last GPO posting day.

Refunds: yes, if returned in original condition and box within 10 days.

Janet Reger

We all know Janet Reger's sexy underwear, which makes regular appearances in sex-and-shopping novels. Some pieces, like black chiffon wraps and lacy nighties, could be mistaken for evening gowns; but her sheer teddies, bustiers and suspenders leave no doubts. There are also surprisingly beautiful plain white pyjamas and robes.

Janet Reger, 2 Beauchamp Place, London SW3 1NG.

Tel: 0171 584 9368. **Fax:** 0171 581 7946.

Price range: £20 to £579. Catalogue, price on request.

Payment: cheque, Amex, Visa, Mastercard, Access, Diners.

Postage & packing: £5.

Delivery: last Christmas orders 1 week before unless stock is out.

Refunds: yes.

Clothes

Artigiano This catalogue probably includes an ideal present for anyone who loves Italian clothes. It is full of crisp tailoring, wonderful colours like strawberry, darkest navy and mint along with the neutrals Italy does so well. The fabrics are the luxurious soft wools, merino and cashmere and silk. There are also leather belts, cotton shirts and trousers – ideal for the elegant businesswoman.

Artigiano, PO Box 1, Yarmouth, Isle of Wight PO41 0US.
Tel: 01983 531881. **Fax:** 01983 531726.
Price range: £15 to £160. Catalogue free.
Payment: cheque, Access, Mastercard, Visa, Amex.
Postage & packing: £3.95 in UK.
Delivery: usually within a week. Express £5 extra, within 48 hours.
Refunds: yes, if returned in original condition within 14 days.

Black Sheep Using Black Welsh sheep and Welsh Mountain sheep, this firm makes tough jerseys in old fishermen's cable, lozenge and diaper patterns. As you'd expect, all are black, brown, grey, natural and marled. The more lively designs use Fair Isle and tartan stripes and checks. As well as sweaters there are hefty socks, hats, scarves and mitts – excellent presents in the deep mid-winter. Rugs, wraps and yarn are available.

Black Sheep, 9 Penfold Street, Aylsham, Norwich NR11 6ET.
Tel: 01263 733142/732006. **Fax:** 01263 735074.
Price range: £3.50 to £120. Catalogue free.
Payment: cheque, Access, JCB, Visa, Amex.
Postage & packing: £1.95 on orders under £10, £3.50 over £10, free thereafter in UK.
Delivery: sent in a week.
Refunds: yes, if returned in 14 days.

Brora Smart and fashionable high-style clothes for the country, in the best wools, cashmeres and tweeds yet in colours and designs which don't look silly on a Highland moor. Nor are they especially seasonal, given the British summer. Plain window-check tweed jackets and waistcoats, simple cashmere sweaters, sleeveless jumpers and a great cashmere T-shirt – good to wear under shirts. Check throws, picnic rugs, tweed bags and hats are also available.

Brora, 344 King's Road, London SW3 5UR.
Tel: 0171 352 3697. **Fax:** 0171 352 1792.
Price range: £13 to £250. Catalogue free.
Payment: cheque, Access, Mastercard, Visa, Switch.
Postage & packing: £3 on orders to £150, £5 up to £300, free thereafter.
Delivery: despatched within a week of order.
Refunds: yes, if returned in 14 days.

Capella Nova Everything you could ever need in waxed cotton, such as crushable hats like boaters and trilbies, capes and coats and a Sherlock Holmes-style caped coat for men and women. There are smocks, breeches and an overskirt plus a child's hat and cape – perfect for Christmas walks.

Capella Nova, 4 Portmans, North Curry, Taunton, Somerset TA3 6NL.
Tel: 01823 490382. **Fax:** 01823 490609. **Mobile** 0378 216037.
Price range: £29.95 to £275. Catalogue free.
Payment: cheque or major credit cards.
Postage & packing: from £5.
Delivery: allow 28 days. Last Christmas orders around 16 December.
Refunds: yes.
Specials: bespoke service.

The Cashmere Company Given the cost of cashmere, it makes sense always to go for the classics, in colour as well as style. If you are buying for a relation or friend, make sure you know exactly what colours they regularly wear. This collection is well thought out, though I would take off gilt buttons in favour of plain mother of pearl.

The Cashmere Company, PO Box 694, Wing, Leighton Buzzard LU7 0YZ.

Tel: 01296 688544. **Fax:** 01296 681030.
Price range: £115 to £425. Catalogue free.
Payment: cheque, Access, Mastercard, Visa, Amex.
Postage & packing: £4.95.
Delivery: allow 28 days.
Refunds: yes, if returned unworn in 7 days.

The Cashmere Store Sweaters, scarves, stoles and coats in cashmere and cashmere mixes. Because this is an expensive and luxurious fabric, the styles tend to be classic and long-lasting. The more eccentric patterns should be ignored in favour of plain knits in the soft colours that cashmere will dye. The reason people buy the yarn is that, weight for weight, it is both softer and warmer than any wool – ideal, therefore, for stoles and scarves.

The Cashmere Store, 254-256 Causewayside, Edinburgh EH9 1UU.
Tel: Freephone 0800 212836. **Fax:** 0131 668 4567.
Price range: £18.95 to £560. Catalogue free.
Payment: cheque, Visa, Access, Mastercard, Amex, Diners, JCB, Switch.
Postage & packing: 1st class postal costs; orders over £250 free.
Delivery: allow 10 days.
Refunds: yes.

Cocoon Beautifully comfortable raincoats made in 60% cotton, 40% nylon fabric silicone treated, which is lightweight but strong; and alternatively in 60% cotton plus 40% tactel with a resin finish. The styles are enveloping, loosely based on trenchcoats, kimonos or swaggers. Colours are mostly neutral but include terracotta, rose pink and ochre along with dark green, navy and soft black, lined with tartan. Look out also for hats, leggings and scarves.

Cocoon, Lomond Industrial Estate, Alexandria, Dunbartonshire G83 0TL.
Tel/Fax: 01389 755511.
Price range: £10 to £240. Catalogue free.

Payment: cheque, Visa, Access, Amex.

Postage & packing: included.

Delivery: normally in 20 days.

Refunds: yes, if returned unworn in 14 days.

Cyrillus This firm was started by a Frenchwoman who couldn't find the clothes she wanted for her children and so decided to create her own collection for all the family – and very stylish it is. The dashing short women's skirts are the right, deep navy, the children's white shorts are nattily below the knee and the cruisewear is in colours just a touch different from the norm, mixing scarlet and pale yellow for instance. The children's nightwear is charming with jolly fish and teapot motifs.

Cyrillus, Wilberforce House, Station Road, London NW4 4QE.

Tel: 0171 734 6660. **Fax:** 0171 734 6661.

Price range: £5 to £213. Catalogue free.

Payment: cheque, Access, Visa, Eurocard, Mastercard, Delta, Switch.

Postage & packing: £2.50.

Delivery: allow 28 days.

Refunds: yes, within 14 days of delivery.

Specials: gift wrapping service.

Elegance This is a German firm which mail orders smart clothes around the world from Finland to Taiwan. The styles are international fashion at its most bland. No English eccentricities here, but clothes you can wear in any world capital or cruise ship. Not to my personal taste but ideal for people who like their fashion straight.

Elegance Fashion & Design (UK), PO Box 41, Nottingham NG9 2NT.

Tel: 0115 967 8123. **Fax:** 0115 922 1170.

Price range: £17 to £600. Catalogue £4.75.

Payment: cheque, Access, Visa, Amex.

Postage & packing: £3.95.

Delivery: allow 28 days. Some clothes can sell out.

Refunds: yes, if returned unworn in 10 days.

Glenalmond Tweed Company Harris tweed in colours and styles you've never seen before – dark sophisticated windowpane checks on black or olive, blue tartans, subfusc herringbones and tweeds zinging with turquoise, orange and scarlet. These are made into bags, cases and a range of clothes from waistcoats to sheepskin-lined slippers, generally edged with leather. The tweed is extremely tough, uncreaseable, warm and the classic styles ideal for long-time country wear. There is also a sea island cotton summer range and a range for men.

Glenalmond Tweed Company, Culnacloich, Glenalmond, Perth, PH1 3SN
Tel: 01738 880322. **Fax:** 01738 880431
Price range: £20 to £400. Catalogue free.
Payment: cheque, Visa, Access, Mastercard, Eurocard.
Postage & packing: £4 in UK.
Delivery: orders by 30 November for Christmas. Supplies may be limited.
Refunds: yes, if returned in 7 days.

Kingshill This is the firm which proved you could sell high fashion at prices up to £500 by mail order. Catalogues come out twice a year with supplements in-between and, as of this year, include French and Italian designers as well as top British names such as Jasper Conran, Nicole Farhi, Paul Costelloe and Amanda Wakeley. There is a slightly cheaper Diffusion catalogue with Artwork, Canovas, I Blues and Fenn, Wright and Manson. Because the designs are chosen to appeal to working girls and out-of-town fashion addicts, they are stylish but not silly. Many, especially the blouses and sweaters and accessories such as belts and handbags, make excellent presents and, because wrong sizes can easily be returned, this is *the* way to buy sumptuous clothes such as ballgowns for the woman in your life.

The Kingshill Collection Ltd, Freepost, Great Missenden, Buckinghamshire HP16 0BR.

Tel: 01494 890555. **Fax:** 01494 866003.

Price range: £25 to £700. £7.50 for main catalogue; £3.50 for Diffusion.

Payment: cheque, all major credit cards.

Postage & packing: included.

Delivery: within 48 hours. Special 24-hour rush service.

Refunds: yes, if returned in 10 days. Also goods on approval if paid for first.

Specials: gifts vouchers in multiples of £50. Gift wrapping service.

Lands' End Loose, casual clothes which work both summer and winter and take you from the garden to country shopping days or casual London weekends. Very much in the American mode with loose cotton shirts and trousers, polos, turtles and sweatshirts and the occasional swirl skirt, these are virtually unisex clothes and almost entirely cotton.

Lands' End Direct Merchants, Freepost LE6187, Pillings Road, Oakham, Rutland, LE15 6NY.

Tel: free 0800 220106. **Fax:** free 0800 222 106.

Price range: £4 to £69.50. Catalogue free.

Payment: cheque, Access, Visa, Mastercard, Amex, Delta.

Postage & packing: £2.95 up to £150, free thereafter.

Delivery: 3 to 4 working days.

Refunds: yes.

Specials: monogramming, gift boxes.

Old Town From deepest Norwich and with a battalion of ancient sewing machines, Old Town recreates Olde Englishe clothes in authentic fabrics. How about a First World War factory worker's dress in check gingham or fall-front jeans as favoured by farmworkers in the 19th century? There are fishermen's smocks, reefers, overall jackets and solid workmen's shirts. Fabrics are chambray, denim, cotton drill and bedford cord; colours are earthy. Extras: heavy-duty button-on striped braces.

Old Town Workwear, 32 Elm Hill, Norwich NR3 1HG.

Tel: 01603 628100.

Price range: £7.50 to £82. Catalogue free.
Payment: cheque.
Postage & packing: included.
Delivery: within a fortnight.
Refunds: yes, if returned promptly.

Polo Neck Designs Following the worldwide success of the T-shirt come these slightly more formal, slightly warmer polo necks, made in the same kind of knitted cotton but with Lycra in the collars and cuffs to make them well-fitting but stretchy. The firm patterns the polos with repeat formal designs such as blue and white or red and black diamonds, blue *fleur de lys* on white and Tattersall checks, and with quirky animals. Suitably, from the home of horse-racing, motifs include colourful jockey caps and horses as well as hedgehogs, elephants and ducks. Sized for women, men and children.

Polo Neck Designs, High Havens Stables, Hamilton Road, Newmarket, Suffolk CB8 0NQ.
Tel: 01638 561114. **Fax:** 01638 667913.
Price range: £10 to £21.50. Catalogue free.
Payment: cheque, Visa, Mastercard, Eurocard.
Postage & packing: £1.90 per order in UK.
Delivery: last orders for Christmas 10 days before.
Refunds: yes.

PS Polos Similar styles to Polo Neck, above, but different patterns, which change around September. Currently there are raspberries and bright teapots on white backgrounds, gingham and hunting and shooting patterns. The children's range has snowmen, dogs and a skiing bear wearing a stetson. There are also twelve plain polos and dickies. The fabric is 55% cotton, 45% polyester with reinforced necks and cuffs to keep their shape.

PS Polos, The Manor Farm House, Chavenage, Tetbury, Gloucestershire GL8 8XW.
Tel: 01666 505720. **Fax:** 01666 503795.
Price range: £14 to £23. Catalogue free.

Payment: cheque, Access, Visa.

Postage & packing: £2.10 for 1 or 2, £4 for 3 or more.

Delivery: allow 10 days. Some patterns sell out around Christmas.

Refunds: yes, if returned in 7 days.

Racing Green Unisex working clothes in the American style which include a neat range of sweatshirts for all weathers in pale greens and dark blues, cotton polo shirts in rainbow shades, jeans and hill-billy check shirts. There are classic cashmeres, too, panamas and bandannas for the summer, nautical capsule wardrobes and accessories for winter cruises. Great presents because they're simple and can be added to. Both men's and women's ranges work well for teenagers and sizes go up to 18.

Racing Green, PO Box 100, Morley, Leeds LS27 0XB.

Tel: 0345 331177. **Fax:** 0113 238 2465.

Price range: £4.50 to £149. Catalogue free.

Payment: cheque, Mastercard, Visa, Amex, Delta, Connect.

Postage & packing: £3.

Delivery: allow 7 working days. 72-hour express for £5 extra.

Refunds: yes, with return form.

Specials: gift vouchers.

Rainforest Clothing Company Waxed jackets go Victorian – using subfusc tartans, waxed cotton in navy, rust and olive lined in wools and silks, the company makes waterproofs in redingotes, wrap coats, dusters and fantails. They are very full, thus fitting easily over wide skirts, sweaters and chunky trousers and, with the bright linings, more formal than most waxed clothes.

Rainforest Clothing Company, Chapel Studio, Ruspidge Road, near Cinderford, Gloucestershire GL14 3YA.

Tel: 01594 825865.

Price range: £25 to £695. Catalogue free.

Payment: cheque, Visa, Access, Amex, JCB.

Postage & packing: included in UK.

Delivery: allow 6 weeks before Christmas.
Refunds: yes.
Specials: clothes made to order and exclusive.

Shetland Knitwear Associates

Shetland Knitwear Associates The front page of the brochure shows the Duke of Windsor wearing a complex patterned Shetland sweater with the necessary accessories: dark tie, flat cap, matching terrier. This is the one to buy along with other old patterns made up into classic sweaters. (Why do men in knitwear catalogues always look such wallies, though?) The babies' shawls, whisper thin in white, are wonderful gifts.

Shetland Knitwear Associates, 31 King Harald Street, Lerwick, Shetland ZE1 0EQ.
Tel/Fax: 01595 692746. E-mail: shetland.knitwear@zetnet.co.uk Worldwide Web: http://www.zetnet.co.uk
Price range: £9 to £325. Catalogue free.
Payment: cheque, Access, Mastercard, Eurocard, Visa.
Postage & packing: £1.80 per garment, 90p per accessory.
Delivery: allow 4 weeks for Christmas. Hand-knitted at home so supplies could be limited.
Refunds: yes, if returned in 14 days.

Shilasdair Using yarn usually spun by hand, from a flock of sheep on Skye, Eva Fleg Lambert and Di Gilpin make bright, complex patterned sweaters. Some, I feel, are too strongly patterned for most people but Skye Stripes in a rich mix of madder, indigo and cochineal is stunning, as are Shoowa, a series of herringbones inspired by African kuba cloth, and Off Beat Squares, a cropped jacket in madder and indigo. You can buy them hand-knitted or in kits. The firm also sells its wonderful naturally dyed yarns. The Moor range is the colour of a Scottish autumn, Lochans are vibrant blues, Heather the shades of ling and Hills are silvery grey and marled.

Shilasdair, Struan Craft Workshop, Struan, Isle of Skye, Scotland IV56 8FE.
Tel: 01470 572284.
Price range: £1.50 to £165. Catalogue free.

Payment: cheque, Visa, Access, Mastercard.
Postage & packing: included.
Delivery: by arrangement.
Refunds: by arrangement.

Wealth of Nations

Wealth of Nations Outfits from around the world collected by Julia Woodham-Smith include both workwear and evening wear. There are plenty of good-looking white cotton shirts from Tibet, Hungary, Mexico and Austria, loose working clothes in neutral shades from Vietnam, Wales and China and brilliant silks from the Far East. Sizes are adaptable but there are also throws and shawls which make excellent gifts. There are ranges for unconventional men and really charming children's clothes like shepherd's smocks and embroidered Portuguese skirts.

Wealth of Nations, Unit 28, The Talina Centre, Bagleys Lane, London SW6 2BW.
Tel: 0171 371 5333. **Fax:** 0171 371 5398.
Price range: £35 to £175. Catalogue free.
Payment: cheque, Access, Visa, Mastercard, Eurocard, Amex, JCB.
Postage & packing: £2.95 by registered post.
Delivery: despatched within 24 hours. Some items may be scarce – ring to check.
Refunds: yes, if returned in 14 days.

Word Out

Word Out Presents for poetry lovers and those who like to feel eyes glued to their backs. This is a range of T-shirts with poems printed on the back. Pick from Lewis Carroll's 'Jabberwocky', ee cummings's lower-case poems, Byron, Stevie Smith and Dylan Thomas. The shirt fronts have pictures of the poet. One magazine called them 'the height of cultural chic' and, if that's your aim, they're for you.

Word Out, 17 Danescourt Road, West Derby, Liverpool L12 8RB.
Tel: none.
Price range: £16.95. Catalogue free, send SAE if possible.

Payment: cheque.
Postage & packing: 75p per shirt.
Delivery: last GPO posting date for Christmas.
Refunds: yes.

Workshop Using the best cottons, linens and silks, the company mails classic but very stylish shirts for women. Most of the styles can be made up in several different colours and most are in plain, textured or lightly striped or checked fabrics. They are shown in the catalogue with jeans, smart skirts and linen slacks proving how very versatile they are. You can't go wrong buying these as presents. There are also women's cufflinks.

Workshop, 1 Garfield Mews, Garfield Road, London SW11 5GZ.
Tel: 0171 738 2525. **Fax:** 0171 738 9477.
Price range: £45 to £225. Catalogue free.
Payment: cheque, Visa, Access, Switch, Debit Card, Amex.
Postage & packing: £3.
Delivery: Christmas orders by last GPO posting date.
Refunds: yes, if returned in 10 days.

Accessories

Connolly This firm makes the leather seats for Rolls Royce and recently began to make what is in my view the world's most luxurious luggage. In the softest, fluid leather and in designs which just hint at the great days of motoring, these are the wallets, card cases, bags, suitcases and washbags for high fliers. Colours are dull black, dark green, blue-black, brown and tan; lining is generally supple cream leather. They're certainly not cheap but give a lifetime's pleasure. There are also silver cufflinks and pens, cashmere clothes, witty driving gloves and, this year, Connolly overalls.

Connolly Limited, 32 Grosvenor Crescent Mews, London SW1X 7EX.
Tel: 0171 235 3883. **Fax:** 0171 235 3838.

Price range: £45 to £2,800 and beyond. 'The sky's the limit,' they say. Catalogue free.

Payment: cheque, Switch, all major credit cards.

Postage & packing: £5 on orders to £250, £10 up to £1,000; £15 over £1,000.

Delivery: 3 working days before Christmas. Some items limited because they are exclusive.

Refunds: yes, if faulty; otherwise exchange or credit note.

Specials: special orders undertaken. Will retrim yachts and private jets, wrap orders in leather.

Denny Andrews You may not thank someone for giving you an apron at Christmas, but they are very useful when cooking in party frocks. Denny Andrews' aprons are really strong in a hefty cotton twill with deep pockets. The range also includes ethnic outfits from the Far East, with kimonos that make excellent summer dressing gowns and are good for lounging. She also does throws, tablecloths and bedspreads.

Denny Andrews, Clock House Workshop, Coleshill, near Swindon, Wiltshire SN6 7PT.

Tel: 01793 762476. **Fax:** 01793 861615.

Price range: £7.50 to £120. Send 3 2nd class stamps for catalogue.

Payment: cheque, Access, Visa.

Postage & packing: as catalogue.

Delivery: Last Christmas orders by 18 December.

Refunds: yes, if returned in good condition but not P&P charge.

Flavell & Flavell You can never have too many leather bags and cases, so they make excellent presents. This firm has a no-nonsense style perfect for good hides and the brass fittings used. There are bucket bags and rucksacks, holdalls in leather and suede including a huge one, twenty-two inches long. Linings may be cotton or more expensive pigskin. This is a small firm which prefers to talk to customers about payment details, colour and leather choices, and welcomes phone calls.

Flavell & Flavell, Keisby House, Main Street, Kirkby Malzeard, nr Ripon, North Yorkshire HG4 3SD.

Tel: 01765 658502.

Price range: £42 to £130. Catalogue free.

Payment: cheque.

Postage & packing: £2.50 per bag.

Delivery: order by end October for Christmas, but later may be possible.

Refunds: yes, if unused.

Gilly Forge Flattering, comfortable, stylish hats. The town range includes the softest fake fur in pull-on styles with upturned brims in leopard, Persian lamb and black and brown furs. A country range mixes tweed with fur under the brim or, for rainy days, dull tartan waxed cotton with fur. All come with Gilly's signature brilliant yellow satin lining and, in my view (since I have two), will suit any age and any face. There are also matching gloves, muffs and fake fur tie collars.

Gilly Forge, 14 Addison Avenue, Holland Park, London W11 4QR.

Tel: 0171 603 3833. **Fax:** 0171 603 2032.

Price range: £48 to £78. Catalogue free.

Payment: cheque, postal order.

Postage & packing: £3.25.

Delivery: aim is 10 days but allow 28.

Refunds: yes, if returned in 14 days.

Hanna Goldman Hanna makes the most beautiful shoes, generally for brides, but these jewelled, embroidered and trimmed beauties are just as perfect for balls or dinner in smart hotels. They are works of art, covered in tiny pearls, silk roses, bows and even shells. Each one is separately made either to her designs, an amalgam of her patterns or your own design, and styles range from high-heeled mules to over-the-knee satin boots.

Hanna Goldman, Studio 4, 10-13 Holly Bush Place, London E2 9QX.

Tel/Fax: 0171 739 2690.

Price range: £195 to £500. Catalogue £3.

Payment: cheque with card.
Postage & packing: £6 average in UK.
Delivery: last Christmas orders by 11 October.
Refunds: yes, if size not correct.
Specials: gift voucher.

Jeremy Law Hand-made deerskin moccasins like the Red Indians wore (with the helpful addition of a strong rubber sole) are the most comfortable shoes in the world. The leather, soft as a glove, is in natural tan only, hand-sewn and with a drawstring to adjust the fit. Shoes are normally hard to size but, though these come from three to twelve, they need not be too accurate. The shoes look very stylish with jeans and trousers and are excellent for older people who have difficulty bending or those with foot problems like bunions and corns. Jeremy Law also sells a range of horn buttons which smarten up dull tweeds and country clothes.

Jeremy Law of Scotland, City Hall, Dunkeld, Perthshire PH8 0AR.
Tel: 01350 727569. **Fax:** 01350 728748.
Price range: 50p to £33. Catalogue free.
Payment: cheque or Visa, Switch, Mastercard, Amex, Diners.
Postage & packing: £3 for moccasins; buttons free for more than 10.
Delivery: Christmas orders by last GPO posting date.
Refunds: goods sent on approval but full refund available.

Margaret Anne Gloves This firm has been making gloves in Derbyshire for over thirty years. They are traditional and practical rather than fashion gloves; most are leather, lined with fleece or wool. There are driving gloves with knitted backs for men and women and chunky pigskin gloves for men. Children have small size mittens. The firm will make other specialist gloves and mitts to order.

Margaret Anne Gloves, 160 Bath Street, Ilkeston, Derbyshire DE7 8FH.
Tel: 0115 930 1073.

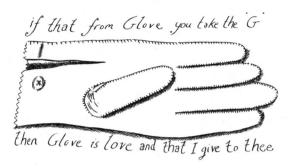

If that from Glove you take the 'G' then Glove is love and that I give to thee.

Price range: £5 to £29. Catalogue free.
Payment: cheque, Amex, Visa, Access.
Postage & packing: included.
Delivery: last Christmas orders by 20 November.
Refunds: yes, for wrong sizes.

McCall This specialist in luxurious, smart (and expensive) hand-made slippers has beautiful designs in red and blue paisley, navy, black and bottle green velvet brocade, a midnight green damask for men and an Oriental carpet design in black, scarlet and yellow for both men and women. There is also a delicious pair of faux leopardskin slippers. All are lined with quilting and come in a purple bag.

McCall, Meadow House, Chapel Row, Bucklebury, Berkshire RG7 6NU.
Tel: 01734 714426/7.
Price range: £78 to £90. Catalogue free.
Payment: cheque, Access, Visa, Mastercard, Eurocard.
Postage & packing: £3.50 per pair.
Delivery: last Christmas orders 20 November.
Refunds: yes, if returned in 10 days.

Mediterranean Imports Just a range of buttons really, but they have great style. There are six hearts in black, red, yellow, white, blue and green, terracotta swirls like Swiss rolls, white buttons with a line of primary colours and little pottery pigs, teddies, fish and rabbits. Specially for Christmas, pick the round red berries and green holly leaves to alternate down a shirt.

Mediterranean Imports, 105 Lowther Road, Brighton, Sussex BN1 6LH.

Tel: 01273 502954. **Fax:** 01273 701467.

Price range: £10.50 a strip of between 4 and 8. Brochure free.

Payment: cheque.

Postage & packing: included.

Delivery: to be agreed.

Refunds: by arrangement.

Original Raised Belt Co Classic leather belts for either sex are made in red or black with raised centres and ornamental stitching, finished with a brass buckle. The leather is good quality and strong.

The Original Raised Belt Co, 2 Blacksmiths Cottages, East Ashling, Chichester, West Sussex PO18 9AS.

Tel: 01243 575399.

Price range: £25.95 to £28.95. Leaflet free.

Payment: cheque.

Postage & packing: included in UK.

Delivery: 1st class post. Hand-made, therefore limited supply.

Refunds: yes.

See also: Cath Kidston (Home Interest), Boden, Cavenagh, Chuffs, The Dufflecoat Company, G-D-S Shirts, Hawkshead, Peta Flint, James Smith, T.M. Lewin, Spencers Trousers (Men's Clothes), Fortnum & Mason, Harrods, L.L. Bean (General Catalogues), Little Treasures, Rachel Riley (Children's Clothes), Rosie Nieper's funny T-shirts (Teenagers).

MEN'S CLOTHES

I suppose there must be men who enjoy shopping and buying their own clothes – but I have yet to meet one. Men seem to be dressed (with maximum annoyance) by their harassed wives or partners in clothes from Marks & Spencer. Instead, therefore, of reaching compromise solutions between the dark navy cashmere sweater and soft olive shirt you know he ought to have and his choice of grey lambswool and pale cream cotton, it's a good idea to buy as a present what you wanted him to have in the first place. As a general rule, I would go for as luxurious a fabric as I could afford in as plain a style as I could find. Luckily, while cashmere is likely to rise in price, silk is getting both cheaper and easier to wash, cotton ever smarter and softer and tweed more carefully coloured and designed.

New man (does he still exist?) is interested in his clothes (as long as he doesn't have to buy them) and is probably willing to try out new fabrics such as silk, pure linen and cashmere. He might even wear a button-down shirt if pushed, but older men are strongly resistant to change. It is useless buying grandpa a soft-tailored denim jacket to replace his old navy blazer and you will never persuade him to change his Tattersall check Viyella shirt for sand-washed silk or to wear yellow socks instead of grey. Don't try – just buy nicer versions of the same old outfits. The furthest he will go is probably a sporty tie and there are plenty of these in the mail-order catalogues.

If there is a trend in men's clothes at present, it is to dress down. The city suit has not been abandoned but even businessmen are beginning to copy America and are wearing more casual clothes on Friday. One supplier listed here offers special Friday shirts. Shoes are becoming more sporty with hefty ridged soles instead of slippery leather and, as everywhere, fabrics are natural.

Younger men might be interested in classic styles in definitely un-classic colours, an idea spearheaded by the designer Paul Smith. Sports jackets come in raspberry, trousers in pale green, suits in soft orange wool or dark grey denim. Firms like Boden and the American L.L. Bean are at the forefront of these changes and can be relied on to spot new ideas which won't die the death of the kipper tie and flared suit.

When buying clothes as presents for men, do ensure that they can be changed. Where clothes are concerned, even the most sweet-natured man can be dogmatic and can take an irrational dislike to the dark aubergine shirt or custard-colour cashmere you have chosen. Best let them change it back to grey – unless you have secret designs on it yourself.

MEN'S CLOTHES – LISTINGS

Clothes

Aviation Leathercraft Does your man have a secret longing to be Biggles or a Dambuster? Aviation Leathercraft sells those high-collared sheepskin jackets, leather and sheepskin flying helmets and glass-lensed goggles which were *de rigueur* among air aces. They also sell leather jackets worn by Tornado and Harrier pilots. The catalogue is pure fantasy and good for women too.

Aviation Leathercraft, Thruxton Airport, near Andover, Hampshire SP11 8PW.
Tel: 01264 772811. **Fax:** 01264 773102.
Price range: £29 to £345. Send 1st class stamp for catalogue.
Payment: cheque, Access, Barclaycard, Mastercard, Visa, Switch.

Postage & packing: £2.50 helmets and goggles; £8 flying jackets in UK.

Delivery: last orders for Christmas by mid November.

Refunds: yes.

Boden   Very much the smart catalogue for the Cotswold set, and the clothes are just what that set wears for play and just a bit of work. Lots of wool, cotton, cords, silk; outfits colourful but not brash, clothes stylish but comfortable, such as soft natural suede jackets and linen shirts. For men and women of all ages and, new this year, children.

Boden, 4 Pembroke Buildings, Cumberland Park, Scrubs Lane, London NW10 6RE.

Tel: 0181 964 2662. **Fax:** 0181 964 2598.

Price range: £10 to £250. Catalogue free.

Payment: cheque, Access, Mastercard, Visa, Amex, Switch.

Postage & packing: £4, 48-hour service extra.

Delivery: about a week.

Refunds: yes.

Cavenagh   Before the Eighties, you could only get really smart shirts in Jermyn Street but then all the boys in red braces had to have them and mail order came on the scene. This company does a limited range including the genuine wide stripe in yellow or red on a blue background along with some slightly more sombre stripes, herringbones and checks for country wear. There are even piqué dinner shirts and ready-tied or untied black silk bow ties. The normal tie range includes patterns of woodland animals, owls, swans and, for the country again, an English setter. The shirts are in good cotton, the ties in silk.

Cavenagh, 5 The Coda Centre, 189 Munster Road, London SW6 6AW.

Tel: 0171 610 2959. **Fax:** 0171 610 2119.

Price range: £28 to £35 for shirts, £12.50 to £25 for ties. Catalogue free in UK.

Payment: cheque, Visa, Mastercard, Amex.

Postage & packing: £4 up to £75, £6 for more.
Delivery: usually 4 days but allow 28.
Refunds: yes, if returned unworn and unwashed.

Charles Tyrwhitt Jermyn Street quality shirts without the trouble of going to London. In the Eighties, these were wide-striped in strong colours; the Nineties have calmed down. Stripes and checks are generally discreet, colours verge on the pastel. When men want to make statements, they do it with ties and cufflinks and the firm sells jokey animal and vegetable ties and yes/no type cufflinks. There's also good luggage.

Charles Tyrwhitt Shirts, 298-300 Munster Road, London SW6 6BH.
Tel: 0171 386 9900. **Fax:** 0171 386 0027.
Price range: £5 to £120. Catalogue free.
Payment: cheque, Visa, Mastercard, Amex, Diners, Switch, Delta.
Postage & packing: £3.50 per order in UK.
Delivery: last orders 7 working days before Christmas.
Refunds: yes, even when worn.

G-D-S Shirts Do you have a clansman among your friends or relations? This firm will make to order in almost any tartan. There are men's and women's dressing gowns and kimonos, shirts in medium or heavy wool, smoking jackets, waistcoats and even bow ties for men and boys. There are over 700 patterns, in shades from bright modern colours to those copied from tartan buried in a peat bog. As well as heavy and medium weight, there is a delicate lightweight fabric.

G-D-S Shirts, 4 Barrock Street, Thurso, Caithness KW14 7DB.
Tel/Fax: 01847 893197.
Price range: £6 to £145. Brochure free.
Payment: cheque, Access, Mastercard, Visa.
Postage & packing: included.
Delivery: last Christmas orders by mid November.
Refunds: no.

Hawkshead   Based in the Lake District, this firm knows all about rugged weather and countryside and its clothes are designed to beat both. There are boots for serious walking, heavy Fair Isle and Norwegian patterned sweaters in bracken, grey and dark green designed to blend with the country, plus weatherproof jackets and waistcoats. Wool is used for basic scarves and gloves and there's a handy range of wellies and belts. Many items are unisex.

> **Hawkshead**, Main Street, Hawkshead Village, Cumbria LA22 0SW.
> **Tel:** 01539 434000. **Fax:** 01539 431100.
> **Price range:** £5 to £59. Catalogue free.
> **Payment:** cheque, Access, Visa, Mastercard, Delta, Switch.
> **Postage & packing:** £2.95.
> **Delivery:** usually within 7 days but allow 28.
> **Refunds:** yes, if returned in 28 days.

Spencers Trousers   Based in the Pennines, where they know a thing or two about bad weather, this firm is famous for its tough trousers. It specialises in tailored trousers, shorts, plus-twos and plus-fours for women and men in traditional fabrics like moleskin (suede-like heavy cotton), cotton corduroy including pale cream and dark olive, wool and synthetics in checks and tartans and good-looking country tweeds which don't frighten the horses.

> **Spencers**, Friendly Works, Burnley Road, Sowerby Bridge, West Yorkshire HX6 2TL.
> **Tel:** 01422 833020. **Fax:** 01422 839777.
> **Price range:** £55 to £85. Catalogue and swatches free.
> **Payment:** cheque, Access, Visa, Eurocard, Mastercard.
> **Postage & packing:** included.
> **Delivery:** allow 7 days.
> **Refunds:** yes.

T.M. Lewin   One of the best shirtmakers in Jermyn Street, Lewin has recently produced a mail-order list of beautiful men's shirts. There is nothing unconventional about the styles, but the choice of deep French blue in a tiny stripe, soft pink and wide-stripe fabrics in blue and white or blue and yellow is delightful. Blue windowpane, Prince of Wales and gingham checks make the transfer between town and country, as does the button-down-collar Friday Shirt. Also dress shirts and ties, whizz-kid braces patterned with zigzags and gold teddies plus jokey ties and cufflinks, as well as silk and cotton shirts and wraps and chemises for women.

T.M. Lewin & Sons, 106 Jermyn Street, London SW1Y 1AE.
Tel: 0171 930 4291. **Fax:** 0171 839 7791. **E-mail:** lewin.and.sons@bbcnc.org.uk
Price range: £25 to £55. Catalogue free.
Payment: cheque, Access, Amex, Visa, Mastercard, Switch, JCB.
Postage & packing: £1.50 for orders under £35, £4 thereafter.
Delivery: last orders for Christmas 18 December; guaranteed special delivery at extra cost 20 December.
Refunds: by arrangement.

Accessories

Bates Gentlemen's Hatters Though hardly anyone wears a bowler today, for die-hards you can buy a black curly brim one here. Or what about an Anthony Eden-type Homburg, shiny black and grey top hats for celebrations and those glam soft felt hats they wore in Thirties movies? There are wide-brim fedoras, straw boaters and tweed deerstalkers, flat caps and eight-piece caps for open-air motoring. How nice if they make a comeback.

Bates Gentlemen's Hatters, 21a Jermyn Street, St James's, London SW1Y 6HP.
Tel: 0171 734 2722.
Price range: £35 to £295. Catalogue free.
Payment: cheque, Visa, Mastercard, Amex, Access, JCB.
Postage & packing: hats £5.50, caps £3.
Delivery: by return.

Refunds: goods exchanged or credit note given. No refund unless faulty.

Chuffs Matching luggage makes travelling more stylish and regular business travellers will appreciate the range of seven items, all in heavy navy cotton with an emerald green trim and customised initials. The range covers spectacle and cassette cases, shoe bags and washbags, suit and dress covers and easily carried overnight bags. The price includes four initials on each.

Chuffs, Robin Hill, Blyth Bridge, West Linton, Peeblesshire EH46 7DG.
Tel: 01721 752237.
Price range: £6.95 to £29.95. Catalogue free.
Payment: cheque.
Postage & packing: included.
Delivery: allow 14 days.
Refunds: no.

The Dufflecoat Company The same firm also runs The Stockbag Company, The Genuine Panama Hat Company, Norfolk Intrepid – The Ultimate Outdoor Hat and The Norfolk Polar Fleece. All are as described and for men and women (children also for dufflecoats). Coat colours are green, natural, navy and bright red. Stockbags are made of strong canvas in olive, navy or tan, leather trimmed, and range from washbags to the largest size bag allowed as airline hand luggage. The panamas, one which rolls and the others like trilbys, come from Ecuador while the Norfolk hat looks more like an Aussie ranch hat.

Specialist Mail Order Limited, 140 Battersea Park Road, London SW11 4NB.
Tel: 0171 498 8811. **Fax:** 0171 498 0990.
Price range: £24.50 to £129.95. Separate catalogues, all free.
Payment: cheque, Access, Visa, Amex.
Postage & packing: included.

Delivery: despatched in 7 days.
Refunds: yes, if returned in 7 days.

Peta Flint 'Has recaptured the art of fine sock making' says her brochure, and these are truly wondrous socks in three styles. Long, medium and short, they have cable knitting where it counts and are knitted to size in five soft moorland shades in wool, cotton and cashmere. Once you've worn them, you won't want nylon ever again.

Peta Flint, 246 Basford Road, Old Basford, Nottingham NG6 0HY.
Tel: 0115 978 2471. **Fax:** 0115 978 4205.
Price range: £15.50 to £28. Catalogue free.
Payment: cheque, Access, Visa, Eurocard, Mastercard, Delta.
Postage & packing: included.
Delivery: last Christmas orders 1 December.
Refunds: yes.

James Smith & Sons Anyone who has been along London's New Oxford Street will know this umbrella firm's unspoilt Victorian shopfront. Less known is the fact that Gladstone and Lord Curzon bought their brollies here. Today, though, the firm will mail order British business brollies with malacca, whangee or root-nose blackthorn handles, large tartan country umbrellas and elegant women's umbrellas with ornate handles and tassels. It also sells canes, silver-topped sticks and even blackthorn shillelaghs.

James Smith & Sons (Umbrellas) Ltd, Hazelwood House, 53 New Oxford Street, London WC1A 1BL.

Tel: 0171 836 4731.

Price range: £30 to £265. Catalogue free.

Payment: cheque, Visa, Mastercard.

Postage & packing: £2.75 for folding umbrellas and sticks; £7.75 for full-size umbrellas and sticks.

Delivery: despatched within 14 days.

Refunds: by arrangement.

Specials: umbrellas, sticks etc made to order and engraved.

See also: Capella Nova, Cashmere Store, Cocoon, Connolly, Cyrillus, Glenalmond Tweed Company, Higginbotham, Jeremy Law, Kingshill, Lands' End, Margaret Anne Gloves, McCall, Old Town, Racing Green, Shetland Knitwear Associates and Wealth of Nations (Women's Clothes), Rachel Riley (Children's Clothes) and entries in General Catalogues.

JEWELLERY

Buying jewellery as a present may not be as hard as buying clothes but it does require a modicum of observation. Does the recipient prefer gold or silver coloured jewellery? If you're going for costume jewellery it should be recognisable as such and should not be trying to mimic the real thing. And there is not much point in brooches and earrings so discreet they are invisible – what about figurative brooches such as cheerful dogs, weird sea-creatures and exotic safari animals? Why not wear a joke on a lapel?

It's also important to consider the size of the recipient. Earrings, brooches and bracelets should not overpower tiny, birdlike women; equally, strapping Amazons are unlikely to welcome chains so fine they mock a sturdy neck.

I am not assuming that jewellery is the preserve of women only. One firm listed here concentrates on earrings, pendants and brooches in the shape of war planes, helicopters and tanks which I presume are intended for men – and why not? I can't see why it is acceptable to flaunt a signet ring (OK for admirals and the like) but not a warship earring (definitely out of bounds). After all, Tudor kings as well as queens dripped with pearls and diamonds. It's just a trend.

Many of the jewellers listed here work to commission and will design special pieces for you; others make unusual pieces for relatively small amounts of money. If, however, you are treating someone to a really expensive piece, do make sure that it can be returned or exchanged. Alternatively, make sure the recipient really wants it. Getting a dull or inappropriate present which costs little is bad enough; when it costs a bomb, it is infuriating.

JEWELLERY – LISTINGS

Amo, Amas, Amat Andrew Macfarlane has taken the beautiful copperplate writing on 18th- and 19th-century documents as the basis for his etchings on pewter jewellery. His range is simple: large, medium and small earrings and cufflinks the size of a new penny. These are one-offs that you won't find anywhere else.

> **Amo, Amas, Amat**, PO Box 225, Taunton, TA4 1BP.
> **Tel/Fax:** 01823 461926.
> **Price range:** £19.95 to £34.95. Catalogue free.
> **Payment:** cheque, Mastercard, Visa, Delta, Eurocard.
> **Postage & packing:** included in UK.
> **Delivery:** within 7 days if possible.
> **Refunds:** if unworn and returned within a week.

Carol Mather A craft jeweller whose best-selling range is silver models of dogs. They come as pendants, brooches with leads, bracelets of doggy medallions, even earrings. The designs include dalmatians, bull terriers, dachshunds and indeterminate shaggy jobs. They are very modern, witty and distinctive, and bound to be much admired.

Carol Mather, 10a Iliffe Yard, London SE17 3QA.
Tel: 0171 252 7524.
Price range: £48 to £116. Brochure with drawings free.
Payment: cheque, Visa.
Postage & packing: £3.50 to £4 registered post.
Delivery: last Christmas orders at start of December.
Refunds: yes.

Christopher Simpson Cufflinks for the whizz kid, top gun and City slicker. Simpson has ranges of shotgun cartridge cufflinks in shocking pink, orange, bright lemon and scarlet; plus sporting cufflinks of little jockey caps, tennis racquets and boxing gloves. There are piggy, elephant and rhino cufflinks and some patterned like sweetcorn and grapes. You can have them plated in gold or silver or hallmarked sterling silver. Some, especially the fruit and animal cufflinks, would be just as good on women's shirts.

Christopher Simpson, Savernake, 61 Clapham Common Northside, London SW4 9SA.
Tel: 0171 350 1741. **Fax:** 0171 350 2334.
Price range: £5.95 to £55. Catalogue free.
Payment: cheque, Visa, Access.
Postage & packing: £1.50 except shotgun links when cost is included.
Delivery: allow 28 days.
Refunds: by arrangement.

Clivedon Collection Pin badges, tie bar and cufflink collection of every kind of plane you can think of from Airbuses to Zeros, helicopters from Chinooks to Apaches, balloons, parachutes, jeeps, tanks and guns. If you want Harrier jets as earrings, a silver charm of a Mini or a scuba diver pin badge, this is your catalogue. They come gold and silver plated, in coloured enamel or, for the Stealth Bomber, in matt black. Quite fun, really.

The Clivedon Collection, Witham Friary, Frome, Somerset, BA11 5HH.

Tel: 01749 850728. **Fax:** 01749 850729.

Price range: £4.20 to £32 but £10 minimum order. Catalogue free.

Payment: cheque, Visa, Mastercard, Switch.

Postage & packing: £1.50 for orders from £10 to £25, £3 for £26 to £50, £6 for £51 to £100, £10 over £100.

Delivery: 2 days after order if by credit card. Cheques must clear.

Refunds: yes, if damaged and reported in 7 days; no refund on earrings and pendants for health reasons.

Cox & Power Modern jewellery which is both strong and understated. Silver and gold mesh necklaces, plain platinum bands with embedded diamonds and hammered rings in gold and silver work as well with jeans as a party dress. The necklace of matt black onyx beads, interspersed with three tiny gold and diamond pendants, brilliantly updates the style of the great 19th-century Italian jeweller Giuliano.

Cox & Power, 95 Walton Street, London SW3 2HP.

Tel: 0171 589 6335. **Fax:** 0171 589 6334.

Price range: from £75 to £4,250. Catalogue free.

Payment: cheque and all major cards (except JCB).

Postage & packing: £6.50.

Delivery: last Christmas orders by 1st week of December.

Refunds: yes, if returned in original condition within 7 days. No for special orders.

Specials: will design to commission.

Hofmann Trading Co The Icis collection is made in Philadelphia and its earrings, brooches and pendants are notable for using coloured metals as though they were red, natural and white gold, enamelled in soft pastels. The jewellery piles alligators on lizards on tortoises on dragonflies; or musical instruments hang from a pair of clarinets. There are piles of hearts for lovers and earrings of dangling elephants. Definitely costume jewellery, the quirkier pieces have undoubted charm.

Hofmann Trading Co, 89 Barnhill, Wembley Park, Middlesex HA9 9LN.
Tel: 0181 904 4716. **Fax:** 0181 908 5083.
Price range: £15 to £35. Catalogue £2.50, refundable with purchase.
Payment: cheque or postal order.
Postage & packing: £2.50.
Delivery: immediate despatch.
Refunds: yes.

C.N.A. Ruff Signet rings are carved in reverse relief to stamp on sealing wax but Ruff can also create rings in full relief (the pattern proud of the surface) and their new technique of 'illusion carving' which looks like etching. As well as working from heraldry, the firm will create jewellery according to people's birth signs, their Chinese year signs, with birthstones or to celebrate wedding anniversaries from paper to diamond. Cufflinks, watch-chain pendants and tie pins can also be custom-made. Most work is done in gold.

C.N.A. Ruff, 9 Solent Way, Gosport, Hampshire PO12 2NR.
Tel/Fax: 01705 580359.
Price range: starts at £100. Catalogue free.
Payment: cheque, banker's draft. 10% deposit required.
Postage & packing: included in UK.
Delivery: Christmas orders by 1 November.
Refunds: no.

Sarah Parker-Eaton Inspiration for this craft jeweller comes from deep sea animals, their fins and tentacles, segmented bodies and pop eyes. Sarah doesn't make botanical copies but creates weird beasts which are both jokey and sinister. She uses gold and silver, oxidising the silver for shade and contrast.

Sarah Parker-Eaton, 33 Honeygate, Luton, Bedfordshire LU2 7EP.
Tel: 01582 431185.
Price range: £24 to £400. Catalogue £1.
Payment: cheque.
Postage & packing: included.

Delivery: last orders for Christmas 1 December. Generally a maximum of 4 weeks.

Refunds: by arrangement.

Specials: all made to order. Discuss with Sarah.

Timothy Lukes A silversmith with an up-to-date range of jewellery for men and women. Tie clips, key rings and cufflinks in the shape of dolphins, hammerhead sharks, whales and mermaids; for women there are nautilus and starfish earrings, octopus, turtle and seahorse brooches, even killer whales and great white sharks. Recent designs are link necklaces with lethal puffer fish, angel fish and octopuses. Plain silver works well in these handsome sea creature shapes.

Timothy Lukes, PO Box 15, St Ives, Cornwall TR26 2YD.

Tel: 01850 471194/01736 793168.

Price range: £15.50 to £160. Catalogue free.

Payment: cheque, postal order.

Postage & packing: £1.50 recorded delivery.

Delivery: last Christmas orders mid November as everything is hand-made.

Refunds: yes.

Specials: any item may also be made in gold. Ask for prices.

See also: top grade jewellery from Fortnum & Mason, Harrods (General Catalogues) and Johnny Loves Rosie for funky stuff (Teenagers).

Chapter Three

HOUSE AND GARDEN

ART AND REPLICAS

It wasn't until the prices of antiques and paintings soared to ridiculous levels that replicas became respectable. Before that, most people wouldn't have dreamt of having fakes around the place. If, however, your friends and relations want their houses to look like the Roman interiors of Pompeii, the 18th-century drawing rooms of the English country house or a cosy farmer's cottage of the 19th century, there are now lots of good repro pieces you can give them.

Rising to the challenge, both new companies and old museums are busily reproducing their wares. Though conservation now dictates that few genuine pieces can be put through the moulding process, many museums have Victorian cast

copies of Egyptian, Greek and Roman antiquities which do just as well and the British Museum has recently brought back a mail-order cast service. Other firms, not bound by conservators, may use objects they have bought or already own. This is the case with Ancestral Collections, which has reproductions of furniture and ornaments from several stately homes.

Modern techniques have made the reproduction of pictures both easier and cheaper. The British Museum offers a very good copy of a Rembrandt drawing of an elephant, for instance. It is generally worth sticking to copies of sketches, prints and drawings rather than oils because they reproduce so much better, being flat on the paper. Otherwise, both metal and pottery copies are lifelike because their ageing can be reproduced too.

This is not the case with wood, which is why reproduction furniture is not such a good idea if accuracy is what you're after.

When you buy any reproduction, check that it really is cheaper than the genuine article. This is often not the case with furniture and certainly not with silver. Check, too, that a real work of art is outside your budget. Abbott & Holder, overleaf, has a huge range of watercolours and drawings by reputable 18th- and 19th-century artists at under £100 apiece which, unlike copies, will keep, if not increase, their price.

Trends in replicas follow trends in antique prices. When the genuine object cannot be bought at a reasonable price yet is in high demand, replicas will start to appear. This is the case with naive art, which has virtually disappeared from the antique shops (and is now copied by Rocket & Rabbit), and the little heraldic keyrings from Burghley House, which never appeared in the shops in the first place. Prints will be a major feature, as will copies of watercolours of house interiors. Indian antiquities will join Egyptian and Greek and copies of Clarice Cliff's Bizarre pottery are already for sale.

ART AND REPLICAS – LISTINGS

Abbott & Holder Not many people know that you can buy an Old Master by post but this company, with a gallery near the British Museum, sends out a regular list of oils, water-colours, sketches and prints to their devoted customers (like me). There may be an oil by Bloomsbury artist Duncan Grant, a drawing by Pre-Raphaelite artist Burne-Jones, or cartoons from the likes of Phil May or Vicky. Obviously, you can't buy pictures unseen (though the list gives brilliant descriptions) and A&H will send on approval if you give a credit card number in advance. Attributions are guaranteed. Money back and a box of chocolates if attribution fails.

> **Abbott & Holder**, 30 Museum Street, London WC1A 1LH.
> **Tel:** 0171 637 3981. **Fax:** 0171 631 0575.
> **Price range:** £25 to £5,000. Free lists sent every 7 weeks.
> **Payment:** credit card, except Amex.
> **Postage & packing:** included.
> **Delivery:** by arrangement.
> **Refunds:** yes, if returned in 2 days, p&p paid both ways. Credit card in advance.
> **Specials:** framing service.

Ancestral Collections A collection from the great houses of Britain including Blair Castle, Burghley, Knebworth and Elton Hall. Castle Howard chips in with a loo brush holder in an artillery shell carrier, Burghley has a coronetted key ring and Blair a wall bracket held up by a cherub given by Queen Victoria. The selection is high quality and exclusive to the firm.

> **Ancestral Collections Ltd.**, The Old Corn Store, Burghley Courtyard, Stamford, Lincolnshire PE9 3JY.
> **Tel:** 01780 482522. **Fax:** 01780 65305.
> **Price range:** £10.99 to £400. Catalogue free.
> **Payment:** cheque, banker's draft, Visa, Access, Mastercard, Switch.
> **Postage & packing:** depends on weight.

Delivery: last Christmas orders 9 December overseas, 17 December for UK.

Refunds: yes, within 10 days, by recorded delivery and with original packing.

Art Room Part of the Past Times stable of mail-order companies, this one specialises in objects inspired by great artists. These vary from straight reproductions of prints, drawings and paintings, like Charles Rennie Mackintosh's architectural drawings and Magritte's surrealist Son of Man painting, to umbrellas printed with Caillebotte's painting of a rainy Parisian day and a melamine tray with Man Ray's photograph 'Violin d'Ingres'. There are books, scarves and hangings along with a whole section of animals in art from Egyptian cats to Dürer's hare. You should find presents here for any adult.

Art Room, Witney, Oxfordshire OX8 6BH.

Tel: 01993 770444. **Fax:** 01995 700749.

Price range: £5 to £600. Catalogue free.

Payment: cheque, postal order, Access, Eurocard, Visa, Mastercard, Amex, diners, JCB, Delta, Switch.

Postage & packing: £2.95 under £30, £3.50 over. Next day express £4.95 extra.

Delivery: 7 days.

Refunds: yes.

British Museum Company A selection of the most popular replicas from the British Museum shop. Egyptian pieces are, deservedly, top sellers. There are tiny figures of jerboas, hippos and cats in the typical blue earthenware, copies of bronze cats (the thirteen-inch high Gayer-Anderson cat at over £350 is quite stunning). The 12th-century Lewis chess set from the Hebrides is world famous. There are replicas of Greek sculpture and casts which include bits of Michelangelo's David. The quality is superb and many make outstanding decorative pieces.

British Museum Company Mail Order, Unit A, Chettisham Business Park, Ely, Cambridgeshire CB6 1RY.

Tel/Fax: 01353 6668400.

Price range: £6.95 to £550. Catalogue free.

Payment: cheque, Mastercard, Visa, Amex, Access, Diners, Eurocard, JCB.

Postage & packing: detailed in catalogue.

Delivery: last Christmas order in UK 11 December.

Refunds: return slip included in delivery.

CCA Galleries

Prints – etchings, lithographs and silk screens – are the firm's stock in trade. The chosen artists are modern but acceptably so (ie not fountains of chocolate and mud footprints). There are English landscapes by artists inspired by John Piper, Annora Spence's naive men, dogs and wheelbarrows in country fields and prints evoking summer holidays on the beach, island and Mediterranean along with still lifes and rather chocolate-boxy nudes. There are also one-off paintings and sculptures.

CCA Galleries, Freepost WD 2823, 8 Dover Street, London W1E 7JZ.

Tel: 0171 499 6701.

Price range: £70 to £3,500. Catalogue free.

Payment: cheque, Access, Visa.

Postage & packing: unframed £8, framed £15.

Delivery: unframed, last GPO Christmas posting date; framed allow at least 3 weeks.

Refunds: everything sent on 45 days' approval. Return within that time.

Debden Security Printing

This is the firm which makes our bank notes and, as a sideline, uses the designs to make a range of prints, paperweights and books on banknotes. The engravings of famous people which appear on our notes – Wellington, Newton, Dickens – are made into prints while the old white fiver (those were the great days of bank notes) turns up in a paperweight. I wouldn't bother too much about the framed bank notes, though.

Debden Security Printing Ltd, Langston Road, Loughton, Essex IG10 3BR

Tel: 0181 508 0045. Credit card hotline: 0181 502 5849.

Fax: 0181 532 0933.

Price range: £2.95 to £235. Catalogue free by telephone or Freepost RM1010.

Payment: cheque, Access, Visa, Mastercard.

Postage & packing: included.

Delivery: within 28 days.

Refunds: if returned in 10 days.

Handmade Designs
Naive art from America and Britain made into prints, wall plaques and cards. Most designs are those square-ended cows, rectangular sheep and pigs like well-stuffed sausages. The cockerels and shire horses are slightly more lifelike. The American pictures also include well-fed cats on chequerboard floors, goats and even a hedgehog family. There are replica birds' eggs and trout flies in specimen cases with old copperplate names and 'faux plates' in MDF designed like old meat plates to hang on the wall.

Handmade Designs, 19 Wilcot Road, Pewsey, Wiltshire SN9 5EH.

Tel: 01672 562640 **Fax:** 01672 563015.

Price range: £1.25 to £140. Catalogue free.

Payment: cheque.

Postage & packing: £3.50.

Delivery: last Christmas orders 13 December.

Refunds: replacement of goods only.

Imperial War Museum
Posters from the Great War (Kitchener pointing – a great image) and postcards from World War II plus ration book bags and packets full of documents of, for example, the Western Front or Normandy Landings. Fascinating and evocative for those who lived through it. There are also books and cassettes on the two wars.

Imperial War Museum Mail Order, Duxford Airfield, Cambridgeshire CB2 4QR.

Tel: 01223 835000 ext. 245. **Fax:** 01223 837267.

Price range: £1.80 to £100. Catalogue free.

Payment: cheque, Access, Visa, Mastercard.

Postage & packing: £1.50 for orders to £7.50, thereafter add 20% to cost.

Delivery: last Christmas order 10 December.

Refunds: yes, if returned with packing and documents within 7 days.

Minton Archive Print Collection

The pottery celebrated its bi-centenary a few years ago and its extraordinary archive of drawings from day one came to light. Minton cups have since turned up on ties and chair fabric and, now, in prints. The meticulously drawn shapes and patterns, carefully hand-coloured, have been taken mostly from the Victorian period. They can be bought framed or unframed.

The Minton Archive Print Collection, 78 Walcot Street, Bath BA1 5BG.

Tel: 01225 422909. **Fax:** 01225 422910.

Price range: £49 to £226. Catalogue free.

Payment: cheque or major credit cards.

Postage & packing: included in UK.

Delivery: allow 28 days. Editions are limited to 850 copies.

Refunds: no.

Museums & Galleries Christmas Collection

A small catalogue of gifts inspired by art rather than reproducing it. William Morris's designs are available as a tapestry kit, for instance, or there's a silk scarf with patterns from early manuscripts in the British Library. The superb cards and gift wrapping are both traditional and unusual, using details from Old Masters, old manuscripts and tapestries.

Museums & Galleries Marketing Ltd, Manor Furlong, Frome, Somerset BA11 4RL.

Tel: 01373 462165. **Fax:** 01373 462367.

Price range: £2.50 to £55. Catalogue free.

Payment: cheque, Visa, Access, Mastercard, Eurocard, Amex, Switch.

Postage & packing: free in UK.

Delivery: last Christmas orders by 10 December.

Refunds: yes, if returned in 14 days.

National Galleries of Scotland The National Gallery in Edinburgh owns the famous Raeburn portrait of a skating clergyman and he turns up on cards, as well as objects like fridge magnets. Other ranges include fine white china with 18th-century prints of chairs and, from the Gallery of Modern Art, weird ideas like handbags made of US numberplates and belts ornamented with beer bottle tops.

National Galleries of Scotland, Unit 24, Beaverhall Road, Edinburgh EH7 4JW.
Tel: 0131 558 3614. **Fax:** 0131 558 9972.
Price range: £2 to £120. Catalogue free.
Payment: cheque, Visa, Access, Mastercard, Amex.
Postage & packing: full details in catalogue.
Delivery: last orders 1 week before Christmas.
Refunds: yes.

The National Trust Most of us are familiar with Trust shops and the mail-order range includes their most popular items. The range is very mixed but the best gifts are those which are replicas of objects found in the houses. The 'Clive for Ever Huzza', an 18th-century electioneering mug and jug in black and pink, are charming as is the replica Leeds creamware. There are good picnic baskets, creels and garden baskets too.

The National Trust (Enterprises) Ltd, PO Box 101, Melksham, Wiltshire SN12 8EA.
Tel: 01225 705676. **Fax:** 01225 706209.
Price range: £3 to £95. Catalogue free.
Payment: cheque, Access, Visa, Mastercard, Amex, Diners, Switch, Delta.
Postage & packing: £1.95 under £15; £3.95 over £15.
Delivery: last orders for Christmas 7 December.
Refunds: yes, if notified within 14 days.

The National Trust for Scotland There's lots of tartan, whisky, clootie dumplings and the like but few replicas. Also featured are objects inspired by Charles Rennie Mackintosh, early board games and early golfing illustrations on boxes and clocks.

The National Trust for Scotland Trading Company Ltd, 5 Charlotte Square, Edinburgh EH2 4DU.
Tel: 0131 243 9393. **Fax:** 0131 243 9302.
Price range: £1.20 to £50. Catalogue free.
Payment: cheque, Access, Visa, Mastercard, Amex, Switch.
Postage & packing: £3.50.
Delivery: allow 28 days.
Refunds: by arrangement.

The Obelisk Collection   Based on antiques and buildings connected with the Irish Georgian Society, this collection has some beautiful objects ranging from a pair of bookends based on an 18th-century casino designed by Chambers to brilliant lemon yellow, black and gold crockery after a print room at Castletown. For children there are faux-ivory old-fashioned hairbrushes and combs, initialled on request, and sumptuous velvet crackers which can be refilled.

The Obelisk Collection, 41 Kensington Square, London W8 5HP.
Tel: 0171 938 2628. **Fax:** 0171 938 4360.
Price range: 70p to £1,349.99. Catalogue free.
Payment: Visa, Amex, Mastercard, Eurocard.
Postage & packing: £3.95 per item per address.
Delivery: allow 28 days.
Refunds: yes, if damaged.
Specials: engraving on silver and faux ivory. Gift wrapping.

Past Times   This is the original mail-order repro service, a very slick marketing operation which has good ideas if you pick carefully. The presents are set out by period, from Roman, Viking and Medieval to 1996's William Morris centenary and a collection inspired by Monet's garden. Some objects are naff but the Victorian auricula collection of six of the fancy perennials and the Victorian lady's straw hat are charming, while the Gothic gargoyle bookends would suit teenagers who are into today's Gothic look. I like the blue glass spiral candlestick, based on a Roman design, too.

Past Times, Witney, Oxfordshire OX8 6BH.
Tel: 01993 770440. **Fax:** 01993 700749.
Price range: £5 to £600. Catalogue free.
Payment: cheque, Access, Eurocard, Visa, Mastercard, Amex, JCB, Diners, postal order, Delta, Switch.
Postage & packing: £2.95 for orders under £30, £3.50 for orders over £30. Next day service £4.95 extra.
Delivery: Last orders for Christmas mid December,
Refunds: yes

Rocket & Rabbit Since naive art of the 19th century has hit the price roof, this firm reproduces the more charming pictures of the period. There are serious children accompanied by large, friendly dogs, little girls in frilly dresses carrying bunches of flowers, luscious bowls of fruit and nuts with birds and insects and charming dog and cat portraits. Each picture is given a special glaze to age it. Because naive artists tended to use thin paint, these reproductions are very lifelike and look best hung in a group of two or three.

Rocket & Rabbit, The Engine Shed, Ashburton Industrial Estate, Ross-on-Wye, Herefordshire HR9 7BW.
Tel: 01989 566797/563015. **Fax:** 01989 768172.
Price range: £27 to £94. Catalogue free.
Payment: cheque, Visa, Access, Mastercard.
Postage & packing: quoted at time of order.
Delivery: 7 to 10 days. Christmas orders by first week of December.
Refunds: normal terms.

See also: Classic Car Art (Enthusiasms).

HOME INTEREST

Fashion writers often say that you should keep an eye on the windows of the smartest clothes shops to know what's really going on. The same applies to interior style – look at the windows or, better still, the mail-order catalogues sent out by the top firms.

A theme which currently runs throughout such catalogues (and throughout the clothes, food, gardening and jewellery catalogues for that matter) is concern for the environment. Shells, pebbles, twigs and berries turn up over and over again with assurances that they are gathered from sustainable sources. Animal patterns are common – elephants and rare breed pigs, for example, travel from T-shirts to earrings to cushions to toys.

The use of natural fabrics is popular. Firms are at pains to point out they are using vegetable, not chemical, dyes. Weaves are deliberately lumpy to indicate hand-weaving and tiny seeds appear in cotton and linen (though the role of silkworms is unmentionable in silk). Animal and farmyard scenes and nostalgic 18th- and 19th-century toiles are popular as patterns.

Nostalgia is the mood of the moment. Some companies hark back to 18th-century Sweden and America; others turn to Edwardian country house kitchens and there's a strong feeling for the Thirties and Forties with Dualit toasters, battleship fridges and pinnies. Even the firms which are promoting new design use recycled, corrugated cardboard for clocks and storage boxes while objects from vases to clocks seem to be sprouting horns in the manner of Philip Starck.

Interior design is very fashionable at the moment and presents for the house are therefore most acceptable. Do, however, check which style the recipient likes. A minimalist will not thank you for a toile de jouy cushion; an 18th-century Swedish fanatic will be at a loss with a brushed aluminium vase with horns.

There is a range of useful books on house style. Some tell you how to use paint or sewing techniques (not worth giving to the rich or unhandy), others detail areas of design like country kitchens, Caribbean interiors or Irish vernacular furniture. Or consider giving a magazine subscription. *House and Garden* is aimed at those who look for clean traditional style with a twist, look to *World of Interiors* for international surprises, *Elle Decoration* is for young modernists. Foreign publications are harder to track down but I recommend *American Architectural Digest* (and its Italian sister *AD*), *Town & Country* and *Martha Stewart Living* and the French *Maison et Jardin*.

HOME INTEREST – LISTINGS

After Noah This firm, which has a shop in Islington, North London, sells a mixture of modern and 1920s items and is in the forefront of wacky design. They went mail order due to popular demand and, last Christmas, the catalogue included items such as resin frames, an eggcup and tiny cruet in a tin and a houseware tin including oven cloth, teatowel, candles, olive oil soap, string bag and a washing-up brush – all in traditional materials. Not to everyone's taste on Christmas day, but certainly to mine. This year promises a larger selection.

After Noah, 121 Upper Street, London N1 1QP.
Tel: 0171 359 4281.
Price range: £7 to £50. Catalogue free.
Payment: cheque, Visa, Delta, Mastercard, Amex.
Postage & packing: £3.50 for 1 item; £6.50 for more.

Delivery: Christmas orders by last GPO posting date.
Refunds: by arrangement.

Annie Cole Traditional Hand Knitting Remember those chunky, bumpy bedspreads hand-knitted for old cottage beds? Annie Cole now recreates them in hand-knitted cotton on fine needles. The technique is called white work and mixes textured and lacy stitches so the pattern is in the knitting, not the colour. All are monochrome and generally white or ecru. You can buy the spreads, shawls, cushion and cot covers in kit form or ready-made. Patterns have lovely names like the architectural Acanthus, lacy Canterbury Bells and heavily textured Garden Plot.

Annie Cole Traditional Hand Knitting, 73 Princes Way, Wimbledon, London SW19 6HY.

Tel: 0181 788 8786. **Fax:** 0181 785 3601.

Price range: £1.95 to £673. Send 4 2nd class stamps for catalogue.

Payment: cheque, Access or Visa. Deposit on ready-mades.

Postage & packing: £3.55 under £100, £5.85 over £100, £6.85 over £200.

Delivery: allow 28 days but normally in a week for kits. Ready-mades up to 3 months.

Refunds: full if kit unopened.

Anta Way north of Inverness, Anta makes its own ranges of original stoneware tartan-painted Ballone crockery, named after the owner's castle, a collection of softly coloured throws using their cleverly recoloured tartan sets and a new children's collection, Antanimals. The rabbit mug, ears and whiskers one side, scut and back legs the other, is great. I use their Ballone ware myself − it goes from Aga or oven to the table without problems and the shapes mould to the hand.

Anta, Fearn, Tain, Ross IV20 1XW.

Tel: 01862 832477. **Fax:** 01862 832616.

Price range: £6 to £65. Brochures free.

Payment: cheque and all credit cards except Amex.

Postage & packing: by weight.
Delivery: Christmas orders by end November.
Refunds: yes.

Bobbins Old-fashioned table and bedlinen revived. Fine cro-
cheted huckaback towels for guests, white woven bedspreads,
lace tray cloths and simple linen union or cotton. When you
use these natural fabrics you will appreciate how much more
pleasant they are than the synthetics which nearly replaced
them.

Bobbins, 24 Bridge Street, Chertsey, Surrey KT16 8JN.
Tel/Fax: 01932 560479.
Price range: £1 to £300. Catalogue free.
Payment: cheque, Visa, Mastercard, Eurocard, Access, Delta.
Postage & packing: £3 for orders over £50, £6 over £100. Huge orders free.
Delivery: usually 1 week, never more than 28 days.
Refunds: yes, if returned quickly.

Bombay Duck Ethnic/modern look for the home with zebra
and cowhide style cushions in black and white, mercury glass,
hundi lamps and a range of anodised aluminium in red, blue,
green and gold from colanders to trays and beakers. Curly steel
furniture of the sort you see in French shops is made into
tables, chairs, shelves and dressers. Stylish and fun.

Bombay Duck, 16 Malton Road, London W10 5UP.
Tel: 0181 964 8882. **Fax:** 0181 964 8883.
Price range: 45p to £1,500. Catalogue £2.50, refundable with order.
Payment: cheque, Visa, Access.
Postage & packing: 10% for orders under £50, free thereafter.
Delivery: last orders for Christmas 14 December.
Refunds: yes.

Brixton Pottery Victorian spongeware – pottery decorated
with shaped sponges – has recently made a welcome reappear-
ance, and Brixton creates the true mix of naive style and

sophisticated colour. Dark olive and navy grapes and vines twine round a bowl, brown snails slither though ochre grass, blue galleons sail spotty seas. Each year sees new patterns and 1996's include a shaggy lurcher dog, mice and nibbled cheese and a formal basket of fruit. Because the method and colour range is consistent, these mugs, jugs, teapots and bowls mix and match neatly.

Brixton Pottery, Hatton Gardens, Kington, Herefordshire HR5 3RB.

Tel: 01544 230700. **Fax:** 01544 231600.

Price range: £7 to £30. Send SAE for catalogue.

Payment: cheque, Visa, Mastercard, Switch.

Postage & packing: 10% on order.

Delivery: last Christmas orders by September.

Refunds: yes, if broken and fragments returned.

Cargo The firm now runs its own printing workshop in Northern Rajasthan where wood blocks up to fifty years old are used to create fabrics, cushions and bedspreads to its own colour mixes and designs. However, patterns are traditional ones used for the first chintzes that came to Britain from India – stylised lotuses, sunflowers, birds, stars and stripes. The colours are bright but controlled such as indigo and pale blue, vermilion and green, blue and turquoise. Because these fabrics are as old as the English country house look itself, they translate perfectly well to this country.

Cargo Furnishings, 23 Market Place, Cirencester, Gloucestershire GL7 2NX.

Tel: 01285 652175. **Fax:** 01285 644827.

Price range: £1.75 to £85. Catalogue free.

Payment: cheque, postal order, Access, Visa, Mastercard, Amex, Connect, Delta, JCB.

Postage & packing: £2.50 postage up to £30, £4.25 to £100 by overnight carrier, over £100 free.

Delivery: last orders for Christmas by 30 November. Generally sent within a week.

Refunds: by arrangement.

Specials: gift service.

Cath Kidston A small range from a bright new designer. Cath has used three of her own designed traditional fabrics and papers – Rose Gingham in blue, green and pink; Fernleaf, a gentle all-over pattern and Bathtime, a 1950s mix of flannel, sponge, bathbrush etc – to create a series of coordinated items for the home. The Fernleaf range has boxfiles, portfolios and notepads, Rose gingham is made into aprons, bedlinen, oil cloth and Bathtime is – unsurprisingly – for the bathroom, including robes, flannels, towels and mats. Buy something to mix and match as a present every year.

> **Cath Kidston Ltd**, 8 Clarendon Cross, London W11 4AP.
> **Tel:** 0171 221 4000. **Fax:** 0171 229 1992.
> **Price range:** £4.50 to £125. Catalogue free.
> **Payment:** postal order, cheque, Visa, Access.
> **Postage & packing:** £3.50 on orders up to £20; £5.50 over £20.
> **Delivery:** within 7 days; if later, they will phone.
> **Refunds:** if notified in 3 days.

Ciel Decor This company sells those brilliantly coloured Provençal cottons which lift the heart in dreary December. They also sell goods made up in the fabrics such as washbags, lavender bags and cushions. From Provence, too, come scented and vegetable soaps, flavoured olive oils and a Vaucluse pot pourri.

> **Ciel Decor**, 187 New King's Road, London SW6 4SW.
> **Tel:** 0171 731 0444. **Fax:** 0171 731 0788.
> **Price range:** £7.95 to £32.90. Catalogue £2.95.
> **Payment:** cheque, Access, Visa, Mastercard.
> **Postage & packing:** £6.95.
> **Delivery:** last Christmas orders 18 December.
> **Refunds:** no, but swatches sent in advance.

Cloakrooms The Americans call these, more aptly, mud rooms and this firm makes accessories for them. There are racks to hold waders, wellies, overshoes and tennis racquets, hat and coat stands, rows of pegs and a gadget to pull off muddy boots. Anyone who has lived in the country in December will know their value. Roller towels and rails, wine racks and doormats with black or red animal silhouettes are also available.

Cloakrooms, Dodbrooke House, Kingsbridge, Devon TQ7 1NW.
Tel/Fax: 01548 853583.
Price range: £3.95 to £110. Catalogue free.
Payment: cheque, Visa, Mastercard.
Postage & packing: each itemised in brochure.
Delivery: last Christmas orders 18 December.
Refunds: yes.

Cologne & Cotton Everyone who visits Cologne & Cotton's shops raves about the pretty bedlinen, coat hangers, delicious scents and soaps from France and the general charm of the styling. The cotton waffle towels, slippers and bath robes, the white lacy pillows and the jacquard tea towels patterned in pastel flowers, fruits and cherubs are luscious presents for long-lasting enjoyment.

Cologne & Cotton, 74 Regent Street, Leamington Spa, Warwickshire CV32 4NS.
Tel: 01926 332573. **Fax:** 01926 332575.
Price range: £1.75 to £200. Catalogue free.
Payment: cheque, Visa, Access, Mastercard, Amex.
Postage & packing: £2.50 under £30, £4.50 to £150, free thereafter.
Delivery: by 48-hour Parcel Force.
Refunds: yes.
Specials: awkward sizes to order.

Damask This company sells really pretty ranges of embroidered bedlinen, smocked nighties, patchwork quilts in pink and cream or rose chintz, botanical specimens embroidered on cushions and a range of napkins embroidered with tiny leeks, carrots and peas. These make collectable presents over several years.

Damask, Unit 7, Sulivan Enterprise Centre, Sulivan Road, London SW6 3DJ.
Tel: 0171 731 3470. **Fax:** 0171 384 2358.
Price range: £1.95 to £410. Catalogue £2.50, refundable on orders over £25.
Payment: cheque, Visa, Access.
Postage & packing: £3 for orders under £100, £6 over £100.
Delivery: allow 28 days but usually within a week.
Refunds: yes, if returned in 2 weeks.

Direct Import Ceramics made in Portugal and Italy include charming lemon and blue Siena pottery and other splashier patterns which are more suited to picnics and rustic meals. In complete contrast, they also have a huge range of elegant Limoges porcelain boxes painted with flowers, botanical specimens and insects. There are others shaped like dogs, turkeys, frogs and a wonderful range of fruit and vegetables such as garlic, broad beans, bananas. Though these boxes have very little use, they are eminently collectable.

Direct Import, Attlepin Farm, Chipping Campden, Gloucestershire GL55 6PP.
Tel: 01386 841923. **Fax:** 01386 841937.
Price range: £1.80 to £95. Catalogue free.
Payment: cheque, postal order, Amex, Mastercard, Visa, Access, Barclaycard.
Postage & packing: £3.95. Limoges boxes free. £5 extra for 24-hour delivery.
Delivery: usually within a week.
Refunds: if returned in 30 days.

DWCD Deborah Reyner moved from fashion to importing natural buttons from Indonesia. This led to ranges of drawer sachets and lavender bags, embroidered cushions in pale olive, old rose cushions and others in cream and white calico embroidered with tiny pockets, buttons and shells. They are modern in conception but have a timeless, subtle beauty.

DWCD, PO Box 5607, London W9 2WR.
Tel: 0171 266 3894.

Price range: £5 to £65. Send A4 SAE 2 x 25p stamps for catalogue.
Payment: cheque, Access, Visa.
Postage & packing: at cost.
Delivery: 14 days but check near Christmas.
Refunds: yes, if returned in 14 days.

Elizabeth Bradley Designs This range of needlework kits in charming Victorian designs, generally on a black background, includes botanical patterns which fill the canvas with daisies, pansies and hollyhocks, often with an added butterfly. There's an animal series of parrots, pugs, a dalmatian on a footstool and naive elephants and lions as well as a Gloucester Old Spot sow and piglets, two fat Suffolk lambs, a Suffolk Punch heavy horse with a hound and a Shorthorn ox. I especially like the Beasts of the Field, taken from Victorian primitive farm paintings. These are excellent designs in subtle colours and there are tiny kits for beginners and travellers.

Elizabeth Bradley Designs Ltd, 1 West End, Beaumaris, Anglesey, North Wales LL58 8BD.
Tel: 01248 811055. **Fax:** 01248 811118.
Price range: £18 to £62. Catalogue free.
Payment: cheque, Visa, Mastercard, Switch, Eurocard, Access.
Postage & packing: included.
Delivery: last orders for Christmas 19 December.
Refunds: if returned unused, in good condition, within 14 days.

Elizabeth Eaton This Chelsea shop stuffed with delightful and useful objects for the home now has a small mail-order catalogue of favourites. The current brochure (out in October) includes stripped willow racks for cheese, fruit or bread and a willow cloche to keep flies from cheeses while they breathe (that's the cheese). I love the little bathing hut money boxes, painted with seaside scenes. The firm will custom-make pleated lampshades which make thoughtful presents.

Elizabeth Eaton, 85 Bourne Street, London SW1W 8HF.

Tel: 0171 730 2262. **Fax:** 0171 730 7294.

Price range: under £100. Catalogue free.

Payment: cheque, Visa, Access.

Postage & packing: each itemised in catalogue.

Delivery: allow 3 weeks before Christmas for last orders.

Refunds: yes, if genuine cause for complaint.

Elmwood Trading Co

Elmwood Trading Co A 'Green' company which uses recycled denim and other fibres with added hemp, grown without pesticide or fertiliser. Using traditional spinning from old textile machines in West Yorkshire, the throws and cushions, in soft indigo, grey and natural checks, handle like rough silk. Other ranges are expected soon.

Elmwood Trading Co, Elmwood House, 11 Bath Street, Dewsbury, West Yorkshire WF13 2JT.

Tel: 01924 456743.

Price range: £20 to £70. Leaflet free.

Payment: cheque.

Postage & packing: included.

Delivery: last Christmas orders by 1st week December.

Refunds: yes.

Farmer John Quilts

Farmer John Quilts In Wales, teased wool is traditionally used for quilts and duvets rather than feathers. It is just as light, good for asthmatics and cheaper to produce. Sally Judd makes everything by hand on her farm using hand-washed wool. There are cot duvets for babies and chair duvets for the old, covered in cotton prints or, by arrangement, your own fabric.

Farmer John Quilts, Gaer Farm, Cwmyoy, Abergavenny, Gwent NP7 7NE.

Tel: 01873 890345.

Price range: £38 to £135. Catalogue free.

Payment: cheque.

Postage & packing: £2.50 for small sizes, £5 for large.

Delivery: allow 2 to 3 weeks. Last orders for Christmas, 5 December as supply is limited.

Refunds: if returned in 10 days, unused.

A Feast of Frames This company sells photo frames to suit all tastes. I like the maple veneer with several slots for family portraits inspired by Victorian frames and Nina Campbell's frame in gold metal like a tassle border. There are self-adhesive montage frames for an ever-changing set of snaps and even fridge magnet frames with designs of Scotties, golfers and musical instruments. There are also good photo albums and fabric noticeboards.

> **A Feast of Frames,** 17 Manchuria Road, London SW11 6AF.
> **Tel/Fax:** 0171 738 9632.
> **Price range:** £4.50 to £95. Catalogue free.
> **Payment:** cheque, Access, Mastercard, Visa.
> **Postage & packing:** £2 on orders to £20, £3.50 between £20 and £85, free thereafter.
> **Delivery:** allow 28 days but phone in emergency and they'll try to help.
> **Refunds:** yes, if returned in 10 days.

Friars Goose Throughout Spain and Portugal, you see tiles used for decorative house numbers and names and for street names. This firm imports frost-resistant tiles from Spain. With blue and yellow decorated borders, they come in all letters and numbers. As well as addresses, they could be made into plaques with a friend's name or memorable date.

> **Friars Goose Ltd,** 52 Sand Street, Longbridge Deverill, Warminster, Wiltshire BA12 7DS.
> **Tel/Fax:** 01985 840991.
> **Price range:** £1.50 to £2.95 each. Catalogue free.
> **Payment:** cheque.
> **Postage & packing:** by arrangement.
> **Delivery:** last Christmas orders by 15 December.
> **Refunds:** yes.

Funky Stuff There's no reason why glasses should have straight stems. These glasses, in matt sky blue, transparent day-glo orange, purple and red and a soft sea-washed green, all come with wobbly stems. Others are printed with giant carrots and sunflowers, seahorses and cacti.

Funky Stuff Ltd, 613b Fulham Road, London SW6 5UQ.
Tel: 0171 371 8788. **Fax:** 0171 371 8312.
Price range: £11 to £60. Catalogue free.
Payment: cheque or postal order.
Postage & packing: £2.50 to £10.
Delivery: last Christmas orders by 1 December.
Refunds: by arrangement. Breakages if returned within 14 days.

Glazebrook & Co Glazebrook has made its mission the recreation of 17th- and 18th-century cutlery patterns. These are invariably comfortable to handle and simple to eat with, unlike modern designs which seem to delight in forks with short teeth and spoons with no bowl. The firm sells the early rat-tail pattern in a matt pewter-like finish along with old English patterns in a more usual mirror finish. There are pistol-grip knives and faux-ivory handled knives with both square and rounded ends.

Glazebrook & Co, PO Box 1563, London SW6 3XD.
Tel: 0171 731 7135. **Fax:** 0171 371 5434.
Price range: £2.30 to £7.50. Catalogue free.
Payment: cheque, Access, Visa.
Postage & packing: included.
Delivery: 3-4 weeks. Last Christmas orders 4 weeks ahead.
Refunds: yes. Samples sent in advance.
Specials: free ash case for 60-piece sets. Silver and silver plate on request.

Global Village Stylish pieces from round the world including sinister African masks, Buddha figures, quantities of baskets and rattan furniture, striking iron vases and beautiful natural marble bowls carved in India. There is hand-blown Mexican glass with brilliant turquoise, yellow and emerald rims, candelabra and Christmas decorations like gilded eggs, glass balls for the tree and multi-coloured metallic crackers.

Global Village, 17 St James Street, South Petherton, Somerset TA13 5BS.
Tel: 01460 241166.

Price range: 95p to £1,000. Catalogue being re-done, leaflets and help on request.

Payment: cheque, Visa, Access, Mastercard, Eurocheque, Switch.

Postage & packing: £4.50 upwards.

Delivery: last orders for Christmas by 1 December.

Refunds: yes.

Glorafilia Updated and well-designed needlepoint classics in kit form – tapestry pictures, cushions, slippers and bellpulls. I love the blue and white range, from 19th-century pottery, samplers and Victorian rugs with blowsy flowers on a staid black background.

Glorafilia, The Old Mill House, The Ridgeway, Mill Hill Village, London NW7 4EB.

Tel: 0181 906 0212. **Fax:** 0181 959 6253.

Price range: £13.95 to £49.50. Catalogue £2.

Payment: cheque, Visa, Mastercard.

Postage & packing: £2.50 for orders under £75, £5 under £100, free over £100.

Delivery: 28 days but usually less.

Refunds: if returned in 7 days.

Glover & Smith Amusing handles provide an instant update for a piece of furniture or a room. For someone setting up home, these lead-free pewter handles and hooks are clever presents. They can transform cheap chests of drawers. There are shells, ammonites, starfish and seahorses plus rabbits' and ducks' heads. The finish is matt, shiny or tinged black.

Glover & Smith, Makers' Cottage, 14 London Road, Overton, nr Basingstoke, Hampshire RG25 3NP.

Tel/Fax: 01256 773012.

Price range: £17.95 to £39.95. Send A5 SAE with 38p stamp for catalogue.

Payment: cheque, credit cards in future.

Postage & packing: included in UK.

Delivery: last Christmas orders by 14 December, 7 December for hand-gilded work.

Refunds: yes, if returned in 14 days.

Handmade Wooden Tray Company Butler's trays are useful to ordinary mortals too, the idea being that the hefty wooden tray can be set on its own legs to make a table. The company makes tables at coffee height and, more useful, at full height as well as a laptop tray with its own cushion – very useful indeed.

The Handmade Wooden Tray Company, Teignbridge Business Centre, Cavalier Road, Heathfield, Newton Abbot, Devon TQ12 6TZ.

Tel: 01626 835174. **Fax:** 01626 835186.

Price range: £24.99 to £325. Catalogue free.

Payment: cheque, Visa, Mastercard, Access.

Postage & packing: included.

Delivery: allow 28 days.

Refunds: yes.

Heathfield Patchwork Hand-sewn patchwork bedspreads in traditional and American patterns such as stylised tulips in pink, green and blue on cream, Luna, which uses traditional shirtings in stripes and checks, blue and white and Sunflower, where whorls of multi-coloured petals are circled with stitching. Any size is available – from cot to kingsize.

Heathfield Patchwork, 163 High Street, Tibshelf, Alfreton, Derbyshire DE55 5NE.

Tel: 01773 872229.

Price range: £17.50 to £79.50. Send large SAE for leaflet.

Payment: cheque, Access, Visa.

Postage & packing: £5.50.

Delivery: Last Christmas orders 1st week of December.

Refunds: yes, if returned in 10 days.

The Holding Company Brilliant storage ideas from American Dawna Walter, whose Chelsea shop at 243-245 King's Road is a wild success. Boxes, baskets, trolleys, canvas wardrobes, holders for unruly childen's toys, even scented cedar coat hangers and shoe trees (you can't have too many). Especially recommended are the drawer tidies which will sort out untidy pairs of socks, toy carts on wheels to keep children's toys in order and an eight-tier tower with added woven baskets to use anywhere from kitchen to bathroom.

The Holding Company Mail Order, Suite 15 Imperial Studios, 3-11 Imperial Road, London SW6 2AG.

Tel: 0171 610 9160. **Fax:** 0171 610 9166.

Price range: £1.75 to £341.95. Catalogue £1.50.

Payment: cheque, Switch, Amex, Visa, Mastercard.

Postage & packing: £4.50 on orders to £100; £6.50 thereafter.

Delivery: last Christmas orders 16 December but 24-hour service for extra charge.

Refunds: if returned within 2 weeks.

The India Shop Indian design first came to Britain in the 17th century and the popularity of its paisleys and chintzes has endured. This company sells cushions with typical tree of life, paisley and mughal animal patterns, woven check throws and geometric wool rugs. There are also hand-made sheesham wood coffee tables and a few presents like dolls, writing paper with incorporated flower petals, aprons and scarves.

The India Shop, 5 Hilliers Yard, Marlborough, Wiltshire SN8 1NB.

Tel: 01672 515585. **Fax:** 01380 728118.

Price range: £2.95 to £305. Catalogue free.

Payment: cheque, Mastercard, Visa.

Postage & packing: included.

Delivery: last Christmas orders 19 December.

Refunds: yes, if returned in 7 days.

In Particular This catalogue offers a choice of the best of British designers – these are really stylish goods for people who care about the latest in design. My preference is for the more subdued designs with decided shapes and the unusual one-off ideas. I particularly like Andrea Maflin's lampshades with old manuscript designs and a collection of clay amphoras and jugs, the cool collection of velvet and calico cushions from DWCD (qv) which should suit any colour scheme and the brilliant tartan ranges from Anta (qv).

In Particular, PO Box 212, Staines, Middlesex TW18 2AS.
Tel: 0701 0702 027. **Fax:** 0701 0701 501.
Price range: £7.50 to £190. Catalogue free.
Payment: cheque, Visa, Access, Delta, Switch.
Postage & packing: £1.95 up to £20, £4.95 up to £150, £8.95 over £150.
Delivery: by post or carrier, allow 28 days.
Refunds: by arrangement.
Specials: gift service.

The Iron Bed Company I was given my very own bed as an eleven-year-old and it was one of my best presents ever – it signified growing up. This company reproduces those Victorian brass-knobbed, black iron beds which made a fashion comeback thirty years ago and have never been superseded. Their simple design and stout construction mean they work in any style of room, from teenager's football poster mode to sophisticated black and white avant garde. A gift that lasts a lifetime.

The Iron Bed Company, Southfield Park, Delling Lane, Old Bosham, Chichester PO18 8NN.
Tel: 01243 574049. **Fax:** 01243 573768.
Price range: £339 to £599. Catalogue free.
Payment: cheque, Access, Visa.
Postage & packing: separate quote via carrier, about £19 on mainland.

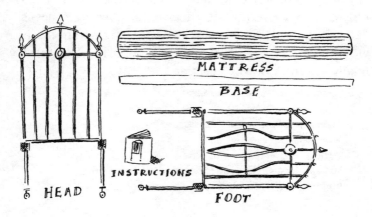

MATTRESS
BASE
INSTRUCTIONS
HEAD
FOOT

Delivery: 4-5 weeks, sometimes faster.
Refunds: yes.

Jerry's Home Store One of London's most exciting and innovative stores offers you American style and bizarre objects you won't find anywhere else. Now there's a burgeoning mail-order catalogue for Christmas. Items are constantly arriving but I know there will be copies of the striped blankets the Hudson Bay Co sold to the Indians, 500-piece jigsaws of Forties pin-ups, a mug like a blackboard for handy messages, lots of animals' presents (already a dog tag like a fire hydrant) and a gingerbread man with the inscription 'He's quiet, he's sweet and if he gives you any grief, you'll bite his head off'.

Jerry's Home Store, 163 Fulham Road, London SW3 6SN.
Tel: 0171 581 0909. **Fax:** 0171 584 3749.
Price range: 50p to £99. Catalogue free.
Payment: cheque, Visa, Amex, Mastercard, Delta, Switch.
Postage & packing: to be quoted.
Delivery: last Christmas delivery, 18 December by post.
Refunds: yes, if returned in a month, with proof of purchase and in good condition.

Joanna's A selection presumably chosen by the owner – very good quality address and visitors' books, notepads, albums and wooden frames in traditional tooled leather and wood. Trays, magazine racks and waste paper bins, skipping ropes, silver-plated mugs and dishes and very useful gingham notice boards with matching criss-cross ribbons combine to make this a very 'English country house' selection.

Joanna's, 20 Upper Wimpole Street, London W1M 7TA.
Tel/Fax: 0171 289 1149.
Price range: £10 to £80. Catalogue free.
Payment: cheque.
Postage & packing: £3 for orders to £20, £5.50 thereafter.
Delivery: last Christmas orders about 15 December.
Refunds: yes, if reasonable and returned in 7 days.

Kingshill Designs Interior designer Sasha Waddell has created a range of Swedish-inspired furniture and accessories for Kingshill which I highly recommend. The chairs, chests, tables and beds, painted soft cream, green, grey and blue, are immediately appealing and, though fashionable, should become classics. The Gripsholm range have delightful curly legs and the Rokoko dining chairs are a curious cross between Queen Anne and French style.

Kingshill Designs Ltd, Kitchener Works, Kitchener Road, High Wycombe, Buckinghamshire HP11 2SJ.
Tel: 01494 463910/440408. **Fax:** 01494 451555.
Price range: £87 to £2,275. Catalogue free.
Payment: cheque, Visa, Access.
Postage & packing: by arrangement with carrier.
Delivery: last Christmas orders by 30 November.
Refunds: yes, if defective.

Lindean Mill Glass This hand-made glass in 24% lead crystal is made into stemmed bowls in stunning colours – sapphire blue, emerald, corn, ruby and purple; beaker glasses with touches of colour on the collar, the stem or slicked around the rim of the glass; and water and wine glasses with the marble flecked patterns of Venetian glass. I am less keen on the candelabra. Each piece is signed and dated.

Lindean Mill Glass, Lindean Mill, Galashiels, Selkirkshire TD1 3PE.
Tel: 01750 20173. **Fax:** 01750 21794.
Price range: £24 to £180. Catalogue free.
Payment: cheque, Visa, Mastercard.
Postage & packing: £10 per order.
Delivery: last Christmas orders by 1 December.
Refunds: by arrangement.

Lloyd Loom Direct This method of making furniture was invented sixty years ago and has recently had a great revival, with early pieces being collected by Thirties enthusiasts. The cord used to weave the chairs and tables is made of paper wrapped round wire, giving it more strength than cane or rattan weaves. Once woven, the whole is sized with glue and sprayed with coloured lacquer in eight colours. Because it is informal and adaptable, Lloyd Loom furniture works well in the house, garden and in conservatories. An extra benefit is that it copes with uneven floors and can be made to suit your decor with added cushions.

Lloyd Loom Direct Ltd, PO Box 75, Spalding, Lincolnshire PE12 6NB.
Tel: 01775 725876. **Fax:** 01775 761255.
Price range: £32 to £450. Catalogue free.
Payment: cheque, Access, Visa.
Postage & packing: £15 per order.
Delivery: within 28 days.
Refunds: yes, if notified within 7 days.

Melin Tregwynt　The Welsh have always created beautiful and comforting blankets but Melin Tregwynt surpasses all. There are two ranges in brilliant colours: the Designers Guild range, by Tricia Guild, mixes scarlet and yellow, a positive rainbow of blue, green, yellow, red and purple with contrast blanket stitch edging and the Brights range – fewer colours but just as strong, again with contrast stitching. Subtler groups of blankets and throws are single checks on a white ground or the traditional reversible diaper of Welsh blankets. All are in pure new wool.

Melin Tregwynt, Tregwynt Mill, Castle Morris, Haverfordwest, Pembrokeshire, Dyfed SA62 5UX.
Tel: 01348 891225. **Fax:** 01348 891694.
Price range: £15.50 to £180. Catalogue free.
Payment: cheque, Access, Visa, Amex.
Postage & packing: £1.50 to £25, £2.75 to £50, £4.75 thereafter.
Delivery: last orders for Christmas 16 December. Later with £5 supplement.
Refunds: yes.

Mildred Pearce This company makes modern ceramics best described as wacky – lots of colour, jokey animals, lascivious drawings on clocks, mirrors, plates and vases (especially note the nude platters with bubbles saying 'Darling! Make love to me this instant!'). Not ideal for strait-laced folk but just the sort of thing to be an antique of the future.

Mildred Pearce, 33 Earlham Street, Covent Garden, London WC2H 9LD.
Tel/Fax: 0171 379 5128.
Price range: £12 to £100. Catalogue free.
Payment: cheque and all major credit cards.
Postage & packing: £2.99 for orders up to £29.99, £3.99 thereafter.
Delivery: up to 28 days. Last Christmas orders 18 November.
Refunds: yes.

Morgan Bellows Why is it so hard to find bellows when they are so useful? These are the Rolls Royce of bellows with brass nozzles so thin that a powerful blast makes smouldering logs glow white hot. They're just as good with recalcitrant coal. Short or long handled, they come plain with green, brown or burgundy leather and brass studs, or painted navy, dark green or black with a foliage border. They can be painted with initials or a crest. There are also candlesticks, wine coasters, bookends and cachepots – all ideal for personalising.

Morgan Bellows, Knockhill, Lockerbie, Dumfriesshire DG11 1AW.
Tel/Fax: 01576 300232.
Price range: £16 to £80. Catalogue free.
Payment: cheque, Access, Visa, Mastercard, Eurocard.
Postage & packing: itemised on leaflet.
Delivery: within 28 days. Ring if urgent.
Refunds: yes.
Specials: custom-made.

Mousehole Craft Shop Something in the Cornish air encourages arts and crafts. This is a small selection of excellent ideas, mostly connected with the sea. There are fierce fish made of old horsehoes, lifelike ceramic seals, a rag cushion cover with a sinister orange crab, pincers poised, and a little ornamental beach hut. Also Peter Perry's painted fish (see page 232 under Cards and Wrapping Paper.)

Mousehole Craft Shop, Brook Street, Mousehole, Penzance, Cornwall TR19 6QY.

Tel/Fax: 01736 731089.

Price range: £6 to £90. Catalogue free.

Payment: cheque, Mastercard, Visa, Access, Eurocard, Delta.

Postage & packing: £3.50 per order.

Delivery: allow 28 days. All pieces hand-made and could be in short supply.

Refunds: yes, if returned with original packing in 7 days.

Mulberry Hall This York shop must hold one of the best collections of good china and glass outside London and most of their stock can be mail-ordered. They sell all the best British porcelain and pottery such as Wedgwood, Spode, Royal Crown Derby, Royal Worcester along with Herend, Ginori and Royal Copenhagen from Europe. Glass and crystal comes from Waterford, Baccarat, Lalique and Stuart. Most of these firms also supply giftware – ornaments rather than tableware – and other gift ideas include Halcyon Days enamel boxes and Georg Jensen silver and jewellery. All is traditional, most in extremely well-known patterns like Spode's blue and white Italian and Ginori's Italian Fruits scattered with plums and strawberries.

Mulberry Hall, Stonegate, York YO1 2AW.

Tel: 01904 620736. **Fax:** 01904 620251.

Price range: £5.95 to £1,995. Catalogue free.

Payment: cheque and all major credit cards.

Postage & packing: under £250 10% of total order to a maximum of £7.50; free thereafter.

Delivery: despatched immediately. Out of stock items notified by return.

Refunds: replacement if notified immediately about loss or breakages.

Special: gift token, gift wrapping.

Nordic Style at Moussie Though Swedish furniture and accessories are terribly smart, I know of only one shop that specialises in them. It is run by two Swedes who mail-order Gustavian furniture, the 18th-century amalgam of French and Scandinavian style which works both in country and town settings. All in painted wood, tables generally have cabriole or bow legs, chairs have a slightly Georgian look and the glass-doored dresser/cupboard would look good in a dining room. There are also oval mirrors with ribboned tops. They plan more mail-order items such as linen, lampshades, fabric and presents soon.

> **Nordic Style at Moussie**, 109 Walton Street, London SW3 2HP.
> **Tel:** 0171 581 8674. **Fax:** 0171 937 6033.
> **Price range:** £4.75 to £3,900. Send large SAE for brochure.
> **Payment:** cheque, Visa, Access, Amex.
> **Postage & packing:** quoted with order.
> **Delivery:** 3-6 weeks.
> **Refunds:** credit only.

The Period House Group A firm which makes nails, hinges and hasps may seem a strange one to recommend for Christmas but these are the most beautiful traditional ones in black iron, designed for traditional country cottages. If you know anyone who lives in a cottage and is keen on DIY, these are perfect presents. They have lovely names: cranked strap hinge, pintle hinge, fish-tail bolt and monkey-tail window catch. Even the nails are called rosehead!

> **The Period House Group**, Plum Tree Cottage, Main Street, Leavening, North Yorkshire YO17 9SA.
> **Tel/Fax:** 01653 658554. **Mobile** 0585 878383.
> **Price range:** £2 to £115. Send 3 1st class stamps for catalogue.
> **Payment:** cheque or postal order.
> **Postage & packing:** £3.50 on orders to £35; £6.50 over £35 and £10 over £100.
> **Delivery:** despatched within 48 hours of payment; urgent orders by carrier at £12 in UK; bespoke orders for Christmas by 28 November.
> **Refunds:** if notified within 48 hours (none for bespoke).

Robert Welch The famous silversmith has also produced several interesting cutlery ranges. One of his most recent – and most interesting – has knife, fork and spoon handles ending in the spiral of the typical ammonite fossil. Earlier ranges, based on Georgian and European silver, have been used in British embassies overseas and are now design classics. Europa, for instance, has the long fiddle and elongated bowl of French cutlery. Unlike a lot of modern cutlery, this is good-looking and practical.

> **Robert Welch Studio**, Lower High Street, Chipping Campden, Gloucestershire GL55 6DY.
> **Tel:** 01386 840522. **Fax:** 01386 841111.
> **Price range:** £1.50 to £600. Catalogue free.
> **Payment:** cheque and all main credit cards except Amex.
> **Postage & packing:** £1.50 small items, £3.50 large.
> **Delivery:** last Christmas orders 18 December.
> **Refunds:** yes.

Sew Far Sew Good Tapestry kits for the beginner in interesting stitches and those for the experienced maker are available here. The patterns are excellent, being bold but pretty. There are flowers on scarlet strips, Corinthian columns with rose bowers, and grapes and pineapples, symbols of hospitality. There are large kits for cushions and tiny ones for spec cases.

> **Sew Far Sew Good**, Copperhill, Westcombe, Shepton Mallet, Somerset BA4 6EU.
> **Tel/Fax:** 01749 831083.
> **Price range:** £12 to £44. Catalogue £1.25, refundable with order.
> **Payment:** cheque, Mastercard, Visa.
> **Postage & packing:** £1.50 per kit in UK.
> **Delivery:** last Christmas order 12 December.
> **Refunds:** yes, if returned unopened in 7 days.

Sewills Reputed to be the world's oldest nautical instrument makers (est. 1800), this firm has a splendid collection of clocks, watches and barometers. Many are still made with proper clockwork movements of the highest quality. In some pieces, the back is crystal to show off the movement, in others the cases are hunter and half hunter. The Manor range includes large-faced tavern clocks, pendulum wall clocks and longcase clocks. Barometers and barographs come in 18th-century-style cases.

Sewills, Cornhill House, 24 Cornhill, Liverpool L1 8DZ.

Tel: 0151 708 7744. **Fax:** 0151 708 6777.

Price range: £20 to £3,000. Catalogue free. Ring 0151 708 0099 and quote HCG96 for Manor Brochure or NCG96 for Nautical Brochure.

Payment: cheque, Access, Visa, Mastercard.

Postage & packing: included for longcase clocks and watches, otherwise between £2.50 and £15.50 including insurance.

Delivery: allow 28 days.

Refunds: yes, if returned in 7 days. 5 year guarantee on instruments.

Special: limited edition, items made to order.

Shaker Desperately fashionable – and pricey – American products based on designs produced by a simple Christian sect. The styles are exceptional and manage to cross the country/town barrier. There are plain wooden chairs which hang from wooden rails, simple tables and curved wooden boxes. A Christmas catalogue includes tree decorations such as animal angels and Noah's Arks (these decorations are convincing perhaps because the original religious fervour somehow remains).

Shaker, 27 Harcourt Street, London W1H 1DT.

Tel: 0171 724 7672. **Fax:** 0171 724 6640.

Price range: £3.95 to £3,999. Catalogue £5, including Christmas supplement from autumn.

Payment: cheque, Visa, Access, Switch, Amex, Connect.

Postage & packing: £5.50.

Delivery: 7-10 days, last Christmas orders before GPO deadline.

Refunds: yes.

Silver Direct Peregrine Pole-Carew believes, as I do, that sterling silver is undervalued in price and generally under-used.

This firm mail orders both good solid sterling and plated pieces. There is silver for the table such as peppermills and toast racks; coasters and wine funnels for drinks and a range for the office including paper knives, calendars and rulers. There are also pretty pill boxes and silver-backed hairbrushes and a range for men including a pure bristle, silver-mounted shaving brush, collar stiffeners and cufflinks. My favourite is a silver travelling peppermill in a leather case. Most pieces can be engraved with initials or crests – prices on request.

> **Silver Direct**, PO Box 925, Shaftesbury, Dorset SP7 9RA.
>
> **Tel:** 01747 828977. **Fax:** 01747 828961.
>
> **Price range:** £5 to £300. Catalogue free on request line 01747 828282.
>
> **Payment:** cheque, PO, Switch, Visa, Access, Visa Delta, JCB.
>
> **Postage & packing:** included.
>
> **Delivery:** last Christmas orders 3 working days before Christmas.
>
> **Refunds:** if notified within 24 hours (excluding engraved pieces).
>
> **Specials:** gift wrapping and third party delivery.

Stuart Buglass Metalwork Stuart makes those curvy French bakers' shelves and wall hangers that cost so much in antique shops. There are heavy single shelves with rails for hanging implements, floor-standing bakers' shelves with curlicues at the top and extremely useful conical pan stands to put near the stove. He does light fittings for candles, chandeliers, standard lamps and wall lights in curly iron or straight candlesticks. The style is traditional but updated – his Arizona candlestick, for instance, carries three lights on branches like a cactus. This plain ironwork looks as good in modern interiors as pre-18th century ones.

> **Stuart Buglass**, Clifford Mill House, Little Houghton, Northampton NN7 1AL.
>
> **Tel:** 01604 890366. **Fax:** 01604 890372.
>
> **Price range:** £5 to £269. Catalogue free.
>
> **Payment:** cheque, Visa, Access, Mastercard.

Postage & packing: £2.95 on orders to £50; £5.95 to £100; £8.95 to £200; free thereafter.

Delivery: within 14 days, but allow 21.

Refund: by arrangement.

Tobias and the Angel If you want to give a present to someone very discriminating, shop here. This is a catalogue which cares about beautiful dusters, red and blue checked or bright yellow fluffy ones; about unbleached scrim for window cleaning and the perfect garden shed. It sells potato dibbers, old wicker laundry baskets and hand-thrown terracotta pots. The owner/designer started as an antique dealer and some items are antiques. I like everything in this catalogue.

Tobias and the Angel, 68 White Hart Lane, Barnes, London SW13 0PZ.

Tel/Fax: 0181 878 8902.

Price range: £1.50 to £2,225. Catalogue £2.

Payment: cheque, Access, Visa, Switch, Amex, Diners.

Postage & packing: at cost.

Delivery: allow 15 workings days. Some items are limited.

Refunds: yes.

Turquaz This company supplies bright-coloured bed and table linen in Indian and Egyptian cotton. Most designs are gingham and madras checks, yellow mixed with bright blue, red with pink and crimson, plus some beige, cream, white mixes. Good setting-up-home presents, as it instantly furnishes a bedroom.

Turquaz, The Coach House, Bakery Place, 119 Altenburg Gardens, London SW11 1JQ.

Tel: 0171 924 3003. **Fax:** 0171 924 6868.

Price range: £12 to £80. Catalogue free.

Payment: cheque, Visa, Access.

Postage & packing: £3.50.

Delivery: last Christmas orders by early December.

Refunds: yes.

Wilchester County American colonial style has recently been sweeping Britain and this family firm makes chandeliers and candle sconces copied from 17th- and 18th-century designs which arrived in the States from Britain and Holland but were adapted to suit the pioneers' simple life and basic tools. They are made of tin and are charming – Bucks County has a conical centre and flat branches ending in candle holders; Westchester is a two-tiered light while the Plantation sconce is a charming collection of tiny hoes, rakes, scythes and spades. Most are made for both real candles and electric light.

> **Wilchester County**, The Stables, Vicarage Lane, Steeple Ashton, Trowbridge, Wiltshire BA14 6HH.
>
> **Tel:** 01380 870764.
>
> **Price range:** £30 to £533. Catalogue £2, refundable against order.
>
> **Payment:** cheque, Access, Mastercard, Visa.
>
> **Postage & packing:** chandeliers £15, sconces £5.
>
> **Delivery:** allow 28 days.
>
> **Refunds:** yes, if returned in 7 days in original condition.

Yellow House This company makes wooden cabinets to hold or display candles and keys, groups of small, unwieldy items and eggs. There are good, solid wooden trays, slope-top writing boxes which can be perched on the lap and old-style wooden cutlery trays. The cutlery trays have two divisions and a central handle which is used to carry the tray while setting the table, and they also work well for shoe cleaning equipment and kitchen knives. All are designed with the utmost simplicity in four wood colours, or seven painted shades either distressed or flat and stencilled. These are genuinely useful objects that you don't miss until you've tried them.

> **Yellow House**, Milepeal Ltd, Pyes Mill, Station Road, Bentham, Lancaster LA2 7LJ.
>
> **Tel:** 01524 262938. **Fax:** 01524 261148.
>
> **Price range:** £5 to £150. Catalogue free.
>
> **Payment:** cheque or postal order.
>
> **Postage & packing:** £3 standard or £5 extra for next day delivery.

Delivery: usually within 7 days but allow 28; last Christmas orders by 23 December with surcharge.
Refunds: yes, if in original condition within 14 days.

See also: Academica for decorative drug bottles (Enthusiasms), Lord Roberts Workshops for splendid traditional brushes (Charities), Hector's Candles for best quality lights (Christmas Trees and Decorations), entries in Kitchenware.

GARDENING

Keen gardeners can never have too many tools, gadgets or plants. However, present-givers should find out what kind of gardener the enthusiast is. Do they grow rows of vegetables such as monster leeks for showing? Or is their style restrained Sackville-West white borders only? Are they greenhouse and annual bedding or hardy perennial fans?

The trend is for designers to be let loose in the garden, taking over from horticulturalists whose main advice seems to be how to dig, manure and propagate. Designers make gardening easier – and present-giving too – for the current passion is for accessories. These include wire topiary frames, conical planters made of willow wands, tiny hurdles to hold back flopping plants and myriads of terracotta pots, preferably old ones or unusual shapes like the square-sided melon pot. The advanced vegetable garden demands such esoteric objects as rhubarb and salsify forcers, glass bell jars and exotic foreign seeds which grow into Italian black cabbage or red Treviso chicory. For the less adventurous, there are fashionable herbs like borage and flat-leafed parsley, most easily grown in the open.

Another major gardening trend is for early and authentically historic plants. Watch out for nurseries specialising in old-fashioned roses, fancy auriculas and ferns. There are others which supply conservatory and house plants for the indoor garden enthusiast. Here the trend is towards strong-featured plants (but not traditional house plants) such as house lime, olive trees and plumbago.

If in doubt about the kind of garden your enthusiast grows and which presents are suitable, look through the relevant gardening magazines. My favourite is *Gardens Illustrated*, which is a newish glossy. Not only does a subscription to it make an excellent present but the magazine itself is full of reader offers – good collections of plants like clematis and irises, hard-to-find books from abroad and high-quality tools such as pruning knives. The magazine also has a regular feature on new products, many of them produced by craftsmen who will send products by mail order or by specialist mail-order firms.

One problem about sending plants as presents is that they usually have to be opened promptly or stored in cool, dark conditions and, in some cases, can only be delivered at unsuitable times of year (ie not around Christmas). Roses, however, are pretty tolerant (though do remember to order in good time in case stocks run out) as, of course, are seeds. If you want to give a specific plant, look in the *Plant Finder*, listed in the Moorland Publishing entry.

Garden accessories are not affected by the delivery problem, instead the problem is often size and fragility. However, makers of hurdles, garden furniture and terracotta pots all have reliable carriers who can deliver to your door – or direct to the recipient. Again, leave plenty of time in ordering – many of these pieces are made to order because they are so bulky to stock.

GARDENING – LISTINGS

Architectural Plants This nursery is run by a clever designer, with all plants chosen for their architectural quality. Many are evergreen with few flowers. Lots of rare house and conservatory plants, and exotics collected from the wild, are included. The plant quality is excellent – my house plants have survived even me. Good for bamboo, yucca, eucalyptus, palms and large-scale trees. All come with provenance and tips for upkeep.

Architectural Plants, Cooks Farm, Nuthurst, Horsham, West Sussex RH13 6LH.

Tel: 01403 891772. **Fax:** 01403 891056.

Price range: £4.25 to £1,000. Catalogue free.

Payment: Visa, Access, Mastercard, Switch, Eurocard, Delta, JCB and Electron preferred.

Postage & packing: £14 minimum for 10 kg, then 36p per kg.

Delivery: order for Christmas up to 2 days before; next day delivery generally on UK mainland.

Refunds: no, unless damaged in transit.

Specials: gift vouchers.

Cottage Garden Roses

John and Teresa Scarman are fanatically interested in the old varieties of roses from the near wild ones grown for their petals and used to make rose water in the middle East to old shrub and climbing roses with evocative names like Gloire de Dijon and Great Maiden's Blush. The nursery will send out vouchers and a catalogue as a present. They also sell their own book, *Gardening with Old Roses* (£16.99 plus £2.50 p&p), and pure Persian rosewater brought back by them from the East in hand-blown glass bottles.

Cottage Garden Roses, Woodlands House, Stretton, nr Stafford ST19 9LG.

Tel: 01785 840217.

Price range: roses £6 each. Catalogue £1.50.

Payment: cheque with order; no credit cards.

Postage & packing: £4 for 5 plants, £5 for 6 to 10, £6 for over 10.

Delivery: allow 28 days.

Refunds: yes.

Specials: gift vouchers.

Countryways Weathervanes

Weathervanes have been used in Britain for over 600 years. While they are ornamental and emphasise good-looking pinnacles or roofs, they also have a function. Gardeners need to know what the wind is doing, as backing or veering can foretell climate changes crucial to planting. These weathervanes are elaborate silhouettes of sailing galleons, pennants flying; of a wavy-haired mermaid or a dolphin with its young. The firm will also work to commission if you want a personalised vane.

Countryways Weathervanes, 25 Bay Crescent, Swanage, Dorset BH19 1RB.
Tel/Fax: 01929 421160.
Price range: £89 but add £15 for special commissions. Catalogue free.
Payment: cheque.
Postage & packing: £8 per weathervane.
Delivery: allow 28 days, more for commissions.
Refunds: yes.

English Hurdle One of the few willow farms left in existence. The Hector family have been growing, coppicing and weaving withies on over 100 acres of Somerset farmland for generations. Everything is woven by hand and therefore can be made to measure. Plain hurdles make excellent fences and backdrops; conical planters (I have six myself) are ideal for climbers from nasturtiums to sweet peas while some of the woven chairs can be ordered green and planted to create a growing willow chair. The Hectors also make a stunning Edwardian-type summerhouse made of twig work laid over wattle and roofed in willow branches.

English Hurdle, Curload, Stoke St Gregory, Taunton, Somerset TA3 6JD.
Tel: 01823 698418. **Fax:** 01823 698859.
Price range: £14.10 to £2,338. Catalogue free.
Payment: cheque, Visa, Access, Mastercard.
Postage & packing: from £7.

Delivery: normally within a month but large items may be longer.

Refunds: yes.

Gardens Illustrated An inspirational glossy magazine taking in gardens worldwide. It features planting maps and product information but is less practical than most. Recent subjects include plant portraits of euphorbias and anemones, growing rhubarb and heavy-duty wheelbarrows. Readers' offers have been garden umbrellas, signed copies of gardening books and special days at featured gardens along with collections of plants featured.

Gardens Illustrated, Freepost SW 6096, Frome, Somerset BA11 1YA.

Tel: 01373 451777. **Fax:** 01373 452888.

Price: currently £19.80 for a year (6 issues). No catalogue.

Payment: cheque, Visa, Amex, Access, Mastercard, Diners, Connect, Eurocard.

Postage & packing: included.

Delivery: on publication.

Refunds: no.

The Heveningham Collection Ironwork furniture is very much in fashion, both indoors and out, but these pieces, designed by Annie Eadie, are notable for their simple style. There is a luxurious chaise longue with back wheels to move it about easily and a plain black iron-framed deckchair with a natural canvas sling. There are matching chairs, stools and tables, shown in the catalogue in conservatories, gardens and beside the pool. There are even standard candelabra for elegant outside meals. She has not made one design error.

The Heveningham Collection by Annie Eadie, Weston Down, Weston Colley, Micheldever, Winchester, Hampshire SO21 3AQ.

Tel: 01962 774990. **Fax:** 01962 774790. **Mobile** 0973 383167.

Price range: £155 to £755. Catalogue £2.50, refundable against order.

Payment: cheque, Visa or Mastercard.

Postage & packing: included for more than two items.
Delivery: 3 to 4 weeks.
Refunds: no.
Specials: own fabric used at extra cost.

Hortus Ornamenti Damian Grounds rediscovered a two-tined fork specially invented by the legendary gardener, Gertrude Jekyll, for weeding. He had it manufactured in the best stainless steel with a brass ferrule and beech handle and packed it into a stout dark green box surrounded by dark green tissue paper. It was such a success, he went on to recreate a Victorian hand trowel and four-tined hand fork, all in the same materials. He does a boxed set of all three and the Ultimate Collection of the three implements in a big wooden box with copper plant labels, a ball of jute string and strong gardening scissors. More launches are expected soon.

Hortus Ornamenti, 23 Cleveland Road, Chichester, West Sussex PO19 2HF.
Tel/Fax: 01243 782467.
Price range: £26.95 to £198. Catalogue free.
Payment: cheque, Access, Visa.
Postage & packing: from £1.95 to £7.95.
Delivery: last Christmas order December 20.
Refund: yes, if damaged.

J.G.S. Metalwork This company specialises in weathervanes made of steel then coated with powdered polyester which is baked on hard to stop rust. There are many shapes from the traditional, boastful cock, running fox and leaping horse (and these are the ones I prefer) to bears fishing for salmon, witches on broomsticks and traction engines. Most are simple black silhouettes but there is a splendid golden cockerel. All come with fixing brackets and instructions.

J.G.S. Metalwork, Broomstick Estate, High Street, Edlesborough, near Dunstable, Bedfordshire LU6 2HS.
Tel: 01525 220360. **Fax:** 01525 222786.
Price range: £15 to £205. Send SAE for catalogue.

Payment: cheque, Access, Visa, Mastercard, Eurocard.

Postage & packing: £2 to £10.

Delivery: from stock for Christmas 19 December, out of stock 3-4 weeks.

Refunds: no arrangements.

Keith Metcalf's Garden Heritage

The Japanese work wonders in small gardens so it's no surprise that their style is catching on in English cities. Keith Metcalf specialises in Japanese garden accessories like bamboo palisades and water spouts and small, heavy granite jars for water features. He has recently added carved marble and granite in Italian and English styles but I haven't yet seen them.

Keith Metcalf's Garden Heritage, The Studio, Braxton Courtyard, Lymore Lane, Milford on Sea, Hampshire SO41 0TX.

Tel: 01590 644888. **Fax:** 01590 645825.

Price range: £150 to £5,000. Catalogue free for Windsor and Roma ranges, £5 for Zen pack.

Payment: cheque.

Postage & packing: subject to weight.

Delivery: by carrier.

Refunds: yes.

Kootensaw Dovecotes

Free-standing and wall-mounted dovecotes in a choice of fifty-seven National Trust colours which are draught- and weather-proofed to be cosy enough to keep the doves happy. You can buy the doves too – 'delightful little creatures...very easy to look after' say the owners. They also sell various dove accessories like homing nets, feeders, food and leg rings.

Kootensaw Dovecotes, Moorcot, Diptford, Totnes, Devon TQ9 7NX.

Tel/Fax: 01548 821415. **Mobile** 0860 173927.

Price range: dovecotes from £195 to £750; doves £35 a pair. Catalogue free.

Payment: cheque, Switch, Access, Visa, Mastercard, Eurocard.

Postage & packing: from 50p for orders of £2.50 to £38 for orders of up to £1,000.

Delivery: 2 to 3 weeks but shorter may be possible.
Refunds: by agreement.

Matthew Eden I hate white plastic in the garden, and these beautiful pieces of furniture are the antidote. Eden produces three basic ranges: the light but strong wirework inspired by Regency designs is made of wire attached to an iron frame; the reeded furniture, again after Regency originals, is made of galvanised iron in hoop designs; then there is solid oak or painted pine furniture designed by Lutyens. Eden also makes a wirework cardholder into which Christmas cards (and, at other times, invitations or postcards) can be stuck and fanned out.

Matthew Eden, Pickwick End, Corsham, Wiltshire SN13 0JB.
Tel: 01249 713335. **Fax:** 01249 713644.
Price range: £20 to £1,050. Catalogue free on request.
Payment: cheques, no credit cards.
Postage & packing: £35 up to 100 miles, £45 if more.
Delivery: by arrangement.
Refunds: yes.

Moorland Publishing Creators of the invaluable *Plant Finder* which lists every plant you can think of and gives relevant nurseries by area. Maps pinpoint them. There is an extremely good bibliography, a helpful guide to names and synonyms. Also helps with spelling plants' names.

Moorland Publishing Co Ltd, Moor Farm Road, Airfield Estate, Ashbourne, Derbyshire DE6 1HD.
Tel: 01335 344486.
Price: £12.99. No catalogue.
Payment: cheque, Access, Visa.
Postage & packing: £1.50.
Delivery: by post.
Refunds: no.

Mr Fothergill's Seeds As you might expect from the name, this seed catalogue is full of old-fashioned flowers which are so hard to find. There are delicious sweet peas like Old Spice and Painted Lady, a poppy like mother of pearl, Angel Wings, and heartsease Johnny Jump Up. There's a selection of wild flower seeds for the fashionable wild meadow look including cornflower, ox eye daisy and harebell. The vegetables are a lively choice: jalapeño chillies, butternut squashes and the amazing strawberry spinach among more ordinary cabbages and carrots. Enjoy yourself picking a selection for the gardener of your choice.

Mr Fothergill's Seeds Ltd, Gazeley Road, Kentford, Newmarket, Suffolk CB8 7QB.
Tel: 01638 751161. Orders: 01638 552512. **Fax:** 01638 751624.
Price range: 89p to £45. Catalogue free, **Tel:** 01638 751887.
Payment: cheque, Access, Visa, Switch.
Postage & packing: included in UK.
Delivery: within 5 days if possible.
Refunds: by arrangement.
Specials: gift voucher, third party delivery.

Museum of Garden History The museum has a small but sprightly shop and its mail-order list reflects that. Like the museum I expect the catalogue to grow rapidly, offering items found nowhere else. An 18th-century print of gardeners at work with solid rollers has been translated into mugs, tea-towels, cotton napkins and a garden planner book. There are Munstead baskets like Gertrude Jekyll used and a charming pair of silver-plated earrings shaped like watering cans. The museum has wrapping paper and tags with old-fashioned tools printed on brown paper and a good range of gardening books which they will post. Talk to them about their stock.

The Museum of Garden History, Lambeth Palace Road, London SE1 7LB.
Tel: 0171 261 1891. **Fax:** 0171 401 8869.
Price range: £1.60 to £29. Send SAE for catalogue.
Payment: cheque, Visa, Mastercard, Eurocard, Amex.
Postage & packing: £3 for up to 3 items, £4.50 thereafter.
Delivery: last Christmas orders 16 December.
Refunds: yes.

Periwinkle Productions Gardening is an ideal subject for videos and this firm has a dozen – and the list is growing – to help with garden tasks like pruning and propagation, as well as with specific plants. These include clematis, roses, soft and tree fruit and notoriously difficult pot plants like African violets. Also how to create hanging baskets and look after the lawn.

Periwinkle Productions, Gardening Videos, Phostrogen Ltd, Dept VO, Deeside, Clwyd CH5 2NS.

Tel: 01553 827247 **Fax:** 01553 827520.

Price: £12.99. Catalogue free.

Payment: cheque and major credit cards.

Postage & packing: included in UK.

Delivery: last Christmas order 7 December.

Refunds: yes, if faulty.

Planta Vera This is a nursery specialising in violas which are highly scented, charming and easy to grow. What better? One of my favourites is Molly Sanderson (they all have names like that) which is a jet black flower with yellow central eye. As so many have girl's names, a present to match a friend would be a lovely idea. Sad to say, there is no Leslie.

Planta Vera, Lyne Hill Nursery, Lyne Crossing Road, Chertsey, Surrey, KT16 0AT.

Tel/Fax: 01932 563011. **Mobile** 0374 499158.

Price range: £2 each with a minimum order of 12. Send £1 in stamps for catalogue.

Payment: cheque.

Postage & packing: £9 for up to 40 plants.

Delivery: the plants go out in April but, for Christmas, order by November and firm will send a special Christmas card.

Refunds: yes, if not received in good condition.

Terrace & Garden Where other firms offer neat willow hurdles and planters, this one has them wild with unclipped tops, wiry extensions to frames and screens that might have come through a hedge backwards. They make little Christmas trees from black twigs with plain glass baubles, discs and spirals which are really for terraces and conservatories but would make sensational indoor Christmas decorations.

Terrace & Garden Ltd, Orchard House, Patmore End, Ugley, Bishop's Stortford, Hertfordshire CM22 6JA.

Tel: 01799 543289. **Fax:** 01799 543586.

Price range: £21.20 to £450. Catalogue free.

Payment: cheque, Access, Visa.

Postage & packing: £2 for orders under £20, £4 for between £20 and £75, free thereafter.

Delivery: by arrangement.

Refunds: by arrangement.

Thompson & Morgan This claims to be the world's largest illustrated seed catalogue at over 225 pages with lots of help-ful, if too perfect, blooms on show. You have to know what you want, as browsing is too overwhelming, but the catalogue is helpfully divided into sections like flowers for fragrance, for windowsills and for cutting. There's also a big vegetable seed section where you will find smart foods like radicchio, striped tomatoes and red spring onions.

Thompson & Morgan, Poplar Lane, Ipswich, Suffolk IP8 3BU.

Tel: 01473 688821. **Fax:** 01473 680199.

Price range: about £1 to £5. Catalogue free.

Payment: cheque, Access, Visa, Switch.

Postage & packing: 95p for orders under £10, thereafter free.

Delivery: seeds at once, plants and bulbs in correct season.

Refunds: yes.

Specials: gift vouchers.

Wadham Trading Company Topiary is a current garden craze and this firm supplies the iron frames needed to control the shape. There are rabbits and giraffes, a cuddly sheep shape and more traditonal urns which look almost as good without planting. Other accessories are iron rose supports, jardinières and ornamental spheres to put each side of the front door. There are also convincing lead-effect cherubs and cisterns, actually made of marble resin.

Wadham Trading Company, Wadham House, Southrop, near Lechlade, Gloucestershire GL7 3PB.

Tel/Fax: 01367 850499.

Price range: £13 to £1,000. Catalogue free.

Payment: cheque, Mastercard, Visa, Access.

Postage & packing: on request.

Delivery: last Christmas orders by 19 December. Later with extra charge.

Refunds: yes, if returned within 7 days.

Whichford Pottery This is the place for terracotta ware. Most is hand-thrown or hand-pressed into moulds and, because it is made in England, is frost-proof. All are guaranteed against frost damage for ten years. Shapes are traditional, urns with swags and garlands, basket ware pots, large Ali Baba and olive oil jars. This is the place to buy the rhubarb forcer, a must for the smart vegetable garden, and small plant pots with saucers for indoor plants.

Whichford Pottery, Whichford, Shipston-on-Stour, Warwickshire CV36 5PG.

Tel: 01608 684416. **Fax:** 01608 684833.

Price range: £3.50 to £1,500. Send 6 1st class stamps for catalogue.

Payment: cheque.

Postage & packing: £15.50 per order in mainland UK, except Scotland and Cornwall which are £20.

Delivery: normally 28 days but more for large pots. Phone for exact time. Supplies can be limited.

Refunds: yes.

Specials: set of 10 charming postcards for £3.95 inc p&p.

Windrush Mill A good general mail-order catalogue to find presents for gardening friends. It doesn't bother too much with plants but concentrates on accessories. These may be foldaway wheelbarrows or hefty log splitters at the practical end, or square terracotta melon pots, tiny willow hurdles to hold back border plants and trowel and fork silver earrings or cufflinks at the ornamental end. There is even a wooden tool store, five foot high, which will tuck into a corner and solve storage problems in small gardens.

Windrush Mill, Witney, Oxfordshire OX8 6BH.
Tel: 01993 770456. **Fax:** 01993 770749.
Price range: £5 to £600. Catalogue free.
Payment: cheque, postal order, Access, Eurocard, Visa, Mastercard, Amex, Diners, JCB, Delta, Switch.
Postage & packing: £2.50 up to £30 orders, £3.50 over.
Delivery: within 7 days in UK, next day service at £4.95 extra.
Refunds: yes.

W Robinson If you have an urge to grow bigger vegetables than anyone else or win prizes at the village fête, get these seeds sent to you as a present. The family-owned firm has been honing its seeds for size since 1860 and can offer the largest red onion in cultivation (it reaches twenty-two inches in circumference), 1lb beefsteak tomatoes and thirty-inch runner beans. There's also Big Max, the giant pumpkin, big enough for Cinderella.

W Robinson & Sons Ltd, Sunny Bank, Forton, near Preston PR3 0BN.
Tel: 01524 791210. **Fax:** 01524 791933.
Price range: £1 to £2.30. Catalogue free.
Payment: cheque, Mastercard, Access, Visa, Amex.
Postage & packing: included.
Delivery: last orders for Christmas 15 December.
Refunds: no.

See also: The Gluttonous Gardener for food plants (Food for presents), Nether Wallop Trading Company for tools and carriers (General Catalogues), WCP Video for plant lessons (Books, Cassettes, CDs and Videos), Gardeners Royal Benevolent Society, Royal Horticultural Society, Soil Association (Charities).

Chapter Four

LUXURIES

This is the section for life's luxuries. Although they are often predictable, they make excellent presents, given that many people rarely buy themselves luxuries and rely on others to give pure pleasure at Christmas.

One trend in this area has been aromatherapy goods. Women always knew that delicious scents worked wonders for the morale but, now that there's a smart new name for it, people take the subject more seriously. Medieval herbalists knew that there was a correlation between the scent of various plants and our health, and the science lingered on in such remedies as balsam for clogged noses and witch hazel for grazes. Now there are scents and oils designed to calm weary Christmas nerves and relax frantic cooks; there are pick-me-up lotions and potions for Boxing Day and for jaded appetites. Scented candles waft perfumed smoke to encourage convivial evenings and there are specially formulated room sprays and candles to evoke Christmas, combining hints of cinnamon, pudding spices and woodsmoke.

In the area of perfume, lighter, more natural scents are increasingly popular. These may recall a single favourite flower like roses or bluebells, the scent of new-mown hay or an orchard of lemons. Lavender water, the English answer to German cologne, is making a welcome comeback. There have always been masculine colognes for men; now there are scents for babies, too. Pets next?

I have also included firms which send flowers. A huge bunch of daffodils or pinks, smelling of spring and arriving on your doorstep in the depths of winter, is a welcome reminder of things to come. You can also order more exotic bunches of flowers by phone. Pick one of the new breed of smart florists like Paula Pryke or Stephen Woodhams in London. A bunch you will be proud of will cost about £30.

Finally, there's a firm which specialises in mail-order cigars for people who enjoy a good smoke at Christmas.

LUXURIES – LISTINGS

Scents, Oils and Cosmetics

Angela Flanders Aromatics Pot pourri for the late Nineties using bark, dried exotic plants, gilded berries and seed pods. Angela has written the definitive book on aromatics and encourages people to develop their own scents from her kits. The scents she mixes are spicy but not overpowering and give rooms a natural freshness. She also sells a French 'moth mouse' to use instead of moth balls, scented candles in scallop shells, burning oils and room perfumes. Everything from lingerie drawers to romantic dinners are improved by her arts.

> **Angela Flanders Aromatics**, The Flower Room, 96 Columbia Road, London E2 7QB.
> **Tel:** 0171 739 7555. **Fax:** 0171 739 7246.
> **Price range:** £9.95 to £19.95. Price list available.
> **Payment:** cheque.
> **Postage & packing:** £2 for orders to £15, £3 over that.
> **Delivery:** last Christmas orders 10 December.
> **Refunds:** usually not applicable.

Aromatherapy Associates Beautifully packaged – in matt black with gold – essential oils for the body, mind and spirit. Juniperberry and grapefruit combine for a stimulating bath oil, pine and eucalyptus spice up winter baths. Petitgrain and camomile are designed to restore the spirit while deep relaxing bath oil – camomile and vetiver – calms a confused mind. All smell wonderful.

Aromatherapy Associates, 68 Maltings Place, Bagleys Lane, Fulham, London SW6 2BY.

Tel: 0171 371 9878. **Fax:** 0171 371 9894.

Price range: £4.95 to £29.95. Catalogue free.

Payment: cheque, major credit cards.

Postage & packing: £2 for 1 or 2 items, £3 for 3 or 4, £4 for 5 or 6; £6 for more.

Delivery: allow 3 weeks.

Refunds: breakages if notified in 24 hours.

Crabtree & Evelyn A traditional perfumier which has recently branched into using modern, avant-garde scents with great success. Along with carnation, damask rose and violet, the enticing scents of vanilla, berries and eucalyptus are available. Each scent comes in a range of products from soap and massage oil to burning candles, foot scrub and pot pourri. Choose a favourite for a special aunt or friend and keep adding to the range, from drawer liners to room spray. There are also bon-bons and Mason's blue and white china in the mail-order catalogue.

Crabtree & Evelyn, Freepost, Customer Services Department, 36 Milton Park, Abingdon, Oxfordshire OX14 4BR.

Tel: 01235 862244.

Price range: £3.95 to £36. Catalogue £1.95.

Payment: cheque, Access, Visa, Amex.

Postage & packing: £3.50.

Delivery: allow 14 days.

Refunds: telephone if damaged.

Culpeper The firm has been going since 1927, long before the current herb craze. It offers herbal remedies and cosmetics. There is a huge list of plant oils for aromatherapy from aniseed to ylang-ylang plus blended massage oils for relaxation, for using after sport and for what it calls 'sexy'. The pot pourri pillows for sweet sleep are filled with herbal mixes and there are soap leaves in jasmine, lavender and rose for careful travellers. This is a lovely list of goodies for men and women, sensibly priced for stocking fillers, plus spices and herbs for the kitchen and a good selection of herbal books.

Culpeper, Hadstock Road, Linton, Cambridge CB1 6NJ.
Tel: 01223 894054. **Fax:** 01440 788196.
Price range: 95p to £19.95. Catalogue free.
Payment: cheque, Access, Visa, Amex, JCB.
Postage & packing: £3.25 for orders under £20; £3.95 up to £50, free thereafter.
Delivery: by Royal Mail/Parcelforce with last GPO posting date for Christmas orders.
Refunds: yes, if genuine.
Specials: gift wrapping.

Czech & Speake The bathroom specialists have recently set up a mail-order service which includes its aromatics and bath-room accessories ranges. The aromatics are traditionally based but with a distinctly modern feel, emphasised by minimalist paper packing coloured like fine granite. Frankincense and Myrrh, an oriental citrus mix, is ideal for Christmas while Grapefruit is fresh and mossy. These scents are used in body and massage oils, shampoos and colognes.

The accessories are more Edwardian – a mix of white porcelain and brass. There are toothbrush holders, wall soap dishes and a splendid bathrack which would make my Christmas.

Czech & Speake Direct, 244-254 Cambridge Heath Road, London E2 9DA.
Tel: 0181 980 4567. **Fax:** 0181 981 7232.
Price range: £5.50 to £150 in these ranges. Separate catalogues free.
Payment: cheque, Visa, Mastercard, Amex, Diners.

Postage & packing: aromatics free in UK, rest by quotation.
Delivery: within 28 days. Last Christmas order a fortnight before; £6 delivery charge for a week before.
Refunds: credit note.

D.R. Harris Set up in 1790, the pharmacy has been selling colognes and flower perfumes ever since. There are classic lavender, rose and English bouquet toilet waters and bay rum aftershave. The skin care ranges use milk of cucumbers, roses and almond oil – all packed in Harris's characteristic Victorian bottles. The range of sponges, loofahs and top-quality shaving brushes make excellent gifts for men – the firm has long supplied diplomats, military and naval officers as well as London dandies and rakes. There is also Harris's Original Pick-Me-Up for use on Boxing Day.

D.R. Harris, 29 St. James's Street, London SW1A 1HB.
Tel: 0171 930 3915/8753. **Fax:** 0171 925 2691.
Price range: £1.95 to £73.60. Catalogue free.
Payment: cheque, Access, Amex, Barclaycard, Eurocard, Mastercard, Visa.
Postage & packing: £1.50 on orders under £11, £6 under £100, over £100 free in UK.
Delivery: won't guarantee Christmas delivery but despatches three times a week.
Refunds: by arrangement.
Specials: gift wrapping service.

Glenelg Candles This company sells all sorts of aromatherapy candles including pale blue lavender to help sore throats and overcome nausea and hangovers; a dark blue rosemary candle to focus the mind after late nights – good for migraine sufferers but bad for some medical conditions; ylang-ylang – a red candle for stress; pale green clary sage which is good against negativity and depression; and eucalyptus which works against colds and chest complaints. Sounds as though all these could help at Christmas. The candles are intended to float alight on water while you relax nearby.

Glenelg Candles, Balcraggie, Glenelg, by Kyle of Lochalsh, Ross-shire IV40 8LA.

Tel: 01599 522313. **Fax:** 01599 522240.

Price range: 55p to £4.55. Send A4 SAE for catalogue.

Payment: cheque, Access, Visa, Mastercard, Eurocard, Delta, Switch.

Postage & packing: at post office rates per order.

Delivery: within 7 days but for Christmas order by 15 November.

Refunds: phone within 24 hours.

L'Artisan Parfumeur There are perfumes, room sprays, burning oils, drawer sachets and soaps in a whole range of scents, notable for their floral and green tones and their innocence. The ranges are based on roses, blackberry, a sun-warmed breeze of leaves and herbs, musky amber, mimosa and fig. You can therefore make your bathroom smell the same as your perfume and use soap and drawer sachets to deepen the fragrance. The firm also sells classic fragrances for women such as orchid, tuberose, citrus and vetiver, sandalwood plus what they call 'a passionate eau de cologne' as well as scent for a baby or rosewood and pear with a touch of praline. For £5, you can get a sample pack of five scents of your choice.

L'Artisan Parfumeur, 17 Cale Street, London SW3 3QR.

Tel: 0171 352 4196. **Fax:** 0171 610 5317.

Price range: £6.50 to £47.50. Catalogue free.

Payment: cheque, Visa, Access, Amex.

Postage & packing: £2.50 for orders to £30, £4.50 thereafter.

Delivery: a week unless out of stock when you will be informed.

Refunds: yes, if defective, exchange if goods not used.

Molton Brown Based in London's South Molton Street, this is one of the smartest cosmetic and scent ranges you can find. There is a sensual range of massage oil, bath foam and 'body satiniser' using the exotic scents of ylang-ylang, orange blossom and jasmine; shampoos and gels and a range of complex make-up brushes. Many products are in small bottles to make up a travel kit. There's also a range for men using the scents cedar, sandalwood and patchouli.

> **Molton Brown by Mail**, PO Box 2514, London NW6 1SR.
> **Tel:** 0171 625 6550. **Fax:** 0171 624 0737.
> **Price range:** £1.50 to £25. Catalogue free.
> **Payment:** cheque, Visa, Mastercard, Amex, JCB, Switch.
> **Postage & packing:** from £2.25. Orders over £50 free.
> **Delivery:** last Christmas orders 19 December.
> **Refunds:** yes, if broken.
> **Specials:** Trial sizes at £1 for 3 if 1 full-size product is bought.

Norfolk Lavender   Some of the most fragrant lavender in Britain is grown in Norfolk and this catalogue comes from a grower who also distills his own scents. There are lotions, talcs, soap and cologne in this most English perfume plus drawer sachets, lavender and beeswax furniture polish and bags of dried lavender flowers to use as pot pourri. Other scents here include rose and jasmine, and lavender for men.

> **Norfolk Lavender**, Caley Mill, Heacham, Norfolk, PE31 7JE.
> **Tel:** 01485 570384. **Fax:** 01485 571176.
> **Price range:** £2 to £35. Catalogue free.
> **Payment:** cheque, Access, Visa, Switch
> **Postage & packing:** £1.75 for 2 items.
> **Delivery:** last Christmas order 19 December. Special delivery for urgent orders.
> **Refunds:** yes.
> **Special:** gift tokens, wrapping service.

Officina Profuma Santa Maria Novella   The pharmacy founded by Dominican monks in 1221 in Florence is probably the oldest in the world and has had plenty of practice in creating soaps, scents, medicines and tonics. There are wonderful shampoos based on lavender, iris and pomegranate from the Italian countryside, aromatics to calm or revive you, one called the Vinegar of the Seven Thieves, and soaps including a strong minty one, seasoned for sixty days, which repels flies. Everything is packed in old-fashioned paper and exudes quality.

Officina Profuma-Farmaceutica di Santa Maria Novella, 117 Walton Street, London SW3 2HP.
Tel: 0171 460 6600. **Fax:** 0171 460 6601.
Price range: £7 to £150. Catalogue free.
Payment: cheque, major credit cards.
Postage & packing: by arrangement.
Delivery: last Christmas orders by end November.
Refunds: by arrangement.

Penhaligon's Both the Prince of Wales and Duke of Edinburgh have given this fine old firm their warrants. It has been going since 1870 but was galvanised into the present quite recently. There are two catalogues, one for their classic scents, the other for wider-ranging presents. The scents are generally light and evocative of an English spring. Bluebell smells like gorgeous hyacinths, Extract of Limes is breathtakingly crisp, while the floral Gardenia, Night Scented Stock, Orange Blossom and Violetta are sweetly romantic. The men's scent range is more complex and spicy but women should also try them. Gifts include beautifully designed silver dressing-table mirrors and brushes for women and mock ivory for men, tiny silver scent bottles for travellers and a range of marble soap dishes, mugs and mirrors. You cannot go wrong with anything here.

Penhaligon's By Request Postal and Gift Service, PO Box 2888, London N4 1NH.
Tel: 0800 716108. **Fax:** 0181 800 5789.
Price range: £13.95 to £395. Catalogue free.
Payment: cheques, Eurocheque, Visa, Mastercard, Amex, JCB, Diners, Eurocard, Switch.
Postage & packing: included.
Delivery: next day on request, otherwise despatched in 2 days.
Refunds: by arrangement.
Specials: bottles, silver, mock ivory engraved. Gift wrapping.

Flowers

Gifts by Post Carnations to your door. You probably don't have time to bother with flowers at Christmas but they bring a touch of spring to winter and, like no other present, say that you care. The busy cook, grandma alone and lovers parted will all welcome the thought. The bouquets range from ten mixed and five spray carnations to a big bouquet of ten mixed and spray carnations and freesias. I recommend making several small vases, by colour, from this bouquet – perhaps in every bedroom.

> **Gifts by Post Ltd**, PO Box 110, Penzance, Cornwall, TR18 4YB.
> **Tel:** 01736 711107. **Fax:** 01736 50248.
> **Price range:** £9.99 to £19.99. Catalogue free.
> **Payment:** cheque, Visa, Access, Switch.
> **Postage & packing:** included.
> **Delivery:** by 1st class post. Guaranteed delivery £2.70 extra.
> **Refunds:** yes.

Groom Bros Guarantee a touch of spring in mid-winter with a box of thirty fresh daffodils delivered in time for Christmas. Thirty daffodils fill three vases and cheer up rooms no end. Also bouquets of carnations and roses can be delivered in December along with amaryllis for spring flowering.

> **Groom Bros Ltd**, Peck's Drove Nurseries, Spalding, Lincolnshire PE12 6BJ.
> **Tel:** 01775 722421/766006. **Fax:** 01775 712252.
> **Price range:** approx £10 to £35. Catalogue free.
> **Payment:** cheque, Access, Visa.
> **Postage & packing:** included.
> **Delivery:** last orders for Christmas 18 December.
> **Refunds:** yes.

Pinks by Post Even in winter, a bunch of delightful, scented pinks can be sent. Though they are in short supply, the firm augments the bunch with freesias and anemones. For a splash of colour in the depths of winter, this is the company to call.

Pinks by Post, 320 London Road, Charlton Kings, Cheltenham, Gloucestershire GL52 6YJ.
Tel: 01242 234961.
Price range: £9 to £20. Catalogue free.
Payment: cheque, Access, Visa.
Postage & packing: included.
Delivery: 1st class post; Christmas orders by last GPO posting date.
Refunds: if lost or delayed, replacement sent.
Specials: regular orders.

Cigars

Percivals This mail-order cigar specialist's list includes Havana Romeo Y Julieta and Rafael Gonzalez. Other cigars come from Honduras and the Dominican Republic and you are given helpful comments about their quality and flavour. There is also a section called Machine Made Continentals. Cigar accessories are included.

Percivals Fine Cigars, Moorside Cottages, Pott Shrigley, Cheshire SK10 5RZ.
Tel/Fax: 01625 572090.
Price range: £11 to £233, minimum order £30. Catalogue free. Freepost envelope included.
Payment: cheque, Visa, Mastercard, Access.
Postage & packing: £2.95 in UK.
Delivery: last Christmas order 12 December. Havanas can be in short supply.
Refunds: yes.

See also: Ciel Decor for Provençal soaps and pot pourri, Cologne & Cotton for soap and cologne (Home Interest), Red Letter Days for top health farms, hotels and make-up and style tuition (Sports), Janet Reger, the queen of sexy underwear, David Nieper for slinky lingerie in silk and satin (Women's Clothes), entries in Drink for fine wines, whiskies etc.

Chapter Five

FOOD FOR PRESENTS

I had great difficulty deciding which of the myriad mail-order firms offering delicious foods to put into this section and which to put into the section on foods to stock over the holiday. Perhaps the best approach is to think of this as a starting point and, if nothing excites you in the list here, then try the Christmas food selections in Part Two where there's masses more.

This selection covers all the firms which sell sweets, candies and chocolates. You can get charming and luxurious boxes of both or even enrol your friends and relations in 'sweetie clubs' which deliver a regular box in the same way as a magazine subscription. You can do the same with kippers – a pair a month – or, in my other section, with boxes of vegetables, fruit or fish.

Producing smoked meat, fish and even garlic seems to be a growth industry. Some smokehouses specialise in sending these as presents; others service cooks with unusual ideas and they are listed in the section on hobbies. Giving smoked trout or salmon (or smoked prawns or venison) is an excellent idea. One firm suggests serving venison with slivers of parmesan and olive oil. It's quite delicious.

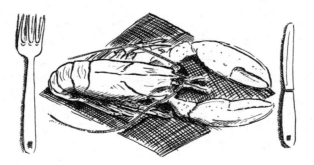

Cake-making is a dying art in the home, particularly now that it's so easy to buy a rich fruit cake cooked by experts in their homes. These come in useful tins and have an extremely long shelf life. Preserves also fall into this category – Wendy Brandon's fine pickles and chutneys feature here because they are particular favourites of mine but plenty of food suppliers have other tempting versions.

Hamper-giving is also on the increase. It's a nice idea (and one used by many businesses to say thank you) because you can never have too much food or wine and the hamper makes a useful memento. Most companies offer their own versions, with prices ranging from less than £30 to £500; others will make up baskets to your choice (and not just of food) while a firm like Panzer's makes a habit of searching out the best fashionable food around to create a gourmet's delight of a hamper.

Do remember though to check a hamper's contents before ordering. Some companies (though not, I hope, any of the ones listed here) produce hampers which contain one or two impressive foods and wines then fill the space with make-weights such as potted crab paste (ugh) and tinned pineapple rings – so beware.

FOOD FOR PRESENTS – LISTINGS

Cakes and Biscuits

Betty's and Taylors of Harrogate Everything you need for afternoon tea from this typically English cafe which has become world-famous. From the Betty's department there are Christmas cakes and fruit cakes in tins (Old Peculier made with Yorkshire's own ale and Earl Grey flavoured with the tea), Christmas biscuits and shortbread, as well as German and Swiss biscuits to commemorate the cafe's Swiss founder. There are also charming hand-made chocolates such as the little teddy with purple and white spotted bow tie. Taylors provide special coffees and teas which they have been blending since 1886.

Betty's and Taylors of Harrogate, 1 Parliament Square, Harrogate HG1 2QU.
Tel: 01423 886055. **Fax:** 01423 881083.
Price range: 70p to £150. Catalogue free.
Payment: cheque, Access, Visa, Mastercard, Switch.
Postage & packing: £5.60.
Delivery: last Christmas orders 8 December.
Refunds: by arrangement.
Specials: gift wrapping, special date delivery.

Collin Street Bakery If you want a cake with a difference, get in touch with this bakery in Texas. The bakery makes 80,000 lbs of cake a day and sends them all over the world including 75,000 to Britain in 1995. 1996 is its centenary. The cake has quantities of pecan nuts in the recipe plus cherries and pineapple from its own plantation. It arrives in a tin illustrated with an old-fashioned house under snow.

Collin Street Bakery, 401 W 7th Avenue, Corsicana, Texas 75110, United States of America.
Tel: 001 903 872 8111. **Fax:** 001 903 872 6879. **E-mail:** collin@airmail.net
Price range: $15.75 to $37.95. Catalogue free.
Payment: major credit cards.
Postage & packing: $4.95, $5.45 and $5.95 for small, medium and large cakes respectively.
Delivery: last Christmas order 5 November.
Refunds: yes.

Dickinson & Morris The firm has been making the Original Melton Hunt Cake since 1854, when it was served to the hunt together with a stiff drink in a stirrup cup. Designed to give energy, it is stuffed with good quality dried fruit, almonds and butter with an added measure of rum. Almonds and glacé cherries stud its top, and each cake comes packed in a special carton. This is a firm favourite round the world, especially among ex-pats who find it a taste of home.

Dickinson & Morris, 10 Nottingham Street, Melton Mowbray, Leicestershire LE13 1NW.

Tel/Fax: 01664 62341.

Price range: £7.20 a cake. Catalogue free.

Payment: cheque, postal order.

Postage & packing: £3.60 in UK.

Delivery: allow 14 days.

Refunds: no.

Specials: gift service.

Goodbrey's Traditional Cakes This firm specialised in baking for its own St Ives tearoom and so has kept old recipes that have become firm favourites. The Penzance and simnel cakes are local to Cornwall, which seems to be the cake-baking centre of England. Penzance includes peel, spice and crystallised ginger and is decorated with a gold band and board; simnel cake is decorated with eleven balls to symbolise the faithful apostles. Their other cakes are Dundee cake with whisky, rich farmhouse with brandy, Guinness cake with green and gold cherries, pecan and Brazil nuts and, the richest of all, Celebration cake with dark fruit and black treacle.

Goodbrey's Traditional Cakes, 8A Longrock Industrial Estate, Penzance, Cornwall TR20 8HX.

Tel/Fax: 01736 332205.

Price range: £10 to £18. Catalogue free.

Payment: cheque, Visa, Mastercard, Delta, Switch, Electron, JCB, Eurocard.

Postage & packing: by weight.

Delivery: last orders 2 weeks before Christmas.

Refunds: yes.

Meg Rivers Cakes and Gifts by Post Cakes for rowers and golfers, sailors and cricketers can be accompanied by a large Royal Worcester teacup appropriately decorated. Meg Rivers also ices cakes to order for children, birthdays or special occasions and there's a zodiac cake to suit your sign. She naturally has a Christmas special and there are even hampers, Christmas pudding and wheat-free cake for those allergic to flour.

Meg Rivers Cakes and Gifts by Post, Middle Tysoe, Warwickshire CV35 0SE.

Tel: 01295 688101 **Fax:** 01295 680799.

Price range: £2 to £55. Catalogue free.

Payment: cheque, Mastercard, Access, Visa, Switch, Connect, Delta.

Postage & packing: Varies, see order form.

Delivery: last Christmas orders by 6 December.

Refunds: by arrangement.

Primrose Hill Cake Company Round or square fruit cakes which include Brazil nuts, walnuts, glacé cherries, sun-dried raisins and sultanas are cooked and then glazed with brandy or rum and come in a green and gold tin. Short-crust mince pies are generally available, though check first – these arrive in a tin decorated with a Victorian toy shop. Cakes to ice yourself can be ordered or the firm will ice for you and include personal messages.

Primrose Hill Cake Company, PO Box 28, Aberdare CF44 YH.

Tel: 01685 812347.

Price range: £1.99 to £10.99. Leaflet free.

Payment: cheque, postal order.

Postage & packing: included.

Delivery: allow 28 days.

Refunds: no.

The edible Christmas tree

Real Cakes Hand-made rich fruit cakes with attitude. Innovative mixtures like the Toddy Cake (honey and whisky) and Devon Cider Cake (apples and apple liqueur) are baked to order. They come in a special Christmas tin which can be used long after the cake is eaten.

> **Real Cakes**, Anne's Park, Cowley, Exeter, Devon EX5 5EN.
> **Tel:** 01392 211286.
> **Price range:** £12 to £20. Catalogue (plus cake sample) free.
> **Payment:** cheque, Access, Visa, Mastercard, Eurocard.
> **Postage & packing:** included.
> **Delivery:** max 14 days, usually less by 1st class post; last Christmas orders by 10 December.
> **Refunds:** full for genuine complaint.

Village Cakes Cake-making is increasingly a lost art at home but there are plenty of keen home bakers who now mail order the longer-lasting English fruit cakes. This firm, based in Cornwall, uses local ingredients to make its cakes special. Ingredients include scrumpy cider, West Country ale and apples, pears, peaches and apricots from local orchards. The Jamaica cake (named after Jamaica Inn) is spiked with rum and the Surfers' Cake includes orange and lemon peel plus Cointreau. There is a special Christmas cake with optional icing and a Medieval Twelfth Night Cake which has brandy, rum, cherry brandy and port added to the recipe.

> **Village Cakes**, Rosemullion, Zelah, Cornwall TR4 9HH.
> **Tel/Fax:** 01872 540644.
> **Price range:** £11.50 to £24.50. Catalogue free
> **Payment:** cheque, Visa, Access.
> **Postage & packing:** £2.95.
> **Delivery:** normally 48 hours, last orders for Christmas, 5 December.
> **Refunds:** no.
> **Specials:** gift cards, third party delivery.

Cheese

The Fine Cheese Co Not your normal cheese hamper. Try the Pair of Wellingtons box: the right foot is made on the Duke of Wellington's estate from Guernsey cows, the left is a fruity wine from Wellington State, South Africa. Then there's the History of British Cheese Hatbox including 11th-century Swaledale, 16th-century Gloucester, Stilton from the 18th and Finn from the 20th. Quirky, but the produce is of the best quality. The deep red hatbox is most handsome.

> **The Fine Cheese Co**, 29/31 Walcot Street, Bath BA1 5BN.
> **Tel/Fax:** 01225 483407.
> **Price range:** £20 to £50. Catalogue free.
> **Payment:** cheque, Visa, Mastercard, Delta, Switch.
> **Postage & packing:** £6.95 per address.
> **Delivery:** overnight carrier. Last Christmas orders by 13 December; last delivery 19 December. Supplies can be limited.
> **Refunds:** only if faulty.

Jeroboams This is a small and select mail-order catalogue from the shop which sells wine, charcuterie but especially good cheeses. The food and wine are packed into special selections for Christmas which make good presents while the food itself works well for the holiday. There are boxes of speciality British cheeses like Appleby Cheshire, Bassett Stilton and the Irish Milleens, a Normandy box of Camembert, Livarot and Pont l'Eveque and jars of Stilton. Also cheese accessories such as a small cheese larder like a tiny meat safe or a raclette machine which melts cheeses at the table. The company offers hampers, hams and foie gras and a very nice glass ice bucket. Jeroboams will also mail order its normal cheese list on request.

> **Jeroboams**, 6 Clarendon Road, London W11 3AA.
> **Tel:** 0171 727 9792. **Fax:** 0171 792 3672.
> **Price range:** £17 to £250. Catalogue free.
> **Payment:** cheque and all major cards.
> **Postage & packing:** 1st class or overnight carrier included.

Delivery: last order around 16 December.

Refunds: yes.

Confectionery

Cavendish Chocolate Company These are rich, beautifully designed and wonderfully made luxury chocolates from a small list of five selections. Some arrive with a bottle of champagne and fifty choice chocolates while the smallest box, the ballotin, holds twenty-seven chocolates (which makes an excellent present).

Cavendish Chocolate Company Ltd, Field End, Long Crendon, Buckinghamshire HP18 9EJ.

Tel: 01844 201660. Order hotline: 01844 201690. **Fax:** 01844 201680.

Price range: £16.50 to £61.35. Catalogue free.

Payment: cheque, Visa, Mastercard.

Postage & packing: included.

Delivery: orders for Christmas by last GPO posting date or guaranteed next day delivery at extra cost.

Refunds: yes if valid.

Chambers Candy Co Specialises in unusual sweeties such as cachous scented with rose, orange blossom and violet, Elizabethan comfits made from sugar-coated seeds (an early breath freshener), strawberries, pecans, coffee beans and raisins dusted with cocoa, plus old-fashioned mint imperials and sugared almonds. There is a choice of nostalgic boxes featuring bears, Wind in the Willows characters and Fabergé eggs – ideal for those tired of chocolates.

Chambers Candy Co, Eagle House, Park Road, Halesowen, West Midlands B63 2RH.

Tel: 01384 424848. **Fax:** 01384 424849.

Price range: £1.25 to £5.99. Catalogue free.

Payment: cheque, Access, Visa, Mastercard.

Postage & packing: £2 on orders to £19.99, £3 up to £49.99, free thereafter.

Delivery: generally within a week.

Refunds: by arrangement.

Charbonnel et Walker The most famous and luxurious chocolates you can find in ranges which are delightfully descriptive of the past – The House Party, The Box at the Theatre, Drawing Room, Les Enfants, After Dinner. The chocolates and other sweets have Edwardian names such as enrobed stem ginger, dusted almonds and crèmes Parisiennes. There are also truffles, cooking chocolate and personalised boxes with a name spelled in foil-covered chocolate letters which is a lovely and unusual idea.

> **Charbonnel et Walker**, One The Royal Arcade, 28 Old Bond Street, London W1X 4BT.
>
> **Tel:** 0171 491 0939. **Fax:** 0171 495 6279.
>
> **Price range:** £3 to £190. Catalogue free.
>
> **Payment:** all major credit cards. Special arrangements for overseas.
>
> **Postage & packing:** £2.50 to £8.
>
> **Delivery:** orders for Christmas before 14 December, otherwise up to 4 days.
>
> **Refunds:** none available.

The Chocolate Club Already 12,000 have enrolled in this most self-indulgent of clubs and you will too, as soon as you order £10-worth or more from their catalogue. There are darkest South American chocolates 'enrobing' hazelnuts and almonds by Valrhona; Ackermann's truffles made with champagne, chocolate-coated nuts such as Brazils, almonds and hazelnuts, while Italy supplies panforte dusted with cocoa and Ricciarelli's real chocolate-coated marzipan. The club has fruit cakes and Christmas puddings, silvered almonds (hang them on the tree) and chocolate-filled prunes. To round off the sugar feast, there's French nougat and Turkish Delight.

> **The Chocolate Club Ltd**, Unit 9, St Pancras Commercial Centre, 63 Pratt Street, London NW1 0BY.
>
> **Tel:** 0171 267 5375. **Fax:** 0171 267 5357.
>
> **Price range:** £5.95 to £27.45. Catalogue free.
>
> **Payment:** cheque, Visa, Access, Diners, Switch, Connect.
>
> **Postage & packing:** £3.50 flat rate.

Delivery: within 14 days.

Refunds: yes.

Specials: club membership, gift service.

The Chocolate Society You can tell how very popular chocolates are as a present by the number of firms which offer them. The aim of the Society is 'To draw attention to the difference between the complex delicacy the world's greatest cooks recognise as chocolate and the low grade, cloying confection which the British consume by the ton every week.' So there! The Society sells Valrhona cooking chocolate (as used by the smart River Cafe in its Chocolate Nemesis) and flakes of drinking chocolate in caddies. These are neat gifts for those who love chocolate but want something different. Conserves and sauces are also sold.

The Chocolate Society, Clay Pit Lane, Roecliffe, near Boroughbridge, North Yorkshire YO5 9LS.

Tel: 01423 322238. **Fax:** 01423 322253.

Price range: £2 to £50. Send 1st class A4 SAE for catalogue.

Payment: cheque, Visa, Access, Mastercard, Switch.

Postage & packing: £5.50 in UK.

Delivery: last orders 10 days before Christmas.

Refunds: yes, if faulty or damaged and returned in 3 days.

Godiva Belgian chocolates are often thought to be the best in the world and Godiva makes them for the Belgian royal family. They look luxurious and come in excellent wrappings. There are neat plain squares in red and silver paper, liqueur chocolates in wooden boxes and even a set of golf ball chocolates. Godiva will custom build a box of the varieties you wish, pralines, truffles, marzipan, fondant and plain squares.

Godiva, 247 Regent Street, London W1R 7AE.

Tel: 0171 495 2845. **Fax:** 0171 409 0963.

Price range: £16 per lb. Gift wrapping from £1.50. Catalogue free.

Payment: cheque and major credit cards.

Postage & packing: from £2.50.

Delivery: 1st class post, last orders 5 days before Christmas.

Refunds: yes.

Specials: keepsake boxes, personalised boxes.

Humphreys Exclusive Confectionery Delicious chocolates are made by David Humphreys in a small shop in the moorland town of Ilkley. He has travelled Europe to get ideas and recipes and the results are rich and sensuous. He also makes novelties such as two-foot high Santas but, as yet, these can only be bought at the shop. The chocolate ranges are traditional English with rose, violet and strawberry creams; Belgique with pralines and marzipan and Swiss truffles flavoured with liqueurs. At Christmas there are marzipan petits fours and 'Christmas puddings' filled with praline and caramel.

Humphreys Exclusive Confectionery, 16 Leeds Road, Ilkley, West Yorkshire LS29 8DJ.

Tel: 01943 609477.

Price range: £4.85 to £26.75. Catalogue free.

Payment: cheque with order.

Postage & packing: included.

Delivery: last Christmas orders the day before last GPO posting day.

Refunds: no, unless faulty.

Specials: boxes made up on request.

Fish

Arctic Salmon Co The buzz word when buying salmon is 'wild', meaning fish which have not been farmed but have led a blameless life at sea. I can't tell the difference in taste but others might be able to. Wild salmon, however, have a much more pleasant life than those kept in pens. All the fish from this company are wild and smoked with beechwood. They come in sides of at least 700g and are ready-sliced. No preservatives are added.

Arctic Salmon Co Ltd, Fourth Floor, 55 South Audley Street, London W1Y 5FA.

Tel: 0171 493 1792. **Fax:** 0171 493 1797.

Price range: £22.60 per side. No catalogue.

Payment: cheque.

Postage & packing: included on UK mainland.

Delivery: within 48 hours of order or to date required.

Refunds: yes.

Dunkeld Smoked Salmon There are lots of smoked salmon firms offering mail order. I chose to include this one because it offers wild as well as farmed smoked salmon and because Delia Smith gets hers here. The smokehouse has been working for two generations, so they should know which fish to pick and how long each should be smoked. No additives are used.

Dunkeld Smoked Salmon Ltd., Springwells Smokehouse, Brae Street, Dunkeld, Perthshire PH8 0BA.

Tel: 01350 727639. **Fax:** 01350 728760.

Price range: £1.25 a tub of smoked salmon pâté to £15.80 per lb wild Tay smoked salmon. Catalogue free.

Payment: cheque, Access, Visa, Switch.

Postage & packing: included at Christmas.

Delivery: last Christmas orders by 1 December.

Refunds: yes.

Summer Isles Foods I once did a kipper tasting and, believe me, there is a huge variation. This firm in the far west of Scotland uses old whisky casks to smoke its kippers and other fish including wild and farmed salmon, sea trout and eel. You can even join its kipper club to be sent two pairs of delicious fat kippers every month for six months. And I bet you'll rejoin. There's also a salmon club which sends different cures, one a month. A hamper of smoked goodies including venison and chicken can also be ordered.

Summer Isles Foods, Achiltibuie, Ullapool, Ross IV26 2YG.

Tel: 01854 622353. **Fax:** 01854 622335.

Price range: £9.50 to £100. Catalogue free.

Payment: cheque, Access, Visa.

Postage & packing: included.

Delivery: last Christmas orders by first Saturday of December.
Refunds: yes.

Ummera Smoked Products

Ummera Smoked Products Wild Irish salmon is the speciality here, smoked over oak chippings. The texture, they say, is firm and tender, unlike the flabby fish which are kept in cages. Nor are the wild salmon given chemical treatment like farmed fish.

Ummera Smoked Products Ltd, Ummera House, Timoleague, Co Cork, Ireland.
Tel: 00 353 23 46187. **Fax:** 00 353 23 46419.
Price range: IR£20 upwards. Catalogue free.
Payment: Access or Visa invoiced in IR punts.
Postage & packing: IR£5.20 on 1kg side. Courier service IR£13.31.
Delivery: allow 2 weeks by post, 1 week by courier.
Refunds: yes.

Hampers

Benoist Baskets The firm has three Royal warrants, supplying the Queen, Prince Charles and the Queen Mother with groceries. Their hampers are notable for the unusual foods included such as artichoke hearts or white tuna in olive oil, Italian pickled onions and almond biscuits, their own conserves and biscuits, English and herbal teas. They are beautifully packed in wicker hampers.

Benoist Baskets, 8-10 Eldon Way, London NW10 7QX.
Tel: 0181 965 9531. **Fax:** 0800 387478.
Price range: £19 to £220. Catalogue free.
Payment: cheque, Visa, Access, Mastercard.
Postage & packing: £6.85 to £11.75 depending on size and area.
Delivery: last Christmas orders 4 December.
Refunds: yes, if lost or damaged.
Specials: discounts on Christmas orders paid for before 1 October.

The Gluttonous Gardener Ned Trier had the clever idea of combining plants and their related food in a kit. There are fourteen on the mail-order list, such as a young olive tree in a terracotta pot along with an excellent bottle of olive oil or a tequila kit of young agave plant, bottle of tequila, fresh lime and salt. His Christmas box, formulated for problem people, has a root-balled Christmas tree and a pudding laced with brandy and port. Other trees include an orange, a bay, a sweet chestnut and a stone pine (for pesto). Altogether a delightful present.

> **The Gluttonous Gardener**, 82 Wandsworth Bridge Road, London SW6 2TF.
>
> **Tel:** 0171 371 0775. **Fax:** 0171 371 8324.
>
> **Price range:** £15 to £45. Catalogue free.
>
> **Payment:** cheque only.
>
> **Postage & packing:** £6, £7 for 24-hour service.
>
> **Delivery:** 48 or 24 hours. Some supplies limited.
>
> **Refunds:** yes.

Hay Hampers This company supplies goodies to corporate customers through its food service and also its sister company, The Vintners Selection, and is thus able to team up good (and interesting) food and drink. I like the idea of the sweet tooth's Christmas hamper of cream sherry, Christmas pudding and all the trimmings plus miniature brandy and fruit cake – a bit incorrect for wine purists but just the job at Christmas. There are also picnic hampers including almost everything you can think of (cold bag for a bottle, for instance) if you decide to picnic over Christmas when cooking gets too much. They come in proper hampers with good-looking cutlery and crockery.

> **Hay Hampers**, The Barn, Church Street, Corby Glen, Grantham, Lincolnshire NG33 4NJ.
>
> **Tel:** 01476 550 420/476/548. **Fax:** 01476 550777.
>
> **Price range:** £10 to £270. Catalogue free.
>
> **Payment:** cheque, banker's draft, Access, Visa, Amex, Diners.
>
> **Postage & packing:** 48-hour delivery £4.99, 24-hour delivery £7.85 on UK mainland.

Delivery: see above but last orders for Christmas on 7 December.
Refunds: replaced or refunded.

Lochengower This smokehouse specialises not only in smoked salmon but also in the mild-flavoured, soft-textured sea trout and venison. These foods are all used in special hampers with a Scottish flavour. The Winter Village Christmas Tin, for instance, includes handmade chocolates, shortbread, Christmas cake, tablet and a clootie dumpling while the Christmas hamper adds smoked salmon, Christmas pudding, mincemeat and lots more. These hampers are well selected.

Lochengower, Kempleton Mill, Kirkcudbright DG6 4NJ.
Tel: 01557 330361. **Fax:** 01557 330385.
Price range: £8.35 to £55. Catalogue free.
Payment: cheque, Access, Visa, Amex.
Postage & packing: included in UK.
Delivery: Christmas orders by last GPO posting date, otherwise 1st class mail.
Refund: yes.

Norfolk Provender Do you know someone who pines for Norfolk and its foods? If so, this is the firm for them. Their hampers include local Elmham wines and punch made to a medieval recipe, Norfolk ham, pickles, chutney and hot honey mustard (deliciously crunchy). There is mincemeat with brandy, brandy butter with stem ginger and wassail cup from Cartwright & Butler, plus local smoked salmon cured in demerara sugar and brandy. They all come in willow hampers or baskets.

Norfolk Provender, Drove Farm Place, Breckles, Attleborough, Norfolk NR17 1 ER.
Tel: 01953 498639/717501. **Fax:** 01953 498639.
Price range: £13.99 to £100. Catalogue free.
Payment: cheque, Visa, Access, Mastercard.
Postage & packing: included.
Delivery: last Christmas orders by 14 December.
Refunds: by arrangement.

Panzer's These hampers are designed to contain the smartest food of the moment, whether it's pink grapefruit marmalade, Fauchon minicrepes or Carluccio's olive oil. There is a stocking hamper with a tapestry teddy bear design filled with chocolates or a galvanised bucket stuffed with champagne, but the firm will also source and make up hampers to your requirements. They have made up Japanese hampers, Thanksgiving hampers and Jewish New Year hampers so if you know someone with a food allergy or a passion for sweets shaped like animals, this is the place.

Panzer's, 13-19 Circus Road, St John's Wood, London NW8 6PB.

Tel: 0171 722 8162/8596. **Fax:** 0171 586 0209.

Price range: from £15. Catalogue free.

Payment: cheques, Access, Visa.

Postage & packing: London £5, mainland UK £10.

Delivery: 24 hours in UK, Christmas orders taken till 23 December, if not a Sunday.

Refunds: no.

Specials: custom-made hampers.

Taylors Traditional Hampers Foodie gifts of all kinds, starting with a series of eight hampers, the grandest of which comes in a dark willow basket and boasts six bottles of booze plus all the traditional hamper fare of Stilton, marmalade, anchovy relish, tea, mustard, Christmas pudding and chocolate plus much more. Then there are open willow baskets containing a bottle plus two goodies like Stilton and anchovy relish, wooden boxes of drink, a special Christmas box and even four picnic hampers including, sensibly, a vegetarian one.

Taylors Traditional Hampers, 31 St Giles, Oxford OX1 3LD.

Tel: 01865 511700.

Price range: £25 to £250. Catalogue free.

Payment: cheque, Visa, Mastercard.

Postage & packing: £7.50 to £25 in UK.

Delivery: by carrier, next day delivery £10 extra.

Refunds: no.

Miscellaneous

Fine Foods from France The firm is run by Britons who want to share the delicacies they have discovered in France, so the French catalogue comes with a glossary. One speciality is foie gras both from geese and ducks along with pâtés and mousses based on this. There is also a selection of cassoulets with goose, sausages, haricots, duck stewed in wine, roast pork, tripe and pâtés of wild boar, hare and pork. The firm will try to source other specialities for you. All come in smartly packaged dark red, blue and green jars, tins and boxes to make handsome presents. There are also hampers.

Fine Foods from France, William Harman, St. Laurent-Lolmie, 46800 Montcuq, France.

Tel: (00 33) 65 31 85 20.

Price range: £1.60 to £63.80. Catalogue free.

Payment: cheque, PO.

Postage & packing: £7 standard, £11 priority.

Delivery: within 10 working days.

Refunds: by arrangement.

Specials: gift hampers. Search service.

Homesmoke A cunning wheeze to smoke unusual foods at home, this is a large bag made from aluminium foil. Put the food inside, fold opening and put in oven, barbecue or even camp fire. The bag is flavoured with oak and thyme with rosemary or bay leaf as alternative flavours. Each bag can only be used once. The company also sells a grow-your-own shiitake mushroom kit.

Homesmoke, Fume International Ltd., 9 Crescent Road, Wokingham, Berkshire RG40 2DB.

Tel: 01734 893097/99. **Fax:** 01734 890906.

Price range: Homesmoke £10.99 for 5; Shiitake kit £15.95. Catalogue free.

Payment: cheque, Visa, Access, Mastercard, Eurocard.

Postage & packing: included.

Delivery: last Christmas order 15 December.

Refunds: yes.

Kileravagh Despite its name, the company smokes food in leafy Kent and will mail order either separate packs of its foods or three different hampers with an excellent choice. Not only is there the traditional smoked salmon, gravadlax and trout on offer but smoked eels, chicken, turkey, duck breasts and venison. The firm also sells special mayonnaise for smoked salmon flavoured with tarragon and lime or the hot Portuguese sauce, Piri Piri, and dill sauce for gravadlax. Even pets are catered for with Posh Pussy and Posh Pooch offcuts.

> **Kileravagh Smoked Foods**, Hedgend Estate, Birchington, Kent CT7 0NB.
> **Tel:** 01843 847086. **Fax:** 01843 848000.
> **Price range:** £3.75 to £75. No catalogue, price list available.
> **Payment:** cheque, Visa, Mastercard.
> **Postage & packing:** included.
> **Delivery:** up to 5 working days before Christmas, generally 24 hour service.
> **Refunds:** yes.
> **Specials:** gift service, flexible orders for hampers.

Quintessentials Europe French foods from the Comtesse du Barry range are available either as packed gifts such as a box of duck and goose foie gras in a metallic hexagonal box, six pâtés and rillettes or even as a presentation dinner for two – for instance, duck bordelais with ceps, pears and brandy soufflé and two half bottles of wine chosen to suit. There is a large range of other French delicacies to order, including cassoulet, salted pork with Puy lentils and lots of terrines and pâtés. Hampers are sent out in pretty boxes of willow, raffia and gingham ribbon.

> **Quintessentials Europe Ltd**, 5a 77 Anson Road, London N7 0AX.
> **Tel:** 0171 580 5068. **Fax:** 0171 637 8683.
> **Price range:** from £1.20. Catalogue free.
> **Payment:** cheque, major credit cards.
> **Postage & packing:** £3 or free for orders over £50.
> **Delivery:** last Christmas orders by 7 December.
> **Refunds:** yes.

Wendy Brandon Most of us no longer have the time or the equipment to make traditonal preserves but Wendy Brandon has. Her preserves are divided into four varieties: the green label covers chutneys and fruit sauces, made without added salt or sugar and including delicious and unusual varieties such as apricot, Kashmiri apple with a spicy Indian flavour and a Jamaican style mango chutney; the orange label is for coarse-cut marmalades made from all varieties of citrus fruit from lemon to kumquat; the red label is for jams, jellies, spiced vinegars and pickles; and the blue is the international range of pickles and chutneys from Europe, India and even Australia (hot piccalilli). You can choose a mixture of preserves (up to eight jars) to pack in a willow tray for a present.

Wendy Brandon, Felin Wen, Boncath, Pembrokeshire SA37 0JR
Tel: 01239 841568. **Fax:** 01239 841746.
Price range: £2.75 to £4.95. Catalogue free
Payment: cheque, Visa, Access, Mastercard.
Postage & packing: £5.75 for any order.
Delivery: last orders for Christmas, December 15. Some preserves in limited supply.

See also: Fortnum & Mason for hampers, food boxes (General Catalogues), Ciel Decor for Provençal specialities (Home Interest) and all food entries in Christmas Food sections.

Chapter Six

SPECIAL INTERESTS AND SPORTS

ENTHUSIASMS

Catalogues devoted to a single interest are not just for fanatics (though they appeal to that category too). These goods will often appeal as general presents. There's a catalogue for wild mushroom collectors which sells beautiful Italian wrapping paper printed with funghi, for instance, or a catalogue of globes – very smart in the country house library. It's a growing area ideally suited to mail-order as you don't often see single-interest shops as obscure as this surviving in the small town high street.

Single-interest businesses may be a bit clubby. The owners are often enthusiasts keen to pass on tips and often just as keen to get ideas from customers. If you want to give a present to a bridge player, for instance, the owner of the playing-card catalogue listed here will be full of good ideas to help. The pharmacist who sells old drug jars will explain their history and the uses of the ointments they once held. If a close friend or family member shares one of these enthusiasms, you will have solved present-giving for life – the catalogues keep evolving as the owner discovers new treats.

ENTHUSIASMS – LISTINGS

Academica Anything to do with decorative pharmacies recreated by a working pharmacist. These include beautiful glass bottles with gilded labels for Latin names. Some are plain for coloured liquids, others in ultramarine Bristol or emerald glass. The firm also imports reproduction maiolica drug jars from Italy. These are painted in brilliant yellow and blue on white or show biblical and military scenes. The quality of the hand-painting is excellent and the range exclusive.

Academica, 57 Brecknock Road, London N7 0BX.
Tel: 0171 485 5924. **Fax:** 0171 485 1217.
Price range: £20 - £400. Catalogue: free on request.
Payment: cheque.
Postage & packing: at cost.
Delivery: 14 days but supplies may be limited.
Refunds: if damaged.

Archers Addicts

Archers Addicts Can't go on holiday without taping affairs at Ambridge? This is the catalogue for such fanatics. There are mugs, T-shirts, a Grey Gables towelling gown, the official map of Ambridge, a replica of The Bull and there's now a weekly synopsis (started in October 1995) of the soap for ex-pats who need to keep tabs.

Archers Addicts, PO Box 1951, Moseley, Birmingham B13 9DD.
Tel: 0121 772 3112. **Fax:** 0121 753 3310.
Price range: 80p to £29.99. Send SAE with C4 envelope for catalogue.
Payment: cheque, Visa, Mastercard, Access, Switch, Delta.
Postage & packing: £2.95 on orders to £19.99; £3.95 to £29.99; £4.95 to £39.99, £5.95 thereafter.
Delivery: last Christmas orders by 12 December.
Refunds: yes.

Brian Jarrett

Brian Jarrett A member of the International Guild of Knot Tyers (yes, really), Jarrett specialises in the old craft of displaying the more complex nautical knots mounted and framed. Each of his designs incorporates white cotton cord in several ordinary knots and the more difficult ones, known as plaits and

sinnets displayed against a navy blue backing. Each knot has a small brass plate engraved with its name. More complex boards can include a central photograph of a famous or decorated sailor or ship. One allows personal insignia to be included.

Brian Jarrett, Villa Rosa, Oakfield Lane, Wilmington, Dartford, Kent DA1 2TE.

Tel/Fax: 01322 227725.

Price range: £20 to £85. Send large SAE for brochure.

Payment: cheque, postal order.

Postage & packing: from £2.50 to £6.25.

Delivery: Christmas orders by last week November.

Refunds: by arrangement.

Classic Car Art

Miniature classic car models are set in an old garage with Shell posters on the wall, the engines on the block, tools scattered around the floor and the whole thing is then framed. Charming gifts for anyone interested in old cars and eminently hangable. Women tend to buy them for men. Cars range from AC to Volkswagen and include Bugatti, Ferrari and Chevrolet Bel Air.

Classic Car Art, Two Hill End Cottages, Hatfield Park, Hatfield, Hertforshire AL9 5PQ (correspondence only).

Tel: 01707 270308.

Price range: £80 to £295. Catalogue free.

Payment: cheque, Eurocheque.

Postage & packing: around £20 apiece.

Delivery: by courier, takes 4 to 6 weeks but allow early November for Christmas as only 500 made per year.

Refunds: no – but look at goods first in the venues printed in the brochure.

Faerie Shop

Need a pair of rainbow wings, a spangled wand or pair of pixie slippers? Yes, you can dress little girls as fairies and little boys as gnomes with the aid of this mail-order catalogue. Also fairy books, cushions, cards and ornaments.

The Faerie Shop Catalogue Ltd, PO Box 604, Marlborough, Wiltshire SN8 3NR.

Tel: 01672 871001. **Fax:** 01672 871003.

Price range: £2 to £32.50. Send stamp for free catalogue.

Payment: cheque, Visa, Access, Mastercard, JCB, Switch.

Postage & packing: £2.95, free on orders over £75.

Delivery: generally 10 days but allow 28. Some goods run short at Christmas.

Refunds: yes, if returned in 14 days.

House of Hamilton

House of Hamilton A collection of all things Scottish including smoked salmon, whisky, tartan, golf and shooting equipment. The smoked salmon was given to President Bush, is used on The Royal Scotsman and is chosen because it's the best available. The whisky is Hamilton's own blend and the sporting accessories are also top of the range.

House of Hamilton, 13 Brewster Square, Brucefield Industrial Park, Livingston, West Lothian EH54 9BJ

Tel: 01506 418434. **Fax:** 01506 418413.

Price range: £4 to £180. Catalogue free.

Payment: cheque and major credit cards.

Postage & packing: £7.05 flat rate.

Delivery: 3 days for salmon. 28 days for rest.

Refunds: yes, if firm is satisfied your complaint is justified.

H.S. Productions

H.S. Productions What Pirelli calendars do for the female body, HS does for the car body. These big glossy productions gloat over each radiator grille, each spoked wheel and shiny badge. They are stunningly photographed and very glamorous. Cars include AC, Morgan, TVR and MG with calendars for Aston Martin, Mini, Range Rover and Rolls in 1997.

H.S. Productions, 74 Dene Road, Northwood, Middlesex HA6 2DF.

Tel: 01923 825121. **Fax:** 01923 835967.

Price range: £7 for posters, £26.50 for calendars but price under review. Catalogue free.

Payment: cheque.

Postage & packing: included.

Delivery: last Christmas orders by end of November. All editions are limited and calendars available from October.

Refunds: yes, if returned in 10 days.

John Ocamster A weird one, this. Ocamster will send you a copy of the wills of John Lennon, Marilyn Monroe, Elvis and John F. Kennedy. Less bizarrely, he will sell you copies of the birth certificates of the Beatles. The wills can run to fourteen pages like those of Elvis and JFK. He does no others – it's not worth the trouble.

> **John Ocamster**, 4 Gurdon Road, Colchester CO2 7PB.
> **Fax:** 01206 575328. No phone.
> **Price range:** £10 for a will; £10 for four birth certificates. No catalogue.
> **Payment:** cheque, postal order.
> **Postage & packing:** included in UK.
> **Delivery:** same day service or when cheque clears.
> **Refunds:** no.

Magic by Post If you're looking for all the gadgets that let you push pencils through coins, pull red hankies through transparent tubes and chop off your own fingers or arms (adults only), then this is the company to get in touch with. You can set your hands on fire, do the three-card trick and make rabbits appear in hats. The range is for both beginners and professionals.

> **Magic by Post**, 167 Winchester Road, Bristol BS4 3NJ.
> **Tel/Fax:** 0117 977 4334.
> **Price range:** £2 to £60. Catalogue free.
> **Payment:** cheque, Access, Visa, Mastercard, Eurocard.
> **Postage & packing:** from £1.60 to £3.60.
> **Delivery:** allow 28 days.
> **Refunds:** yes.
> **Special:** join the Magic Club for an extra £5.

The Maritime Company Seafaring and yachting objects make great presents and are currently highly fashionable indoors – just look at the prices paid for antique pond yachts. This mail-order catalogue is new from the Past Times stable and has all the hallmarks of its efficiency and smart service. Ideas vary from practical binoculars and pocket knives to ornamental ships' models, barometers and candles shaped like colourful lighthouses.

The Maritime Company, Witney, Oxfordshire OX8 6BH.
Tel: 01993 770450. **Fax:** 01993 700749.
Price range: £5 to £600. Catalogue free.
Payment: cheque, postal orders, Access, Eurocard, Visa, Mastercard, Amex, Diners, JCB, Delta, Switch.
Postage & packing: £2.95 orders under £30, £3.50 for over.
Delivery: within 7 days or next day express in UK for £4.95 extra.
Refunds: yes.

Millington Marketing Your aid to winning the lottery, or at least enjoying the attempt. The British Lottery Ball Pack has a set of one-inch balls colour-coded like those on BBC, five displays to set up your numbers in order and a special pen to write the numbers. All in a black bag. Ideal for someone who has everything but a lottery win.

Millington Marketing, PO Box 49, Saffron Walden, Essex CB11 3NH.
Tel: 01799 513174. Fax 01799 513247.
Price: £12.99. Send SAE for brochure.
Payment: cheque, postal order.
Postage & packing: included.
Delivery: last Christmas order 12 December.
Refunds: yes, if damaged.

Mycologue Everything for the mushroom maniac including posters, cards, wrapping paper, prints to frame, books and videos on mushroom identification and hunting. Then there are foraying knives with compasses in case you get lost and rulers to measure your finds, woven willow mushroom baskets and life-like model mushrooms to convince the world your foray was fruitful. Finally, what about a little silver lapel pin so other mycologists can identify and discuss hunts with you?

Mycologue, 47 Spencer Rise, London NW5 1AR.
Tel: 0171 485 7063. **Fax:** 0171 284 4058.

Price range: £5 to £40. Catalogue free.
Payment: cheque or postal order.
Postage & packing: included.
Delivery: orders for Christmas by last GPO posting date.
Refunds: for faulty goods, credit for non-faulty goods.

Nauticalia Anything to do with the sea from a Royal Navy sword and scabbard to bosun's whistles and models of cannons. There are barometers, brass bulkhead chronometers renowned for excellent time-keeping and lots of books about the romance of seafaring. Though a single-interest catalogue, there's something here to suit many people.

Nauticalia Ltd, Ferry Lane, Shepperton, Middlesex TW17 9LQ.
Tel: 01932 253333. **Fax:** 01932 241679.
Price range: under £10 to over £1,000. Catalogue free.
Payment: cheque or any credit card.
Postage & packing: £2.95.
Delivery: within 10 days; next day delivery, £7.50 extra.
Refunds: yes.
Specials: proportion of proceeds go to Maritime Trust.

A Pack of Cards A fine selection of playing cards and bridge accessories. The cards are backed with Florentine or tartan patterns, portraits of Elizabeth and Essex, old-fashioned cricketers and golfers and can be personalised. There is even a set of children's cards to get them hooked early. Also score cards, pencils and recipe books of meals to serve at bridge parties.

A Pack of Cards, Hollins Hill House, Utkinton, Tarporley, Cheshire CW6 0JP.
Tel: 01829 760549.
Price range: £1.50 to £60. Catalogue free.
Payment: cheque, Mastercard, Access, Visa.
Postage & packing: £1.50 on orders to £15; £2.50 between £15 and £25, £3.25 thereafter.
Delivery: last Christmas orders by GPO deadline.
Refunds: by arrangement.

Replogle Globes This firm has been selling globes since 1930, ranging from those huge ones on wooden stands that are found in country house libraries to a 4.7-inch diameter globe of the world to be held in the hand. There are star map globes which light up to show pin-point stars against the heavens and a twelve-inch globe of features of the moon. The globes are fine without exception but in my view some of the stands are less so. Pick those which are least obtrusive. There are also colour prints of the world seen by satellite.

> **Replogle Globes**, Thanet Globe Emporium, 2-3 Orange Street, Canterbury, Kent CT1 2JA.
>
> **Tel:** 01227 450055. **Fax:** 01227 760548.
>
> **Price range:** £15 to £7,900. Catalogue free.
>
> **Payment:** cheque, Visa, Mastercard.
>
> **Postage & packing:** £3.25 orders under £25, up to £12.50 to £999, over £1,000 free.
>
> **Delivery:** overnight carrier. Some globes in short supply.
>
> **Refunds:** by arrangement.

See also: Sewills for barographs, barometers, chronometers (Home Interest), Video Plus and Talking Pages Direct for loads of single interest tapes, WCP Video for falconry, birds of prey (Books, Cassettes, CDs and Videos), Roger Alsop for car portraits, Wright & Logan for ship portraits (Personalised Presents), Dolls' House Catalogue for miniature furniture etc, Teddy Bears of Witney for a huge range of old and new toy bears (Children).

CHARITIES

Buying presents, gift wrapping and cards from charities poses different questions from buying other gifts. When you select from a charity catalogue, do you want to support the particular cause or charity in general? Many causes earn most of their money over Christmas and the number of charity catalogues grows every year. And charity Christmas cards have virtually taken over from those produced by stationery firms.

Some causes are ideal for gift catalogues. People keen on birds not only support the RSPB but find the gifts relate to their interest; the same is true of Survival which tries to protect vanishing tribes worldwide. Guide Dogs for the Blind's catalogue is animal based, as is the RSPCA's. The NSPCC, in contrast, has cleverly emphasised stocking fillers in its catalogue and is the natural mail-order catalogue choice to solve this aspect of Christmas shopping.

Unlike other companies, charities need to keep their administration and production costs in check. The glossy and glitzy productions of some firms' literature would be out of place in this context so the catalogues tend to be produced on limp paper. You need just a bit more imagination to choose presents from them.

Most catalogues cover a wide range of items: food, cards and wrapping paper, trinkets, soaps and accessories such as scarves and gloves. Many charities contract out the work of selecting products and publishing a catalogue to seasoned mail-order firms like Innovations. When you order from the catalogues, you will generally be dealing with these businesses and not directly with the charities.

CHARITIES – LISTINGS

Action Research This charity funds medical research into areas such as how to treat children with burns and why those with sickle cell disease are more likely to have strokes. It has a small catalogue but everything in it is in good taste and useful, with a bias towards stationery. There are also Christmas cards and wrapping paper.

Action Research, Nancegollan, Helston, Cornwall TR13 0TR.
Tel: 01209 831456. **Fax:** 01209 831995.
Price range: £3 to £30. Catalogue free on request to the above address or charity's head office at Vincent House, Horsham, West Sussex RH12 2DP.
Payment: cheque, Access, Visa.
Postage & packing: from about £1.25.
Delivery: last orders for Christmas 16 December.
Refunds: yes, if returned in 14 days.

British Heart Foundation This catalogue is full of cards, wrapping paper, gift-tags and presents which tend to be jokey, such as musical socks, wine-stained T-shirts and shocking pink car radios. The foods – mince pies, milk chocolate puddings, cakes – do no harm, the Foundation says, taken in moderation.

British Heart Foundation Catalogue, Euroway Business Park, Swindon, Wiltshire SN5 8SN.
Tel: 01793 420000.
Price range: £1.95 to £65. Catalogue free.
Payment: cheque, Access, Visa, Mastercard, Amex, Diners.
Postage & packing: £3.25.
Delivery: last Christmas orders 12 December.
Refunds: yes.

Countrywide Workshops Everything in this catalogue is made by disabled people, either by single craftsmen working on their own or from charity or local authority sheltered work-shops. The real Shetland Fair Isle waistcoats, the wooden nativity and Noah's ark sets for children, the hand woven willow baskets and rocking cots are all beautifully made. The catalogue also has an amazing array of brushes from the Lord Roberts Workshops which I think make an inspired present if carefully chosen – not the loo brush, perhaps, but the banister brush and grate brush, both in old-fashioned shapes.

Countrywide Workshops Charitable Trust, 47 Fisherton Street, Salisbury, Wiltshire SP2 7SU.

Tel: 01722 326886. **Fax:** 01722 411092.

Price range: 20p to £2250. Catalogue free but donations welcome.

Payment: cheque, Access, Visa, Diners, Switch.

Postage & packing: £1.50 as donation.

Delivery: 28 days.

Refunds: complete guarantee.

Gardeners Royal Benevolent Society As this charity interests gardeners, the gifts include strong gardening gloves, tools (go for the Felco secateurs, the best you can find), stout carry-alls and gardening books. There are also cards, gift wrapping and Christmassy paper napkins.

GRBS (Enterprises) Ltd, Bridge House, 139 Kingston Road, Leatherhead, Surrey KT22 7NT.

Tel: 01372 373962. **Fax:** 01372 362575.

Price range: £2 to £25. Send SAE for catalogue.

Payment: cheque, Access, Visa, Mastercard, Switch.

Postage & packing: detailed on form.

Delivery: allow 28 days.

Refunds: yes.

Guide Dogs for the Blind Association Charities working for animals have an easy time at Christmas, as their cards, calendars and wrapping paper simply use charming pictures of the relevant beast. Thus we have images of the breeds used as guide dogs such as setters, Alsatians and labradors, in every pose. There are also doggy toys, doormats, T-shirts, ovengloves and toys, brushes and beanbags for dogs.

Guide Dogs for the Blind Association, PO Box 20, Tanners Lane, Barkingside, Ilford, Essex IG6 1QQ.
Tel: 01268 524948. **Fax:** 01268 520230.
Price range: £1.50 to £65. Catalogue free.
Payment: cheque, Access, Visa.
Postage & packing: scale in catalogue.
Delivery: last Christmas orders by 1 December.
Refunds: yes, if returned in 28 days.
Specials: personalised Christmas cards and stationery.

Help the Aged All the profits of the charity go to the elderly with problems, and the catalogue has a bias towards their comforts. There are pill organisers, special pillows, a gadget to help pull on tights, walking sticks and wheeled shopping baskets. There's a clever selection of cassettes from the BBC with old favourites like Joyce Grenfell, 'Round the Horne' and Alistair Cooke's 'Letter from America'. General items include cards, calendars, food and children's toys.

Help the Aged (Mail Order) Ltd, PO Box 28, London N18 3HG.
Tel: 0181 807 8074.
Price range: £1.99 to £40. Catalogue free (write to Mail Order Dept, Help the Aged, St James Walk, Clerkenwell Green, London EC1R 0BE. **Tel:** 0171 250 0253 **Fax:** 0171 250 4474).
Payment: cheque, Visa, Access, Mastercard.
Postage & packing: £1.95 for orders under £10; free thereafter.
Delivery: last Christmas orders by 10 December.
Refunds: yes.

Lord Roberts Workshops If you, like me, love old-fashioned brushes, this is the place to look for presents. There are seventeen different household brushes – hard-bristle scrubbing ones and soft banister ones, brooms for indoors and out and long-handled ones for baths. All are made by disabled servicemen at an Edinburgh factory patronised by the Queen and Queen Mother.

Lord Roberts Workshops, 6 Western Corner, Edinburgh EH12 5PY.

Tel/Fax: 0131 337 6951.

Price range: £2.30 to £90. Catalogue free.

Payment: cheque, Visa, Access.

Postage & packing: included.

Delivery: allow 28 days.

Refunds: by arrangement.

NSPCC The charity has had the bright idea of specialising in stocking fillers (lamentably spelt 'fillas' in its catalogue). There are sections for toddlers, teenagers (including temporary tattoos and Christmas earrings, spell-checkers, pocket translators and fridge magnets) and key-rings for grown-ups. There are also cracker fillers and wrapping paper. The charity has had a lot of fun finding jokes and games to create a selection unlike any other.

NSPCC, Stockingfillas, Euroway Business Park, Swindon SN5 8SN.

Tel: 01793 410080. **Fax:** 01793 520035.

Price range: 50p to £18. Catalogue free.

Payment: cheque, Access, Visa, Delta.

Postage & packing: £1.99.

Delivery: last Christmas orders by 11 December.

Refunds: yes.

Notting Hill Housing Trust A catalogue that's different from most with a bias towards home gifts such as chair throws, cushions, curtains and colourful glass bottles. It is small but selective.

Notting Hill Housing Trust, Aspen House, 1 Gayford Road, London W12 9BY.

Tel: 0181 563 4888. **Fax:** 0181 563 4899.

Price range: £1 to £30. Catalogue free.

Payment: cheque, Visa, Access.

Postage & packing: £3.50.

Delivery: last Christmas orders 11 December.

Refunds: yes.

People's Trust for Endangered Species This charity, working to help wildlife, has a small catalogue. T-shirts, aprons, bags and so on are printed with animals; there are some good books on the subject plus items such as hedgehog boxes, seeds for butterfly-attracting plants and cards to help children identify animals' tracks. Cards and gift-tags are also available.

People's Trust for Endangered Species, 15 Cloisters House, 8 Battersea Park Road, London SW8 4BG.
Tel: 0171 498 4533. **Fax:** 0171 498 4459.
Price range: 99p to £17. Catalogue free.
Payment: cheque, Visa, Mastercard, Eurocard.
Postage & packing: included.
Delivery: a few days but allow longer at Christmas.
Refunds: yes.

Queen Elizabeth's Foundation for Disabled People The charity gives support and help for disabled people learning new skills. Its catalogue has a good selection of general cards along with calendars and crackers, as well as food, stationery, kitchen equipment, soap, garden tools and games. If you want to support its cause, you will find something here to buy.

Queen Elizabeth's Foundation for Disabled People, Retail Trading Office, Oaklawn Road, Leatherhead, Surrey KT22 0BT.
Tel: 01372 843616. **Fax:** 01372 842761.
Price range: £2 to £33. Catalogue free.
Payment: cheque, Access, Visa, Mastercard.
Postage & packing: under review.
Delivery: last orders for Christmas 1 December.
Refunds: yes.

Royal Horticultural Society This charity has a nicely chosen general catalogue with some connection with gardening. There is crockery patterned with flowers, gardening books and videos, pot pourri and small garden tools such as secateurs and pruning knives. Simple but charming cards are available.

RHS Enterprises, RHS Garden, Wisley, Woking, Surrey GU23 6QB.

Tel: 01483 211320.

Price range: £3 to £45. Send SAE for catalogue.

Payment: cheque, Mastercard, Access, Visa, Amex.

Postage & packing: £1 for orders under £5, up to £5 between £30 and £100, free thereafter.

Delivery: allow 28 days.

Refunds: yes, if returned as new in 14 days.

Royal Opera House Neil Bottle, known for his beautiful printing on silk, has been commissioned by the ROH to create both silk squares and hand-made ties and bow ties. He has used themes from the building and musical scores – a treble clef, swooshing lines of music, the handsome portico and Corinthian capitals – to print on red and cream silk, with overtones of slate, olive and deep blue. Charming and elegant.

Royal Opera House, Postal Sales, Covent Garden, London WC2E 9DD.

Tel: 0171 495 0550. **Fax:** 0171 495 4050.

Price range: £29.50 to £125. Catalogue free.

Payment: cheque, Mastercard, Access, Visa, Amex.

Postage & packing: included.

Delivery: allow 21 days.

Refunds: by arrangement.

RSPCA Naturally most of the gift ideas in this catalogue involve animals, especially cats and dogs but also birds, hedgehogs, farm animals and more exotic elephants and tigers. If you want to support the charity, you should be able to find something here. Cards and gift wrapping are available.

RSPCA Trading Ltd, PO Box 46, Burton Upon Trent DE14 3LQ.

Tel: 01283 506125.

Price range: £1.99 to £42.99. Catalogue free, **Tel:** 01283 506122.

Payment: cheque, Switch, Delta, Visa, Mastercard.

Postage & packing: to be confirmed.

Delivery: last Christmas orders by mid December.

Refunds: yes, if returned in 14 days.

Royal Society for the Protection of Birds In this catalogue, there are lots of cards of birds (and angels), crackers, wrapping paper and tags, napkins, tablecloths and candles for Christmas day. Present ideas mostly relate to birds – bird mugs and trays, T-shirts with birds, flappy puffin toys – for all the family. And, of course, bird boxes, feeders, baths and food.

> **Royal Society for the Protection of Birds**, The Lodge, Sandy, Bedfordshire SG19 2DL.
>
> **Tel:** 01767 680551. **Fax:** 01767 682118.
>
> **Price range:** 50p to £99. Catalogue free on request to RSPB Sales Ltd, Queensbridge Works, Queens Street, Burton on Trent DE14 3LQ.
>
> **Payment:** cheque, Switch, Access, Mastercard, Delta, Visa.
>
> **Postage & packing:** up to £3.35.
>
> **Delivery:** up to 21 days unless personalised when allow 28 days.
>
> **Refunds:** yes, depending on complaint.

Soil Association This charity, dedicated to good farming practice, has a list including masses of books from *Goat Husbandry* to *Story of the Potato*. There are a few cards, shopping bags and labels for re-using envelopes. You can also buy copies of their directory of farm shops and vegetable box schemes.

> **Soil Association**, Mail-Order Department, Organic Food and Farming Centre, 86 Colston Street, Bristol BS1 5BB.
>
> **Tel:** 0117 929 0661.
>
> **Price range:** 50p to £15. Catalogue free.
>
> **Payment:** cheque, Mastercard, Access, Visa.
>
> **Postage & packing:** 50p on orders to £3, £1.50 to £10, £3 up to £20, £4 thereafter.
>
> **Delivery:** last Christmas orders by 5 December.
>
> **Refunds:** by arrangement.

Survival This charity, concerned about the survival of endangered tribes worldwide, sells goods based on tribal designs and artefacts. There are boomerangs, aprons and bags based on Amazonian rock drawings and interesting stick figures by bushmen. Also cards and gift wrapping with the same themes.

Survival, Nancegollan, Helston, Cornwall TR13 0SU.
Tel 01209 831831/831456. **Fax:** 01209 831995.
Price range: £1.95 to over £100. Catalogue free.
Payment: cheque, Visa, Mastercard, Switch, Delta.
Postage & packing: £2.95 for orders up to £15; £3.95 there-after.
Delivery: last Christmas orders 11 December.
Refunds: yes, if returned in 28 days.

Traidcraft This company, which encourages fair trade with the Third World, sells nativity sets from Peru and Tanzania, decorative seagrass stars from the Philippines and gilded moon and star baubles from Bali. In the gift range, there are brilliant blue and yellow primitive guinea fowl from Zimbabwe, plus marbled and batik covered stationery. Good for unusual ideas.

Traidcraft, Kingsway, Gateshead, Tyne & Wear NE11 0NE.
Tel: 0191 487 1001. Order line: 0191 491 0855. **Fax:** 0191 487 0133.
Price range: £1.25 to £55. Catalogue free.
Payment: cheque, Visa, Mastercard.
Postage & packing: £2.99 up to £25, £3.99 over £25, free over £75.
Delivery: last orders for Christmas 15 December; express (£5.50) 20 December.
Refunds: yes, if returned in 14 days.

WaterAid The charity is devoted to getting safe water to Third World country communities. Its catalogue is a curious mix of goods connected with water: plant pots, taps, watering cans, drinking glasses and waterproof rugs. Bathroom ideas include soapdishes patterned with seahorses, vases pressed with ammonite patterns and starfish towel hooks. Nicely chosen.

WaterAid Trading Ltd, Forest Side, Newport, Isle of Wight PO30 5QW.
Tel: orders 0990 539081, catalogues and enquiries 0990 539141.
Price range: £2.50 to £50. Catalogue free, though SAE would help.
Payment: cheque, Access, Visa, Mastercard.

Postage & packing: £1.80 up to £7, £3.40 from £7 to £59.99, thereafter free.

Delivery: last Christmas orders 13 December.

Refunds: yes, if returned in 14 days.

See also: Museums and National Trust and National Trust for Scotland (Art and Replicas)

SPORTS

I have to own up – sports leave me cold, although even I started to get enthusiastic about some of the amazing presents you can buy mail order.

Calendars which do for sports cars what Pirelli does for girls, soap that won't harm mountain streams or a do-it-yourself dental kit for those trekking through the Taklamakan desert (the world's most horrible place) can be found. There are clothes which defy even the Scottish midge (the world's most voracious insect) and a marvellous firm called Red Letter Days, the mail-order equivalent of *Jim'll Fix It* which can fix you a session with a professional footballer or a trip on the Orient Express.

Even the least sports-conscious men have hidden longings to drive steam trains, pilot World War II fighters in flak jackets and glass goggles or potter along in a vintage car. They can, they can. You can give vouchers for all of these or for balloon rides, sky-diving and kart racing.

It all sounds petrifying to me, but I know lots of people just waiting for the chance to do something dangerous. You probably do too.

SPORTS – LISTINGS

Activities

Acorne All sorts of derring-do by voucher. You can give a balloon ride, a sky-dive, or a parachute jump. You can give people the chance to have a go at piloting a plane, gliding a glider or hovering in a helicopter. Give them twenty minutes of Biggles in a Tiger Moth or commanding a jumbo (in a simulator, thankfully). Acorne also offers a voucher where the recipient picks his own peril and, as over 140 locations accept these vouchers, it shouldn't be too hard to find something of interest.

Acorne Air Sports, Wycombe Air Centre, Booker, Marlow, Buckinghamshire SL7 3DR.
Tel: 01494 451703. **Fax:** 01494 465456.
Price range: £51 to £361. Catalogue free.
Payment: cheque, Access, Visa, Diners, Amex.
Postage & packing: included.
Delivery: up to last GPO posting day.
Refunds: not available.

Bespokes You may not be able to buy your man an E-type Jag or Ferrari 308 GTS but you can hire him one for a day, a weekend or a week from this firm. They also have Alfa Romeo Spiders, Mercedes 230SL and the Aston Martin DB6 and V8. Just imagine a week's holiday in the Highlands in one of these superb and beautiful machines. Cars can be delivered to and collected from you by arrangement.

Bespokes, 127 High Road, Bushey Heath, Hertfordshire WD2 1JA.
Tel: 0181 421 8686. **Fax:** 0181 421 8588.

Price range: £138 to £1,310; or on application. Catalogue free.

Payment: cheque, major cards except Amex.

Postage & packing: not applicable.

Delivery: By arrangement. Advance gift-vouchers allow recipients to pick dates and cars.

Refunds: by arrangement.

Specials: only drivers between 25 and 65 with valid licences.

Castle Combe Skid Pan & Kart Track Gift vouchers for this company which does exactly what it says. Children over ten and over 4ft 6in tall are eligible for the kart-track practice sessions; the kart racing proper is for anyone over fifteen. Skid pan driving is for driving licence holders only.

Castle Combe Skid Pan & Kart Track, Castle Combe Circuit, Chippenham, Wiltshire SN14 7EX.

Tel: 01249 782101. **Fax:** 01249 782161.

Price range: £15 to £705. Brochure free.

Payment: cheque, Visa, Access.

Postage & packing: postage of voucher included.

Delivery: orders by last GPO Christmas posting date.

Refunds: not applicable.

Delta Racing and Aviation Professional instructors teach enthusiasts the skills of motor racing at two Yorkshire tracks and another in Essex, so gift vouchers would work over much of England. Drivers are taught lapping skills and are driven by professionals at racing speeds. The aviation days use Tiger Moths and T-6 Harvards. With dual controls and dressed in WWII flying gear, there is at least twenty minutes in the air plus group photo and cockpit photo.

Delta Racing and Delta Aviation, 2 South View, Maunby, North Yorkshire YO7 4HF.

Tel: racing 01845 587415, aviation 01845 587507. **Fax:** 01845 587507.

Price range: racing £125 to £185, aviation £185 to £425. Catalogue free.

Payment: cheque, Amex, Access, Visa.

Postage & packing: included.

Delivery: lst class post, fax up to Christmas Eve for faxed voucher in return. Days are limited.

Refunds: no.

Drive it all Complete beginners and veteran rally drivers alike use this track in specially prepared rally cars. The treated gravel surface combines fast and slow corners and varying surface conditions but it is without trees and ditches and therefore safe.

Drive it all, Enstone Business Park, Church Enstone, Oxfordshire OX7 4NP.

Tel: 01608 678339. **Fax:** 01608 678639.

Price range: from £109 but gift vouchers of any amount. Brochure free.

Payment: cheque, Visa, Mastercare, Amex.

Postage & packing: included unless Post Office Special Delivery for Christmas.

Delivery: by post.

Refunds: not applicable.

Specials: gift vouchers.

Great Central Railway This company gives you the chance to be an engine driver of a steam train (under supervision of course) on the main line between Loughborough and Leicester. Gift vouchers are also available for lunch and dinner in the first-class restaurant cars of the Master Cutler and Charnwood Forester trains.

Great Central Railway, Great Central Road, Loughborough, Leicestershire LE11 1RW.

Tel: 01509 230726. **Fax:** 01509 239791.

Price range: £6.75 to £1,250. Catalogues free.

Payment: cheque, Visa, Visa Delta, Mastercard, Access.

Postage & packing: postage of vouchers included.

Delivery: allow a week.

Refunds: sometimes exchanges.

Mid-Hants Watercress Line Almost every man has a secret longing to drive a steam train, and the Watercress Line makes this a reality. You can drive or act as fireman on the footplate or tackle the steep gradient between Alton and Alresford for up to eighty miles, an all-day trip. For those less energetic, the line serves Sunday lunch or luxury five-course dinner on the train. In the run-up to Christmas, children can meet Santa on board.

Mid-Hants Watercress Line, The Railway Station, Alresford, Hampshire SO24 9JG.

Tel: 01962 733810. **Fax:** 01962 735448.

Price range: 20p to £1,500. Send A5 SAE for catalogue.

Payment: cheque, Visa.

Postage & packing: not applicable.

Delivery: not applicable.

Refunds: no.

Specials: advance booking. Vouchers by arrangement.

Red Letter Days Beat the sound barrier in a Russian fighter aircraft, drive a 1928 Bentley, train with football professionals or be a TV presenter, circus clown or llama trekker. Why not take the Orient Express or Concorde or spend time relaxing at Champneys? Whatever you dream about can come true if Red Letter Days can manage it.

Red Letter Days Ltd, Melville House, 8/12 Woodhouse Road, North Finchley, London N12 0RG.

Tel: 0181 343 8822. **Fax:** 0181 343 9030.

Price range: £21 to £5,000. Catalogue free.

Payment: cheque, Access, Visa, Amex, Switch, Edge, Credit Charge/Credit Charge Gold, Delta.

Postage & packing: included. Special delivery add £6, express service £12.

Delivery: within 10 days or last GPO posting date for Christmas.

Refunds: some for vouchers. Not for booked days.

Silverstone Rally School The school offers gift vouchers to those wanting to rally drive. They will take on anyone with a full driving licence who can change gear – no previous experience is needed. The Introductory Course includes two practice sessions and a chauffered rally drive by the instructor; the Clubman's Course has an extra – driving at speed on the skid pan.

Silverstone Rally School, Silverstone Park, Northamptonshire NN12 8TJ.
Tel: 01327 857413. **Fax:** 01327 858285.
Price range: £95 to £199. Catalogue free.
Payment: cheque, Access, Visa, Switch.
Postage & packing: included.
Delivery: 1st class post, last GPO posting date for Christmas.
Refunds: vouchers can be transferred.

Equipment

Bugwear If you have ever been in the Highlands in June, you'll know about the midges. The Highland firm, Bugwear, has come up with lightweight insect-proof clothing which is also showerproof and ideal for all kinds of outdoor sports, especially fishing. The cotton-polyester blend has areas of fine mesh for ventilation and the sleeves, jacket bottoms and trousers are elasticated. For extreme situations there's a kind of beekeeper's mesh hood which zips on to the jacket front over the face. The firm recommends its baseball cap, with logo of cross bug, to keep the mesh off the face.

Bugwear Ltd., Drummond Street, Comrie, Perthshire PH6 2DS.
Tel: 01764 670033. **Fax:** 01764 670958.
Price range: £7.50 to £49.95. Catalogue free.
Payment: cheque, Mastercard, Visa.
Postage & packing: included.
Delivery: last Christmas orders by 1 December.
Refunds: yes, if returned within 14 days.

Camplyon Charles Wright started by selling an extremely nifty combined golf club carrier, the Cadette, which is lightweight and ideal for women golfers, as well as holding tees and balls. Then came the StepSac, which is not only a coolbag for your picnic and a rucksack but also converts into a seat or stool to get a head above everyone else at the races. Finally, and incongruously, he sells belts made by the Indians in Guatemala with intricate designs laid on to leather. Each costs £12, of which 50p goes to a charity for the street children in Guatemala city.

Camplyon Trading Company Ltd., PO Box 444, Ashbourne, Derbyshire DE6 2ZZ.

Tel: 01335 324600. **Fax:** 01335 324375.

Price range: £12 to £39.95. Catalogue free.

Payment: cheque, Visa, Mastercard, Switch, Delta, JCB.

Postage & packing: included.

Delivery: by post or Parcel Force, allow 10 days; for Christmas by 48-hour carrier except for belts when an extra charge may be made to ensure delivery.

Refunds: yes.

Dolphin Enterprises We all know that golfers get obsessional and that golfing wives feel more like widows. This firm has a set of cartoon table mats that make the point. I particularly like the rainy scene with fishermen sitting glumly on the bank while a wet but smiling golfer says 'Look at those idiots – fishing in this weather'. The present for the golfer with everything.

Dolphin Enterprises, 68 Tremadoc Road, Clapham, London SW4 7LP.

Tel/Fax: 0171 498 7465.

Price range: £27. Brochure free.

Payment: cheque.

Postage & packing: included.

Delivery: allow 28 days.

Refunds: yes.

Explore Trader This company caters to the inveterate and adventurous traveller and sells items ranging from a personal mosquito net (why share?) to biodegradable soap to avoid polluting streams in the wild. It also sells a DIY dental kit to repair fillings when you can't find a dentist and a mountain first-aid kit of dressings, zinc oxide tape and antiseptic wipes. Equally useful is the book *Stay Healthy Abroad* and videos of whitewater rafting in Peru, crossing deserts, rainforests and mountains.

Explore Trader, 1 Frederick Street, Aldershot, Hampshire GU11 1LQ.

Tel: 01252 316016. **Fax:** 01252 315935.

Price range: £2.99 to £69.95. Catalogue free.

Payment: cheque, Access, Mastercard, Visa, Connect, Switch.

Postage & packing: £2.50 up to £50, £3.95 to £100, free thereafter.

Delivery: 10 days, or 28 if not in stock.

Refunds: yes, if returned in 10 days with explanation.

Specials: vouchers for adventurous places.

Farlow's of Pall Mall Established in 1840, this is London's oldest fishing shop – and supplier to the Prince of Wales – with a huge selection of tackle and clothes. The mail-order choice is smaller but includes top-flight trout and salmon rods, fly boxes, reels and lines. There is smart country clothing in tweed and waxed cotton for men, women and children as well as gloves, socks and handwarmers.

Farlow's of Pall Mall, 5 Pall Mall, London SW1Y 5NP.

Tel: 0171 839 2423. **Fax:** 01285 643743.

Price range: 50p to £500. Catalogue free in UK.

Payment: cheque, Access, Mastercard, Amex, Visa, Delta, Connect.

Postage & packing: £1.50 for packets, £3 for parcels

Delivery: 7 to 10 days.

Refunds: yes, if returned at customer's expense.

Field & Trek Clothes for energetic sports such as mountaineering, canoeing, cycling and hard walking can be found here. There's a huge range of boots, as well as camping equipment, maps, altimeters and sleeping bags for the worst conditions. Backpacks, snowshoes, sandals for the desert, mountaineering axes and inner, middle and outer layer thermal and lightweight clothes are all in the catalogue, which also offers helpful advice.

Field & Trek, 3 Wates Way, Brentwood, Essex CM15 9TB.

Tel: 01277 233122. **Fax:** 01277 260789.

Price range: £1 to £720. Catalogue £1.95. Also free winter catalogue in September.

Payment: cheque, F&T Budget card, JCB, Visa, Access, Mastercard, Eurocard, Amex, Delta, Connect, Switch.

Postage & packing: details in catalogue.
Delivery: 24 and 48 hour service.
Refunds: yes, return with covering letter to sales manager.

John L. Chapman & Co

Traditional country bags and luggage, especially for shooting and fishing. There are game bags with net pockets and rubberised interiors, padded vinyl and fleece-lined gun covers, luggage ranging from garment carriers to rucksacks and country handbags in tweed and linen. All are beautifully finished with leather straps and bindings, brass fittings and webbing shoulder straps.

John L. Chapman & Co Ltd, Gallery House, Harraby Green Business Park, Carlisle CA1 2SS.
Tel: 01228 514514. **Fax:** 01228 515758.
Price range: £20 to £300. Catalogue free.
Payment: cheque.
Postage & packing: £2 to £4 on size of bag.
Delivery: Christmas orders by 1st week December.
Refunds: yes, as long as in new condition.

John Jaques

Splendidly boxed sets of the more esoteric games. Jaques is known for its croquet sets but was making billiard balls 200 years ago. A newly launched gift box collection includes convertible snooker/dining tables, table tennis, chess and bridge sets, archery, carpet croquet and even baseball sets including a baseball bat, leather balls, baseball gloves (to fit anyone from ten upwards) and, of course, two baseball caps. An inspirational catalogue.

John Jaques & Son Ltd, 361 Whitehorse Road, Thornton Heath, Surrey CR7 8XP.
Tel: 0181 684 4242. **Fax:** 0181 684 4243.
Price range: approx £15 to £,500. Catalogue free.
Payment: cheque.
Postage & packing: by arrangement.
Delivery: 2-3 days.
Refunds: yes, with agreement.

Pedometers International As well as pedometers, there are stopwatches, compasses for people and cars, magnifiers for rallying, measure tapes and accessories such as altimeters, barometers and personal alarms for sale here.

Pedometers International Ltd, 13/14 James Watt Close, Drayton Fields, Daventry, Northamptonshire NN11 5RJ.

Tel: 01327 706030. **Fax:** 01327 71633.

Price range: £2.75 to £175. Catalogue free.

Payment: cheque, Visa, Mastercard.

Postage & packing: £1.95.

Delivery: 1st class post.

Refunds: by arrangement.

Riders and Squires of Kensington This company specialises in all forms of riding equipment and clothes but focuses particularly on polo and children, exporting to over fifty countries worldwide. The firm has no catalogue but works through personal contact, sending high-quality tack to enthusiasts. Knowing the number of small girls who pass through the pony phase – some never leaving it – a good riding equipment supplier is invaluable.

Riders and Squires of Kensington Co Ltd, 8 Thackeray Street, London W8 5ET.

Tel: 0171 937 4377. **Fax:** 0171 937 7335.

Price range: £10 upwards. No catalogue, all arrangements by phone.

Payment: cheque and major credit cards.

Postage & packing: by arrangement.

Delivery: by arrangement.

Refunds: by arrangement.

Specials: overseas and export orders. Helpful advice.

Salmon & Trout Association Even the most dedicated fisherman may still need a river map of his special beat and this company has them for the Dee, Spey, Tweed, Carron and Shin. There are salmon and trout boxer shorts, car mascots and fishermen's knives and field kettle. The association has a huge list of fishing videos such as *The Enigmatic Sea Trout* and *The*

Educated Trout (I think they're serious) along with fishing books to record true lengths and weights.

The Salmon & Trout Association, c/o Mr. W.H.A. Davies, Field Secretary, 29 Neales Close, Harbury, Warwickshire CV33 9JQ.
Tel/Fax: 01926 612661. **Mobile** 0860 858468.
Price range: 95p to £31.95. Catalogue free.
Payment: cheque, postal order, Visa.
Postage & packing: £3.25 per parcel.
Delivery: allow 28 days.
Refunds: yes, if returned in 14 days.

Sam de Teran A choice of black, red and cream ski outfits, lined with Goretex Windstopper, which are windproof and water resistant as well as warm and soft can be bought here. Some are trimmed with artificial fur, like black beaver on the red and black outfits or cream mink on the cream. All, except those with fur, are fully washable. As well as full suits, jackets and pants, there are wool hats plus polo necks for warmth underneath. The items can also be seen at the London shop which operates the mail-order side.

Sam de Teran, 151 Fulham Road, London SW3 6SN.
Tel: 0171 584 0902. **Fax:** 0171 589 9906.
Price range: £29 to £320. Catalogue free.
Payment: cheque and major credit cards.
Postage & packing: £3.50 per item.
Delivery: allow 6 weeks.
Refunds: by arrangement.

Snow + Rock Everything for the skier – and Christmas is the ideal time to give it. The catalogue changes every year to mirror the latest fashions so there is up-to-the-minute ski wear along with warm gloves and socks, skis themselves, roof racks to carry all the equipment and books on the subject. Gear for all the family here.

Snow + Rock Mail Order Department, 99 Fordwater Road, Chertsey, Surrey KT16 8HH.
Tel: 01932 569569. **Fax:** 01932 569589.

Price range: £8 to £1,400. Catalogue free.

Payment: cheque, Access, Visa, Mastercard, Amex, Switch.

Postage & packing: £2.25 on orders under £35 £2.25, £4.50 thereafter.

Delivery: 48 hours or 24 hours at extra cost.

Refunds: yes, if returned as new in 14 days with packing.

See also: L.L. Bean for trainers, sportswear (General Catalogues), Godiva for golf-ball chocolates, Meg Rivers Cakes for sportsmen's cakes and matching teacups (Food for Presents), House of Hamilton for golfing and shooting equipment, H.S. Productions for car posters and calendars (Enthusiasms), Super Tramp for trampolines (Children), Aviation Leathercraft for pilot's gear, Spencers Trousers for shooting and golfing trousers (Men's Clothes), Christopher Simpson, Clivedon Collection for sporting cufflinks, pins (Jewellery).

PETS

Pets are perhaps the easiest family members to choose presents for. They don't expect anything, can't complain and are instantly grateful for the tiniest gift. Remember when choosing a present for your pet – whether a super-intelligent collie or a less bright hamster – that all animals' priorities are the same: first, food; second, comfort; third, fun.

This makes present-choosing easy. Your pet will appreciate all offers of food, preferably in the quantity that it can appreciate – neither a single choc drop nor a sack of meal but something which offers instant gratification with the promise of more. Then, trade up. A dog which normally has petfood or boiled entrails might appreciate pheasant breast; a cat faced with tinned herring would brighten up at the sight of fresh poached salmon and a parrot shriek with pleasure at real mango. Use your imagination. The manufacturers are now taking as much interest in creating good instant meals for pets as for people. This is a real trend.

If you prefer to offer comfort, a change of nest would be appreciated – a new clean bean bag or cushion, an offering of the best straw, some reeds – whatever is appropriate.

Once your pet has had its food and bedding (bedding includes such things as cosy blankets for the car and sofa, waterproof picnic rugs, catmint stuffed cushions and perfumed hay for the travelling cage), it will turn its attention to fun. Recent experiments have shown that zoo animals can beat boredom if they are given the kind of toys the jungle would afford and this is the way to discover what your pet will play with.

You might think a cat would spit out the toy mouse once it discovered that, instead of flesh, there was mouse-scented synthetic filling inside but you would be wrong. Many cats will play for hours with a phoney mouse or even a piece of paper on a string. My dog, given a series of fluffy toys each Christmas, has tossed a woolly lamb around for days without damaging it and now sleeps surrounded by as many soft toys as Christopher Robin. One, for some reason (perhaps it was too cheap) he tore to pieces, taking the eyes out first. A glovepuppet like a striking cobra he still treats with commendable caution.

A recent trend is to make animals into fashion objects as shown by models walking dogs on the catwalk. Manufacturers such as Burberry now offer dogs and cats ever grander outfits and cosmetic companies have also jumped on the bandwagon with a range of herbal shampoos designed for dogs with sensitive skins and unruly hair. Since some pet owners will stop at nothing in pampering their pets, can we expect in future shiny lip lotion for dogs, cuticle remover for cats and scale cream for snakes along with Dogga Karan, Issey Miaoyaki and Armani-dillo designer pet ranges?

DOGGA KARAN

ARMANI-DILLO

ISSEY MIAOYAKI

Do pay attention to the experts before buying unsolicited presents for unknown animals. It can be safer to stick to products made specially for the animal concerned. As a tip, hamsters enjoy locust beans and chocolates, rabbits take to milk or yoghurt drops and birds (as well as bears) enjoy a honey snack. If in doubt, contact one of the mail-order firms which specialises in treats for pets. You may not know what a pet iguana enjoys, but they probably do.

PETS – LISTINGS

Bones Dog and Catalogue I love this catalogue for its quirky humour, photographs of real pets – Lily the lovely lurcher, Gordon the curious cat – and marvellous presents for pet and owner from all over the world. Germany exports a pet picnic box with food and water compartments and a new edible mixed grill including steak, tomato and a carrot all in rawhide chews. Your cat gets a bespectacled mouse-size vet to savage or a sisal pyramid house to scratch and hide in. There are handmade soaps, flea bandannas and homeopathic remedies too.

Bones Dog and Catalogue, The Upper Mill, Coln St Aldwyns, Cirencester, Gloucestershire GL7 5AJ.
Tel: 01285 750007. **Fax:** 01285 750100.

Price range: £1.95 to £86.50. Catalogue free.

Payment: cheque, Access, Visa, Mastercard, Eurocard, Visa, Connect, Delta.

Postage & packing: £2.95 an order excluding beds which are £5 more for small and medium beds and £7.50 for larger sizes. If a bed alone is bought the price is £5.

Delivery: last orders for Christmas 18 December though up to 23 December for extra fee.

Refunds: yes, if returned within 14 days.

Boston Birdhouse Company

Bird boxes and feeders designed like little clapboard houses are a common sight in America, and this company has brought them to Britain. Imagine a whole set of pastel-coloured bathing huts fixed to the wall or grouped like a village on poles, or the Nantucket Tit Colony which is a high-rise of four tit boxes. Other styles are Cape Cod Clapboard and Vermont Cabin birdhouses. The feeders look like New England village stores or Maine barns. They are charming, make an excellent gift for the garden and the birds will flock.

The Boston Birdhouse Company, Old Plough Cottage, Epping Road, Roydon, Essex CM19 5HT.

Tel: 01279 792581. **Fax:** 01279 792282.

Price range: £14.50 to £89. Catalogue free.

Payment: cheque, Access, Visa, Mastercard, Eurocard, Delta.

Postage & packing: £3 per address, orders over £50 free.

Delivery: last Christmas orders 16 December.

Refunds: if returned in 14 days, unused and with original packing.

Ciapparelli Cats

Luigi Ciapparelli is an oral surgeon who invented the Catsedan for his own cats and now sells them by public demand. The sedan is like a garden swing seat with a metal frame and suspended padded bed. It can be put by a radiator or zipped into a ventilated travelling case which can be secured by a car seat belt. The bed is a soft cream and the travelling cover royal blue, the whole the size of a small suitcase with strong handles.

Ciapparelli Cats, 277 Southend Road, Shotgate, Wickford, Essex SS11 8QA.

Tel: 01268 764286. **Fax:** 01268 561632.

Price: £49.95. Send SAE for catalogue.

Payment: cheque or postal order.

Postage & packing: £5.95.

Delivery: Christmas orders by 10 December; otherwise allow 28 days.

Refunds: if returned undamaged in 28 days.

George's of Chelsea This shop is in Cale Street, round the corner from Harrods, and it's *the* place for the smart Knightsbridge dog. It is also the Sloane Rangers' stamping ground and, predictably, offers custom-made waxed doggy jackets to match your Barbour and such Sloaney jokes as a Downing Street cat or dog flap made to order. They will make collars and leads to order – even with your crest – bookends, waste paper baskets etc with pictures of your pets, plus baskets and beds to match.

George's of Chelsea, 6 Cale Street, London SW3 3QU.

Tel: 0171 581 5114. **Fax:** 0171 581 5941.

Price range: custom-made items all quoted. Catalogue free.

Payment: cheque, major cards.

Postage & packing: quoted when ordering.

Delivery: quoted when ordering.

Refunds: not when made specially.

Natural Friends It's hard to believe the number and variety of pet beds this firm offers. They come as pyramids, square boxes, round baskets and flat cushions in a choice of rich kilim-like fabrics in dark orange, burgundy and dark green, plus tartans. There are dog bones made of nylon and poly-urethane which defy the busiest teeth as well as flying discs and frisbees. The firm is unusual in offering presents for ferrets (which apparently are increasingly popular) including collars, vitamin supplements and ferret shampoo – a job which I would not like to undertake. An associated company, Acorn Supplements Ltd (same address, details as below), offers natural pet remedies such as multi-vitamin supplements and remedies for unhealthy coats.

Natural Friends, PO Box 103, Robertsbridge, East Sussex TN32 5ZT.

Tel: 01580 881222. **Fax:** 01580 881444.

Price range: £1 to £51.69. Catalogue free, would appreciate 25p stamp.

Payment: cheque, Visa, Mastercard.

Postage & packing: £1 on orders up to £10, £1.50 to £30, over £30 free.

Delivery: Christmas orders by first week of December.

Refunds: yes, if returned in 14 days.

The Nuttery Christmas is the ideal time to start encouraging wild birds to your back yard or garden. The Nuttery makes handsome bird feeders: some, like little iron parrot cages, are designed to be squirrel proof (which means large birds like magpies are also put off), others are like small hanging flower baskets designed for the suet cakes which the tits love. Bird feeders make a lovely present for friends, the elderly – and the birds.

The Nuttery, 42 Dene Road, Northwood, Middlesex HA6 2DA.

Tel: 01923 829592. **Fax:** 01923 836506.

Price range: £5.95 to £29.95. Catalogue free.

Payment: cheque, Access, Visa, Mastercard.

Postage & packing: £2.95.

Delivery: last Christmas orders before 18 December.

Refunds: yes, if returned undamaged in 28 days.

Over the Top Textiles If you assume that you will never get your pet to stay on the floor and leave the chairs unmarked, then this is the company for you. It specialises in all forms of sheets, bean bags, snuggle and towel to keep your pet and your best sofa apart (and that goes for the car, too). There are luxurious white pure wool furry blankets, heavy-duty pet sheets in four sizes coloured cream, olive, cool grey and buff, fitted and loose covers for car seats and even quilted pads for post-operative dogs. New to the range is a dog duffle which looks more like a giant laundry bag into which you insert the beast. Its three layers make it warm and drying.

Over the Top Textiles, Barley Hill House, Chadlington, Oxon OX7 3NU.
Tel: 01608 676625. **Fax:** 01608 676484.
Price range: £5.95 to £127.95. Catalogue free.
Payment: cheque, Access, Mastercard, Connect, Switch, Delta.
Postage & packing: up to £3.25.
Delivery: until a few days before Christmas but stock may be short by then.
Refunds: yes if undamaged and clean.

Waggers This catalogue is for the pet who likes his comfort. It has a range of beds stuffed with hollow fibre which is allergen-free, washable, warm and fire-resistant. The beds are thick, free-standing cushions, there are also basket liners, car boot beds, a soft 'snuggler' to stretch over a basket and a cotton towelling bag into which to zip a wet dog. I've never managed it but some dogs seem to love this. There is even a willow travelling hamper for the dog.

Waggers, Comfy Pet & People Products, 2-4 Parsonage Street, Bradninch, near Exeter, Devon EX5 4NW.
Tel: 01392 881285. **Fax:** 01392 882188.
Price range: £3.50 to £49.50. Catalogue free.
Payment: cheque, Visa, Mastercard, Access.
Postage & packing: £1.50 for orders under £10, then by degrees.
Delivery: guaranteed Christmas orders 2 weeks in advance.
Refunds: yes, on return by registered post.
Specials: gift service.

Winna The firm makes beds and rugs for pets. The beds are filled with a hollow fibre duvet with an outer cover of tough poly-cotton designed so the hairs don't stick. They close with Velcro and are easily washed. There are also flatter rugs for car seats and sofas plus a waterproof-backed picnic rug. The colours are very smart: Black Watch or Lindsay tartan, or dark blue and green with red piping.

Winna Pet Beds, Henley Old Farm, Henley, Dorchester, Dorset DT2 7BL.

Tel/Fax: 01300 345210.

Price range: £15 to £47.50. Send SAE for catalogue.

Payment: cheque, Access, Visa, Mastercard.

Postage & packing: £6.50 per order.

Delivery: last orders for Christmas 7 December.

Refunds: if returned unused.

See also: Jerry's Home Store (Home Interest), Kileravagh for pet snacks (Food for Presents), Graig Farm for pet snacks (Christmas Food, Meat and Poultry), Kootensaw Dovecots (Gardening), Letterbox for personalised dog and cat bowls (Children), Barclay & Bodie, Flights of Fancy for bird lovers, Harrods for pet Christmas stockings and toys (General Catalogues), Guide Dogs for the Blind, People's Trust for Endangered Species, RSPCA, Royal Society for the Protection of Birds, and all animal charities for gifts related to specific animals (Charities), Carol Mather for doggy brooches (Jewellery).

PART TWO

CELEBRATING CHRISTMAS

Chapter One

DECORATIONS AND STATIONERY

CHRISTMAS TREES AND DECORATIONS

Christmas decorations are as subject to fashion as any kind of interior design. Recently, the emphasis has been on restraint – natural accessories and lots of greenery for example. People are increasingly choosing simple Christmas tree decorations – white lights, silver or transparent baubles and so on. Top florists make swags of dried flowers and fruit in soft neutrals to hang around the fireplace and ivy and fir to twine through the banisters. Candles everywhere are 'in'.

Of course, if you have young children, you can forget restraint. Pzazz is what counts. All hell breaks loose if Christmas trees aren't decorated with an array of coloured baubles, presents, fairies and multi-coloured lights and surrounded by enticing presents. Streamers and balloons should festoon every room to complete the 'look' (not to mention fake snow on the window panes).

Alternatively, if you have a flair for design or you have nimble fingers, go ahead and make your own decorations. Magazines often have good ideas though they're sometimes complex. Shop windows are also a good source of inspiration as they follow the latest trends.

CHRISTMAS TREES AND DECORATIONS – LISTINGS

Balloon City This company sells helium balloons by post, including a red and silver 'Merry Christmas' balloon. They also do lots of other messages on heart-shaped or round balloons in gold, silver and bright colours. Balloons can be ordered in a candy-striped box with ordinary unfilled balloons and other party items such as blow-outs and confetti, Godiva Belgian chocolates, a bottle of champagne or Scotch, a box of Floris soap or even Zinnia toilet water. The company also sells packs of ordinary balloons to blow up.

> **Balloon City**, 65/66 Woodrow, Woolwich, London SE18 5DH.
> **Tel:** 0181 856 5222. **Fax:** 0181 488 0424. **E-mail:** michael@balloonc.ftech.co.uk
> **Price range:** £11 to £42. Catalogue free by Freepost LON7512.
> **Payment:** cheque, Access, Visa, Amex, Switch.
> **Postage & packing:** included.
> **Delivery:** last Christmas order 20 December.
> **Refunds:** yes, if damaged.

The British Christmas Tree Growers' Association 12 Lauriston Road, Wimbledon, London SW19 4TQ. Tel: 0181 946 2695. Fax: 0181 947 0211. Send an SAE to Tony Richardson, the secretary, and he will send a list of growers who sell direct to the public. He also gives advice on how to care for your tree.

Chatsworth A complete selection of Christmas decorations originally intended for the restaurant trade. They stock fake but natural-looking fir wreaths and swags which you can add to, crackers, tinsel and shimmer garlands, realistic fake Christmas trees and flickering lights. There are 22-inch high Father Christmas and snowman balloons with feet and 36-inch high Santa Bear and Banana Face as well as hats, masks, blow-outs and streamers. These are neither elegant nor beautiful but they're good for a party.

Chatsworth, 31 Norwich Road, Strumpshaw, Norwich
NR13 4AG.
Tel: 01603 716815. **Fax:** 01603 715440.
Price range: £2 to £200. Catalogue free.
Payment: cheque, postal order, Visa, Access, Amex, Diners.
Postage & packing: £7.50 on orders under £300.
Delivery: allow 28 days but less with surcharge. Cut-off date
for Christmas 1 December but 10% discount on orders paid for
by 30 September.
Refunds: yes, if damaged or not delivered.

Cherie Colman Designs This company makes ready-made
card hangers with scrunchy tartan bows at the top and a fall of
ribbon on which to attach the cards. Cherie Colman initially
made them for herself but went into business after finding that
others wanted a way to make their cards look good (and not
fall over). They look splendid and make instant Christmas decorations.

Cherie Colman Designs, 23 Calbourne Road, London
SW12 8LW.
Tel: 0181 675 9847. **Fax:** 0181 265 3775.
Price range: £11.50 to £19.95. Send A4 SAE for catalogue.
Payment: cheque.
Postage & packing: £2.50 on orders up to £50, £5.50
thereafter.
Delivery: 1 week from order, last Christmas orders by 18
December. Supplies may be limited.
Refunds: yes.

English Stamp Company Decorative stamps for use on
walls but they work just as well on wrapping paper, home-
made crackers, paper hats and decorations. There are suns
and stars, lyres, cherubs and wreaths and a whole slew of
fruits from grapes to pineapples, the traditional symbol of
hospitality. The firm also sells the tools needed to do-it-yourself such as paints in gold and silver and good strong
colours, a useful roller and a complete kit. There is a special
Christmas range with wise men, holly, ivy and fir tree plus a

children's range with tractors, trawlers and good stripey or spotty animals. Why not decorate a child's room as a present?

The English Stamp Company, Sunnydown, Worth Matravers, Dorset BH19 3JP.

Tel: 01929 439117. **Fax:** 01929 439150.

Price range: £2.95 to £12.95. Catalogue free.

Payment: cheque, Visa, Access, Amex, Diners and Switch.

Postage & packing: included.

Delivery: allow 1 week for Christmas, generally within 1-2 days of order.

Refunds: when faulty.

Specials: custom-made stamps.

Hector's Candles

Hector's Candles Hector's great-grandfather started the church candlemaker Hayes & Finch but Hector has gone one step further by wrapping the candles in blue tissue and sending them in smart brown boxes. The candles justify it. Some have 25% beeswax and smell delicious; others are 100% paraffin. The pure beeswax versions fill a room with the scent of honey. There are eight sizes from six to eighteen inches but if your candelabra or chandeliers are an odd size, candles can be specially made to fit. The firm is also planning to sell candle holders and accessories.

Hector's Candles, PO Box 8254, London W6 0BZ.

Tel: 0181 741 9708.

Price range: £6 to £28 per box. Catalogue free.

Payment: cheque, Visa, Delta, Switch, Mastercard, Eurocard.

Postage & packing: £4.50 on orders less than £50, £6 thereafter.

Delivery: within 21 days.

Refunds: yes, if returned in 10 days.

Specials: gift service.

Panduro

Panduro A huge catalogue of over 10,000 items which, apart from food, virtually does Christmas for you. There are tree decorations, spray paints, labels and stickers of Santa Claus, angels, wreaths, advent calendars and Christmas cards, wrapping paper, string, gift boxes and sealing wax. Then you can get the necessary materials to make your own Christmas figures – from mice in bed to little match girls – or sprays of dried flowers, and berries and so on. This Scandinavian company has some slightly strange products (very few robins, for instance) and the sheer quantity is boggling but there's a helpful index.

Panduro Hobby, Freepost, Transport Avenue, Brentford, Middlesex TW8 8BR.
Tel: 0181 847 6161 **Fax:** 0181 847 5073.
Price range: 85p to £195. Catalogue £2.95.
Payment: cheque, postal order, major cards.
Postage & packing: generally £2.95 a parcel.
Delivery: last Christmas orders by 12 December.
Refunds: if damaged and returned in 14 days.

Smallwood Christmas Trees Direct

A choice of five conifers – Norway Spruce, Scots Pine, Blue Spruce, White Fir and Noble Fir – can be bought rooted, sawn, blocked or potted from this catalogue. They range from eighteen-inch 'desktop' trees (a growing trend apparently) to eighteen-foot trees, ordered whenever you like and delivered when it suits you. In emergencies, trees can be delivered, installed and even decorated for you. Once the holiday is over, the firm will take your tree away and use it as mulch on the farm. They also sell holly wreaths, mistletoe, swags of ivy and fir, all fresh and boxed. Wonderful.

Smallwood Christmas Trees Direct, Upper Munderfield Farm, Bromyard, Herefordshire HR7 4SA.
Tel: 01885 400323. Orders Freephone: 0800 413092. **Fax:** 01885 400317.
Price range: from £7. Average, 6-ft Norway spruce, £29 delivered. Catalogue free.
Payment: cheque, Access, Visa.
Postage & packing: included.
Delivery: last Christmas orders up to 20 December.
Refunds: yes.
Specials: trees as presents; free greenery with tree orders before 1 December.

Specialist Crafts This company's huge catalogue is a good source for glues, modelling kits, paper and board (if you want to make your own cards and decorations) and figures for the tree or around the home. There are candle-making kits, glitter kits and masses of different paints – from acrylic to fluorescent. Also a good source of presents for children with hobbies like finger painting or photography.

> **Specialist Crafts**, PO Box 247, Leicester LE1 9QS.
>
> **Tel:** 0116 251 0405. **Fax:** 0116 251 5015.
>
> **Price range:** a few pence to £700. Catalogue £3.75 refundable against orders over £30.
>
> **Payment:** cheque, postal order, Visa, Mastercard.
>
> **Postage & packing:** from £1 for orders under £5 to £5 over £50. Over £130, free.
>
> **Delivery:** usually within a few days but 24-hour service at extra charge.
>
> **Refunds:** by arrangement.

See also: Paperchase (Cards and Wrapping Paper), Spotted Duck (General Catalogues), Global Village, Tobias and the Angel selling decorations (Home Interest), Lakeland Plastics (Kitchenware), Obelisk Collection for reusable velvet crackers (Art and Replicas), WCP Video for Jane Packer's video on Flowers for Christmas (Books, Cassettes, CDs and Videos), Magic by Post for balloons (Enthusiasms), Terrace and Garden for twig Christmas trees and glass decorations (Gardening), Angela Flanders Aromatics for Christmas scents and candles (Luxuries), Frog Hollow for party balloons etc (Stocking Fillers). Virtually all the charity catalogues offer crackers, cards, decorations and wrapping paper.

CARDS AND WRAPPING PAPER

Fashions in Christmas cards change. Whereas once it was smart to deliver huge, glossy glitter-covered jobs, today we feel happier helping charities or sending something more personal. All the listings in the Charities section have cards, as do many museums, and all offer plenty of variety in style and price. Otherwise, I have listed cards which are works of art and frameable as such. Suppliers of attractive wrapping paper and – more important – of all the gubbins for sending parcels safely are also listed. Bubblewrap and padded bags are a real boon, as is good quality tissue paper which makes the most mundane present into a treat.

If you want to send family cards talk to your local printer – generally the smaller and more personal they are, the better. Each year I have an old family photograph printed in sepia on cream card, leaving the greetings to be hand-written. The printer does the work in days and delivers it to my door. Any cards left over from Christmas I send people throughout the year.

CARDS AND WRAPPING PAPER – LISTINGS

Arona Khan The expert who did gift wraps for stores like Hamleys and Bentalls of Kingston reveals her trade secrets in a book, *Wrap It Up*. It is full of excellent ideas which are clearly explained. If, like me, you find it hard to wrap the simplest shape, you need her guidance. There's help on mastering basic skills like wrapping awkward shapes and more advanced techniques like making fancy bows.

> **Arona Khan**, Gift-Wrapping Consultancy, 3 Sevington Street, London W9 2QN.
> **Tel:** 0171 289 2439. **Fax:** 0171 286 0679.
> **Price:** special price for readers of £7.95 (a saving of £3). No catalogue.
> **Payment:** cheque.
> **Postage & packing:** included in UK. £2 for overseas.
> **Delivery:** last orders by 16 December.

Refunds: by arrangement.

Specials: Arona will sign the book.

Carousel Accessories

Carousel Accessories This firm, which supplies wrappings and display stands to the antique trade, found the public also wanting the wrapping service and has just organised a mail-order catalogue. They will deliver bubble wrap in quantity, strong brown parcel paper, sticky tape for parcels and coloured tissue paper. Also crisp and beautiful acid-free tissue paper (good for clothes, for works of art, silver) in black and white. Just what we've been waiting for.

Carousel Accessories, PO Box 10, Langport, Somerset TA10 9TW.

Tel: 01458 250587. **Fax:** 01458 252655.

Price range: everything under £15. Send SAE for catalogue.

Payment: cheque, Visa, Access, Mastercard.

Postage & packing: £1.50 on orders to £15, £3.50 up to £30, £5 over £30.

Delivery: last Christmas orders by 10 December.

Refunds: exchange or credit. No p&p refund.

Engraved Greetings

Engraved Greetings Roger Rolfe is a graphic designer who combines 18th- and 19th-century engravings into cards of his own design. These are high definition, all in black and white and without any kind of message. I find that, in a sea of coloured cards, these unusual and stylish monochromes stand out well. There are four styles: Grecian Muses, who look like statuesque Victorian girls; Versailles Flora, an ornate vase full of flowers; Classical Symmetry, a building design in a fancy frame; and Ordering the Muse, involving an angel bossing workers in an art gallery. He also sells stick-on French herb and spice labels for jars.

Engraved Greetings, 284 Dyke Road, Brighton, East Sussex BN1 5BA.

Tel/Fax: 01273 553073.

Price range: £5 for 4 different subjects, or 5 same subject. No catalogue.

Payment: cheque to Frank Ainscough (trading as Engraved Greetings).

Postage & packing: included.

Delivery: by return, 1st class.

Refunds: no.

Falkiner Fine Papers This firm supplies artists and craftsmen with beautiful hand-made papers. To wrap presents in this may seem an outrage because it is so beautiful (although not as expensive as it looks) but, if you want to achieve a special effect, this paper is worth it. There are textured Japanese papers with the grass still visible, reversible silver and gold, snakeskin paper and hand-marbled paper. Actually, I'd be happy with the paper as a present and forget the rest.

Falkiner Fine Papers, 76 Southampton Row, London WC1B 4AR.

Tel: 0171 831 1151. **Fax:** 0171 430 1248.

Price range: around £1 to £5 a sheet. Send C4 36p SAE for catalogue.

Payment: cheque, Visa, Mastercard.

Postage & packing: on application.

Delivery: last Christmas delivery as GPO last posting date. Some paper in short supply.

Refunds: no.

Paperchase From the shop which really understands about paper, there now comes a mail-order catalogue. It has a selection of cards chosen from charities, beautiful wrapping paper in the latest fashions and excellent tree decorations and crackers.

Paperchase, 213 Tottenham Court Road, London W1P 9AF.

Tel: 0171 580 8496. **Fax:** 0171 637 1225.

Price range: 80p to £40. Send large SAE for catalogue. Available from October.

Payment: cheque, Access, Visa, Mastercard.

Postage & packing: from £2.50. Orders over £100 free.

Delivery: allow 3 weeks. Express delivery available.

Refunds: yes, if faulty.

Peter Perry Designs Cards which are works of art and, says Peter, often framed afterwards. He cuts fish and seabirds from slim pieces of wood, paints in their scales or feathers and sticks them on to high-quality card paper. He also sells the painted wooden fish and gulls with a seascape background in frames and the most marvellous Cornish harbour village in painted wooden blocks which you can arrange to your liking. Less a child's toy, more a potential heirloom.

> **Peter Perry Designs**, S.P.G. Perry, Stile Cottage, Trevithal, Paul, Penzance, Cornwall TR19 6UQ.
>
> **Tel/Fax:** 01736 731846.
>
> **Price range:** cards £5, fish in box £24, harbour village £80. Catalogue free.
>
> **Payment:** cheque.
>
> **Postage & packing:** approx £1.20 for set of cards, £2 for fish, £6 for harbour.
>
> **Delivery:** cards allow 2 weeks, last Christmas orders for harbours early November. Hand-made so limited supply.
>
> **Refunds:** by arrangement.

See also: entries in Christmas Trees and Decorations. Mycologue for mushroom wrapping papers (Enthusiasms), Handmade Designs for naive art cards, Museums & Galleries Christmas Collection, National Trust and National Trust for Scotland (Art and Replicas). See entries under Charities; most do cards and wrapping paper.

Chapter Two

CHRISTMAS FOOD AND DRINK

GENERAL FOOD CATALOGUES

The supermarkets keep making noises about mail order or delivering orders to the door and some small schemes have been tested. It's bound to come, as people would love to save the time spent on a weekly out-of-town shop and avoid the hassle. But, to date, no workable scheme has been introduced nationwide. Meanwhile, lots of the small shops which once delivered have been put out of business by the supermarket giants. In their place are dedicated mail-order firms which will provide almost any foods, at a price (though it's harder to get people to deliver the boring bits like washing powder and dog food). The supermarkets' problem is to find a workable catalogue of what they sell when the list is so vast and changes so often; the smaller companies have to work hard to convince the public that they are reliable.

It is possible to have all the foods you need delivered to your door – but you'll probably have to deal with a handful of firms to do so. The day can't be far off when one firm will oblige but life will be more boring. These general catalogues provide foods that you rarely find on supermarket shelves, especially in less sophisticated areas.

GENERAL FOOD CATALOGUES – LISTINGS

Carluccio's The Italian shop run by this well-known cook and mushroom enthusiast is a delight and the mail-order catalogue, produced only at Christmas, mirrors his enthusiasms.

There are hampers like the Piccolo Gourmet to introduce you to Italian cooking at its best which includes pasta, polenta, sundried tomatoes and special olive oil from Liguria, a box of groceries from Southern Italy with chillis, char-grilled artichokes, biscuits made with wild fennel and salted baby peaches. There's a special mushroom knife with a brush at the end and a rare Crutin cheese presented with its own knife. Everything is beautifully packed.

Carluccio's, 28a Neal Street, London WC2H 9PS.

Tel: 0171 240 5710. **Fax:** 0171 497 1361. **E-mail:** carluccios@cix.compulink.co.uk..

Price range: £12.49 to £165. Catalogue free.

Payment: cheque, postal order, Visa, Amex, Mastercard.

Postage & packing: phone for quote.

Delivery: from November by next-day courier but not guaranteed from 18 December.

Refunds: no.

Clark Trading Company A small general catalogue of food, mostly Mediterranean. The idea is to stock your store cupboard with pâtés, cassoulets and various luxury game stews from France along with the best ingredients such as Carnaroli rice, saffron, good pasta, the ubiquitous but still delectable olive oils and balsamic vinegars from Italy. Their specials include caviar, smoked sturgeon, jamon serrano, the best paprika and sweet quince cheese. The catalogue is a good source for special meals which need no preparation over Christmas.

The Clark Trading Company, 17 Southbrook Road, Lee, London SE12 8LH.

Tel: 0181 297 9937. **Fax:** 0181 297 9993.

Price range: £2.75 to £68. Catalogue free.

Payment: cheque.

Postage & packing: £2.95 up to £75, otherwise free.

Delivery: last Christmas orders by 17 December but helpful over panic measures.

Refunds: yes.

Specials: hampers.

Fine Food Club For an annual membership fee (currently £12.50) you get access to specialist food producers who normally won't sell direct or to major stores. The list includes bacon and ham from Dorset, Chewton Mendip cheddar, chutneys, smoked foods and English wines. There's an enthusiastic newsletter. Orders are sent off monthly on a fixed date.

> **Fine Food Club**, 33 Elvendon Road, Goring-on-Thames, Reading RG8 0DP.
> **Tel:** 01491 875175/873227. **Fax:** 01491 873227.
> **Price range:** £1.10 to £51.75. Send SAE for initial enquiry.
> **Payment:** cheque, Visa, Mastercard.
> **Postage & packing:** £6.95 up to 25 kg.
> **Delivery:** order 7 December for despatch 19 December. Some items limited stock.
> **Refunds:** credit notes.
> **Specials:** gift parcels custom-made.

The Food Ferry This company covers central London only (regrettably). Apart from a special Christmas list including fresh stuffing, nuts and stem ginger and raised pies, they supply fresh meat, fish, vegetables and fruit (the hardest items to get mail order), prepared meals and cocktail eats. Babies and pets are catered for – and so is the washing-up.

> **The Food Ferry Company**. Telephone only.
> **Tel:** 0171 498 0827. **Fax:** 0171 498 8009.
> **Price range:** normal grocery prices. Catalogue free.
> **Payment:** cash, cheque, Visa, Mastercard, Switch, Delta. Accounts negotiable.
> **Postage & packing:** no charge on first order; flat £4.11 for each subsequent delivery.
> **Delivery:** last orders for Christmas 23 December. Generally, each area has specified delivery day.
> **Refunds:** yes, if still resaleable and returned in 48 hours.

Morel Bros, Cobbett & Son Excellent general list of packed foods including pastes such as Patum Peperium and anchoiade, relishes, mustards (both English and French), truffles and caviar. Especially good on peppercorns and salts including fleur de sel, salt with seaweed and large grain sea salt, black, pink, green pepper, Szechuan pepper and allspice. Also tea and coffee, jams and chocolates.

Morel Bros, Cobbett & Son, Unit 7, 129 Coldharbour Lane, London SE5 9NY.

Tel: 0171 346 0046. **Fax:** 0171 346 0033.

Price range: £1.75 to £150. Catalogue free in UK.

Payment: cheque, Visa, Access, Mastercard, Amex, Switch.

Postage & packing: £3.95.

Delivery: last Christmas orders 15 December.

Refunds: yes, if faulty and returned in 10 days.

Teesdale Trencherman A small catalogue stuffed with the best of the kind of foods you can't generally buy outside big centres. Johnny Cooke-Hurle looks out for top-quality producers like Ashdown Smokers who smoke fish (eel, trout, haddock, kippers), sausage, poultry, bacon and quail eggs; the Merchant Gourmet for Camargue red rice, marrons and mustard fruit chutney and Fayre Game, Britain's largest quail farm, which provides oven-ready birds, quail eggs – an excellent standby over the holiday because they are so pretty – and game in season. It's a personal selection which should appeal to perfectionist cooks.

Teesdale Trencherman, Startforth Hall, Barnard Castle, Co Durham DL12 9RA.

Tel/Fax: 01833 638370.

Price range: £2.75 to £187.50. Catalogue free (includes recipes).

Payment: cheque, Visa, Access.

Postage & packing: from £2.50 on orders below 1lb.

Delivery: order by 10 December; later orders till 20 December but stocks may go.

Refunds: no.

Specials: will make up hampers to order. Gifts with messages.

See also: entries under Food for Presents.

MEAT AND POULTRY

I get tired of people saying that the British only care about cheap meat. It's not true – just look at the way we fell on properly cured bacon which didn't exude white gunge. If cooks are offered cuts and cures which are tasty, they will buy them if they can afford to.

A further proof is the rise and rise of the mail-order meat business. Most firms offer meat from animals which are well-treated and raised without risky additives to their feed; many are free-range or come from old-fashioned breeds like the Gloucester Old Spot pig, which almost died out before we remembered how good its bacon tasted. Other firms have gone back to traditional cures for ham and bacon (which beat the supermarket traditional cures by miles). Jack Scaife's bacon,

Kangaroo

Pig

Alligator

Emu

exported to embassies worldwide, was a revelation to me. Sweet and tangy, it is how bacon ought to be.

The same has been true for poultry. There are firms on this list who have worked hard at breeding turkeys, geese and ducks for taste rather than weight. Their success has been phenomenal. Although turkey has never been my favourite Christmas bird – we always have goose – that is because, in recent years, most birds have been bred to taste like dry bread. The bronze turkeys listed here, approximating to the wild American turkeys, are an entirely different bird.

If you want to try something new for Christmas, Barrow Boar will sell you a peacock for Christmas dinner – or alligator, locust or kangaroo for that matter. Plenty of other firms offer wild boar, venison cuts, game and goat. Smoked meat, other than ham, is also common.

Do try some of these old-fashioned and unusual meats – before Christmas if they make you nervous. They make the cook's job easy.

MEAT AND POULTRY – LISTINGS

Barrow Boar You won't have seen a catalogue like this before. Wild boar is the least exotic bit. Try kangaroo, ostrich, bison and peacock for a start. Then branch into alligator or crocodile. Or, to be really ordinary, try the wild rabbit, guinea fowl or wild duck in season. Or emu. Or goat. Or boar and bison sausages ... And you can always try locusts on guests who overstay their welcome ...

Barrow Boar, Foster's Farm, South Barrow, Yeovil, Somerset BA22 7LN.
Tel: 01963 440315. **Fax:** 01963 440901.
Price range: £1.75 to £19.29 for 500kg. Catalogue free, SAE welcome.

Payment: cheque, Visa, Access, Mastercard, Eurocard.
Postage & packing: generally £8.50.
Delivery: last Christmas order, 2 weeks before.
Refunds: by arrangement.
Specials: gift card service.

The Country Victualler This small company specialises in a narrow range of hams, pâtés and terrines, smoked food and Christmas pudding, and it's none the worse for that. The Alderton ham, invented by an old colonel, is cured to a secret formula and glazed with marmalade; the Victuallers Ham is cooked with honey and Guinness and glazed with marmalade. Pâtés are of coarse pork or wild boar, either en croûte or with juniper berries; smoked foods include chicken, turkey and duck. The Christmas pud is from a 19th-century Yorkshire recipe including fresh lemon, apple and breadcrumb as well as normal dried fruits. All are delicious.

The Country Victualler, Winkburn Hall, Newark, Nottinghamshire NG22 8PQ.
Tel: 01636 636465. **Fax:** 01636 636717.
Price range: from £30. Catalogue free.
Payment: cheque, Visa, Access, Mastercard, Amex.
Postage & packing: £10 for orders under £50, otherwise free except where post office surcharges.
Delivery: 24-hour carrier service.
Refunds: yes.

Derek Kelly Turkeys This company is famous for its KellyBronze turkey, the bronze-feathered bird that is the original American native. The bird was an overall winner when Anton Edelman did a turkey taste in 1995. He described it as moist and meltingly sweet as well as nutty. Delia Smith also endorsed the bird. Kelly turkeys are additive free, and grown to maturity on fresh straw with access to open woodland. Their diet has no growth promoter. If you want to sample the taste before Christmas, there is a special offer day on the first

Saturday of October when bulk packs are sold if you apply in advance.

Derek Kelly Turkeys, Springate Farm, Bicknacre Road, Danbury, Essex CM3 4EP.

Tel: 01245 223581. **Fax:** 01245 226124.

Price range: £4.10 per lb to £8.43. Brochure free.

Payment: cheque.

Postage & packing: included.

Delivery: order by 5 December for delivery on 22 December. If it fails to arrive by 7pm, ring and a replacement will be sent.

Refunds: yes.

Specials: free recipes, £1 voucher and set of place cards with each turkey.

Dukeshill Ham As traditional butchers are put out of business by the supermarkets, it becomes gradually more difficult to find regional hams, cured in the proper way. This company specialises in England's different ham recipes. There is Wiltshire ham, the most popular, which is smoked or cured in brown sugar and is mild in flavour. York hams are both drier and saltier, cured in the way country houses once used, and matured for over ten weeks. Shropshire black starts off like York ham but is then infused with a delicious mix of molasses, herbs and juniper. It is the sweetest of the three and sold only at Christmas. The firm also does an air-dried Parma-type ham to eat raw with fruit. The English hams can be ordered on the bone for drama and York and Wiltshire cures in smaller quantities and sliced.

Dukeshill Ham Co Ltd, Deuxhill, Bridgnorth, Shropshire WV16 6AF.

Tel: 01746 789519. **Fax:** 01746 789533.

Price range: £6.50 to £70. Catalogue free.

Payment: cheque, Visa, Access, Amex.

Postage & packing: included.

Delivery: by overnight 24-hour carrier or Parcel Force.

Refunds: no.

Eastbrook Farm Organic Meats Over 1,000 acres of land – owned by the Church of England – have been managed by the Browning family for forty years. They have been farming organically since 1986, and the Eastbrook range includes their own smoked Wiltshire ham and bacon, lamb grazed on wildflower meadows and free-range poultry. The list also includes sausages, organic cheeses, humanely treated veal and well-hung beef.

Eastbrook Farm Organic Meats, Eastbrook Farm, Bishopstone, Swindon, Wiltshire SN6 8PW.
Tel: 01793 790460. **Fax:** 01793 791239.
Price range: approx £6 to £30 per kg. Catalogue free, SAE appreciated.
Payment: cheque, Visa, Access, Mastercard, Switch.
Postage & packing: £10 on orders under £35, £8 to £75, £4 to £150 orders, free thereafter.
Delivery: Christmas orders before 2 December. Some foods in limited supply.
Refunds: by arrangement.
Specials: farm visits encouraged.

Fletchers of Auchtermuchty Venison is growing in popularity, both fresh and smoked. The secret is to get it tender and that means farmed rather than wild. John Fletcher is a vet who farms his herd organically in paddocks on an upland farm. The products vary from delicious hot and cold smoked venison and a selection of joints, casseroles, game pie mix, venison haggis and sausages. The smoked venison is perfect treated like bresaola, drizzled with olive oil and topped with shavings of parmesan – or teamed with left-over cranberry sauce or jelly. The meat is vacuum packed, giving a shelf life of one to two weeks, and the smoked meats last longer. Venison is unusual enough to be festive and the smoked varieties and casseroles need no preparation.

Fletchers of Auchtermuchty, Reediehill, Auchtermuchty, Fife KY14 7HS.
Tel: 01337 828369. **Fax:** 01337 827001.

Price range: £10 to £100. Catalogue free.

Payment: cheque, Visa, Mastercard, Eurocard.

Postage & packing: £8.95 for overnight carrier, orders over £80 free. Smoked foods by post £2 plus postage cost.

Delivery: generally overnight but, for Christmas, order by beginning of December to allow meat three weeks to hang.

Refunds: yes. Carriage refunded if late, order refunded in full if food doubtful.

Goodman's Geese Since Judy Goodman started to rear geese ten years ago, her flock has grown from 100 to over 3,000. She added 750 bronze turkeys in 1991 and now rears over 1,000. She has won numerous awards for her poultry and her business. The birds are free range and sold oven-ready. She includes goose recipes – necessary as no two cookbooks agree on times.

Goodman's Geese, Walsgrove Farm, Great Witley, Worcester WR6 6JJ.

Tel: 01299 896272. **Fax:** 01299 896889.

Price range: goose about £6.50 per kg, turkeys about £5.10 per kg. Catalogue free.

Payment: cheque in advance.

Postage & packing: approx £10 per bird.

Delivery: overnight carrier. Birds can be in limited supply so order September or October.

Refunds: no.

Graig Farm If you are worried about how your meat is reared and how humanely slaughtered, buy from this farm. The animals are not given drugs, growth promoters or animal offal, they are fed organically and humanely slaughtered. The meat also tastes better. The farm sells chicken like it used to taste, free-range bronze or white turkey, duck, wood pigeon and guinea fowl. Meats include wild venison, rabbit, goat and wild boar along with more normal meats and mutton. Also sold are local cheeses, dolphin-friendly trawled fish from St Helena, organic Christmas cakes and baby food as well as local wild honey. A recipe book on how to cook the rarer foods is also available.

Graig Farm, Dolau, Llandrindod Wells, Powys LD1 5TL.
Tel: 01597 851655. **Fax:** 01597 851991.
Price range: 56p to £32. Catalogue free.
Payment: cheque, Visa, Mastercard, Eurocard.
Postage & packing: free for orders over £40, under that at cost.
Delivery: Christmas orders by late November. Supplies, especially organic turkeys, may be limited.
Refunds: yes, if reasonable.

Heal Farm Meats

Old-fashioned breeds are used for superb fresh and cured meat and poultry. Gloucester Old Spots, Tamworths and British Lops are among the pigs; beef is from North Devon cattle; Shetland, Ryeland and Southdown produce the lamb. Rouen cross ducks, bronze turkey, guinea fowl and pheasant are on offer, as are special joints, ready-to-cook stews and curries and home-cured West Country hams and bacons. Rearing and killing is humane and additive-free by the farm.

Heal Farm, Kings Nympton, Umberleigh, Devon EX37 9TB.
Tel: 01769 574341. **Fax:** 01769 572839.
Price range: £5 to £24 per kg. Catalogue free.
Payment: cheque, Access, Visa.
Postage & packing: £8.50 per minimum order of £25.
Delivery: overnight courier.
Refunds: no.

Hereford Duck Company

These are dedicated duck breeders, using the Rouen as the base of a bird bred specially for flavour and raised in apple orchards. The ducks are not fed any antibiotics, hormones, enzymes or animal protein and are killed humanely, too. Because the Trelough Ducks are not fatty, the skin should not be pricked and owner Barry Clark recommends a glaze of clear honey and water left on the skin overnight. Other recipes come with the package. The Trelough duck was voted the best in Britain by Albert Roux after a tasting competition. More recently, Mr Clark has started to rear chickens and the Devereux is a typical French farmyard bird, reared free range and again without harmful additives. The firm also sells duck eggs, giblets, confit and smoked duck breast.

Hereford Duck Company, Trelough House, Wormbridge, Hereford HR2 9DH.

Tel: 01981 570767. **Fax:** 01981 570577.

Price range: £2 to £14 per lb. Ducks are £2.50 per lb, chickens £2.10. Price list free.

Payment: cheque, postal order.

Postage & packing: £10 for orders under £25, £6 to £49.99, £4 to £99.99, free thereafter.

Delivery: by carrier.

Refunds: no.

Specials: overnight stays amid ducks. Duck for supper, eggs for breakfast.

Holme Farmed Venison

The animals are naturally reared though not wild. The farm offers cuts of meat low in cholesterol along with sausages and burgers. There is also a range of smoked venison and three pies, notably the venison, Stilton and orange one, and ready-cooked casserole in red wine with celery, walnuts and redcurrants.

Holme Farmed Venison, Thorpe Underwood, York YO5 9SR.

Tel: 01423 331212. **Fax:** 01423 330855.

Price range: £1.35 to £12.40. Catalogue free.

Payment: cheque, Visa, Access.

Postage & packing: £4 under £20, £6 thereafter.

Delivery: order on Monday, despatch Wednesday.

Refunds: yes, if immediate return.

Jack Scaife

Bacon cured the proper way by Chris Battle of Jack Scaife butchers is despatched regularly to the House of Lords, Fortnum's, British embassies worldwide and Annabel's nightclub. Chris had been curing his own bacon for breakfast for thirty years and experience shows. The bacon, which comes from Berkshire cross large white pigs which are slaughtered late in life, is lightly sweet and crisps up well. It is matured in a space designed to feel like a Yorkshire farmhouse cellar and hung for up to nine days. The firm also mail orders oak-smoked and unsmoked hams, home-made sausage such as Cumberland and honey roast pork, old-fashioned black pudding and dry-cured ox tongue.

Jack Scaife Ltd, The Factory, Mill Lane, Oakworth, Keighley, West Yorkshire BD22 7QH.
Tel: 01535 647772. **Fax:** 01535 646305.
Price range: £1.90 per lb to £3.15. Price list free.
Payment: cheque with order.
Postage & packing: £3.20 for up to 2lb then by weight to £5.70 for up to 60lb.
Delivery: allow 7 days.
Refunds: no.

Macsween This Edinburgh firm has been noted for its haggises for over forty years and is now on the third generation of experts. Haggises, which come from cocktail size to ceremonial chieftain, are vacuum packed and will keep up to four weeks in a fridge or a year in a freezer. There is also a vegetarian haggis, which I can't think Rabbie Burns would like, and some Scottish specialities such as clapshot pie, Lorne sausage and fruit pudding.

Macsween of Edinburgh, Bruntsfield, Edinburgh EH10 4ES.
Tel: 0131 229 1216. **Fax:** 0131 229 9102.
Price range: from £7.85 but under review. Catalogue free.
Payment: cheque, credit cards except Amex, Delta, Switch.
Postage & packing: included.
Delivery: usually next day, allow a week.
Refunds: yes, if genuine.
Special: some countries refuse entry to haggis. Firm is moving so address may change.

Pipers Farm Everything is reared, they say, to improve the taste of the meat and poultry. Traditional breeds are reared slowly on grass; the meat is hung the requisite time. No additives are fed. Bronze turkeys can be bought ready-stuffed with apricots, nuts and herbs; ham is ready-cooked on the bone. Chicken may come boned and stuffed or plain dressed. They also offer beef, lamb, mutton and pork, venison, bacon, sausage and burgers.

Pipers Farm, Langford, Cullompton, Devon EX15 1SD.
Tel: 01392 881380. **Fax:** 01392 881600.
Price range: £3.35 to £24.09 per kg. Catalogue free.
Payment: cheque, Access, Visa.
Postage & packing: £10 standard on £40 minimum order.
Delivery: overnight courier mainland UK. Food can run out so order early.
Refunds: by arrangement

Rannoch Smokery Wild red deer, which need to be culled periodically, are used to make the most delicious smoked venison which should be eaten with just a touch of lemon juice or with scrambled eggs. It also makes excellent nibbles at parties and the firm suggests ideas. Each carcass is checked by a vet and the best cuts brined and smoked with oak chips from whisky barrels. There is also a smoked venison pâté, smoked chicken, duck and pheasant and fresh venison steaks.

Rannoch Smokery, Kinloch Rannoch, by Pitlochry, Perthshire PH16 5QD.
Tel: 01882 632344. **Fax:** 01882 632441.
Price range: £1.30 to £14. Send SAE for catalogue.
Payment: cheque with order, Visa, Mastercard.
Postage & packing: £1.45 per 250 gms.
Delivery: Christmas orders by 1st week December.
Refunds: by arrangement.

Real Meat Company Animals reared for this company are subject to independent checks on their welfare and conditions by student vets from Bristol. Once the animals are humanely slaughtered, they are hung for the correct time; ham and bacon is cured the old-fashioned way and sausages are made from proper cuts of meat. Along with normal cuts of beef, pork and lamb, there is Wiltshire bacon and ham, sausages and burgers. At Christmas, the firm sells turkeys, large chickens, ducks and geese and special packs. The Festive Pack contains a goose, leg of lamb, gammon joint, bacon, sausage, Stilton and Cheddar. All you need for the holiday at £98.

Richard Guy's Real Meat Company Ltd, Warminster, Wiltshire BA12 9AZ.
Tel: 0345 626017. **Fax:** 01985 218950.
Price range: £2.29 to £98. Catalogue free.
Payment: cheque, Visa, Access, Switch.
Postage & packing: £3.95 per order.
Delivery: within 24 hours.
Refunds: by arrangement.
Specials: special offers. Ring for details.

R & J Lodge Selling in West Yorkshire where they don't tolerate anything less than the best, this firm is noted for its outstanding pies and bacon. The pies are hand-raised and include pork, turkey and ham and game pie (hare, mallard, venison and pheasant cooked in red wine). There's dry-cured bacon from pigs reared humanely in the Derbyshire Dales and cheese from specialist farms around the area.

R & J Lodge, Greens End Road, Meltham, Huddersfield HD7 3NW.
Tel: 01484 850571.
Price range: £15.95 to £38. Catalogue free.
Payment: cheque with order.
Postage & packing: included.
Delivery: overnight courier but allow 4 working days.
Refunds: no.

Swaddles Green Farm Not only does the farm sell organic geese, turkeys, ducks and chicken to a very high standard, it also offers poultry and meat ready prepared for grand meals. There is the monumental three bird roast: turkey stuffed with goose, stuffed with duck which is stuffed with stuffing. This will feed forty for Christmas dinner. There is a pork joint stuffed with Christmas fruits, beef and lamb also stuffed, plus cooked hams, pies and charcuterie. One order will feed the family for the entire holiday.

Swaddles Green Farm, Hare Lane, Buckland St Mary, Chard, Somerset TA20 3JR.

Tel: 01460 234387. **Fax:** 01460 234591.

Price range: £2.50 to £130. Catalogue free.

Payment: cheque, major credit cards.

Postage & packing: £10 for orders under £40, £5 under £80, free thereafter.

Delivery: overnight carrier.

Refunds: no.

Specials: reminder service to nudge you when you forget to order.

Traditional Farmfresh Turkeys This organisation will advise on which of their members will mail-order to your door.

Traditional Farmfresh Turkeys, 5 Beacon Drive, Seaford, East Sussex BN25 2JX.

Tel: 01323 899802. **Fax:** 01323 899583.

See also: Fjordling, Inverawe Smokehouses (Fish), Fine Foods from France, Kileravagh, Quintessentials Europe (Food for Presents).

FISH

Smoking has been used as a preservative since medieval times, as it dramatically increases the shelf life of all kinds of fish, meat and poultry. Some smoked foods have a reputation for luxury while others are considered more run-of-the-mill but the pecking order is slowly reversing. Smoked salmon, once a great luxury, has become steadily cheaper as fish are farmed. Kippers, once an everyday breakfast food, are now sought by gourmets as herring stocks reduce. The trend is to bring back regional variations in curing and smoking fish, to do away with the ugly yellow dyes for cod and halibut and to experiment with fish that have not traditionally been so treated. Smoked prawns are very popular and smoked cod's roe makes a fine British answer to taramasalata.

As the interest in food increases in Britain and as farmers and fishermen become more concerned with the taste, the range of smoked foods is widening. Salmon, trout and mackerel are old friends but herrings now turn up as bloaters and red herrings, as well as kippers, while Arbroath smokies join finnan haddock. There are delicious smoked eels, prawns and mussels to buy and oily smoked halibut to slice like salmon. Smoked fish makes an ideal meal around Christmas because it's either ready to eat or simply needs boiling. Alternatively, add it to soup, rice or pasta or copy a British breakfast idea and serve smoked fish with scrambled eggs and bacon for brunch.

Even fresh fish, which spoils so fast, can now be bought by mail order, thanks to vacuum packing, dry-ice containers and overnight carriers. Mail-order firms don't bother with mundane cod and sole but concentrate on luxurious shell-fish and crustacea. Fish is an excellent Christmas standby because it cooks fast and provides an antidote to the rich foods on offer. It freezes well for short periods and unfreezes fast so when the parcel arrives, just pop it in the freezer until required.

FISH – LISTINGS

Brown & Forrest This company smokes salmon the traditional way which involves smoking the sides for twelve to eighteen hours over an oak fire. Smoked eel caught locally, smoked trout and smoked poultry breasts are also sold as well as smoked loin of pork (kasseller) which is marinaded in salt, honey and spices and then smoked over oak chippings. A Parma-type ham cured for up to eight months by air-drying makes a no-work starter when paired with an exotic fruit such as mango and figs rather than the ubiquitous melon.

Brown & Forrest, Thorney, Langport, Somerset TA10 0DR.
Tel: 01458 251520. **Fax:** 01458 253475.
Price range: £4 to £40. Catalogue free.
Payment: cheque, Visa, Access.
Postage & packing: included.
Delivery: by return or on specified date for gifts.
Refunds: yes.
Specials: hampers, special days watching smoking in action.

Fjordling An excellent selection of traditional and unusual smoked fish and meat includes halibut, river eel and Fjordling smoked trout to a Norwegian recipe as well as mackerel, salmon and kippers. There is smoked lamb, thin beef fillet (eat with thin brown bread and a good horseradish sauce), smoked turkey, duck, chicken and Cheddar cheese. All are smoked over oak to Norwegian methods. To sample some of the products, there's a mixed pack.

Fjordling Smokehouses, Dunstable Farm, West Winterslow, near Salisbury, Wiltshire SP5 1SA.
Tel: 01980 862689. **Fax:** 01980 863944.
Price range: £2.10 to £38. Catalogue free.
Payment: cheque, Access, Visa.
Postage & packing: included.
Delivery: 48 hours from despatch, excluding Monday.
Refunds: by arrangement.

Inverawe Smokehouses While many of the smokehouses specialise in sending presents (look them up in the Food for Presents section) this one is more for the dedicated cook. It not only sells an interesting range of smoked fish from the family-owned netting rights on the Awe – eel, halibut, kippers and smoked Loch Etive trout – but also smoked meats like ham, venison and beef. It can supply virtually all the ingredients for a dinner party (eg smoked duck with pears and kiwi fruit, Loch Etive fresh trout fillets with dill sauce, mince pies and brandy butter, cheese and biscuits at a cost of £53.85 if you take six portions). It sells Aberdeen Angus beef, cheeses, bacon and Christmas hams, cakes, preserves and puddings – in fact, you need go no further than this one firm for all your Christmas food apart from vegetables.

Inverawe Smokehouses, Taynuilt, Argyll PA35 1HU.
Tel: 01866 822446. **Fax:** 01866 822274.
Price range: £7.95 to £120. Catalogue free.
Payment: cheque, Visa, Access, Mastercard, Switch.
Postage & packing: included for smoked products. £3.95 for up to 3 gourmet items, £1.90 up to six, free thereafter.
Delivery: Christmas orders by 12 December.
Refunds: no.
Specials: freezer packs, standing orders, monthly offers, finds and recipes, gift vouchers.

Ghillies A fish merchant with a limited but well chosen range of Scottish fish for gourmets. There are oysters by the dozen, fresh langoustines, whole fresh salmon and a choice of Loch Fyne or Ullapool kippers. You can try Orkney marinated herrings in either sweet or rollmop cures (a legacy of the islands' Scandinavian links) and smoked salmon from Wester Ross. Since so many of these foods never reach the fishmonger (they're sent off to France) this is an opportunity to be grasped.

Ghillies, No 1 The High Street, Nairn, Ross IV12 4AG.
Tel: 01667 456900. **Fax:** 01667 455800.
Price range: £2.50 to £24. Catalogue free by Freepost IV 1208.
Payment: cheque, Access, Visa.
Postage & packing: £6.50 up to £20, free thereafter.
Delivery: 24-hour carrier.
Refunds: yes, if not in good condition.

Loch Fyne Oysters Not only oysters are supplied but three different smoked salmons – mild, golden, which takes twice as long, and kiln-roasted – plus gravadlax. Also smoked eels, trout, mussels and hard-to-find smoked cod's roe. Fresh fish include the oysters from Loch Fyne's rocky coast, grit-free mussels grown on ropes, langoustines, fresh salmon and queen scallops. The tubs of herring marinade from rollmop to sweet tomato are worth trying. Every order includes a free product guide and serving suggestions.

> **Loch Fyne Oysters Ltd**, Clachan Farm, Cairndow, Argyll PA26 8BH.
> **Tel:** 01499 600264. **Fax:** 01499 600234.
> **Price range:** £1.90 to £32. Price list by phone.
> **Payment:** cheque, Switch, Access, Visa, Mastercard, Diners.
> **Postage & packing:** £5.95, free for orders over £100.
> **Delivery:** next day on mainland.
> **Refunds:** if notified within 48 hours of receipt.
> **Specials:** gift boxes.

Mackenzies The smoking method of this firm is secret but no preservatives are used. Along with smoked salmon, they also smoke haddock (uncoloured), Wensleydale, Cheddar and Northumberland cheeses, ham and prawns which are delicious. They will also smoke to order if you have some abstruse cooking wish.

> **Mackenzies Smoked Products**, Unit 1, Wood Nook Farm, Hardesty Hill, Blubberhouses, North Yorkshire, LS21 2PQ.
> **Tel:** 01943 880369. **Mobile** 0378 604619.
> **Price range:** £1.95 to £7.90 per lb. Catalogue free.
> **Payment:** cheque.
> **Postage & packing:** postage rates.
> **Delivery:** last Christmas order, 15 December.
> **Refunds:** never been asked.

See also: Fish entries in Food for Presents.

HERBS AND SPICES

I was recently given a meal of free-range chicken cooked with oriental spices on a bed of roast red peppers. The plain chicken tasted totally different and a simple meal was turned into a treat. There is a growing trend to inventing new dishes with cross-cultural connections and at its centre is California, where a strong eastern influence, a major wine trade and a lack of tradition is creating the most interesting food in the world.

The secret lies in the spices. Recipes I have recently copied from West Coast cookbooks have used Japanese rice vinegar, toasted sesame seeds, lemon grass and Szechuan pepper. All these are readily available by mail order and provide flavours which are exotic but not too extreme.

Other firms are using spices with the exotic vegetables now available in Britain to make new blends of old chutneys, preserves, relishes and marmalades. These can, of course, be served with cold meat or for breakfast but they can also be used in cooking. Marmalade makes an excellent glaze on ham or adds an interesting flavour to pork casserole; chutneys and fruit sauces spice up dull sauces. I also recommend using the whole range of hot chilli sauces now available in almost everything savoury.

HERBS AND SPICES – LISTINGS

The Bay Tree Food Company Highly unusual home-made relishes, chutneys, jams and marmalades. Try the caramelised apple compôte with thyme, cranberry and raspberry vinegar relish with turkey, or Boxing and Festive chutneys, the first with apricot to liven up old turkey, the second sweeter and fruitier. Also spiced oranges for the cold ham. Many come in reusable Parfait jars as an extra bonus.

The Bay Tree Food Company, Perridge House, Pilton, Shepton Mallet, Somerset BA1 2RQ.
Tel: 01749 890195. **Fax:** 01749 890196.
Price range: £3.45 to £10. Catalogue free.
Payment: cheque, major credit cards.
Postage & packing: £5 per order, orders over £100 free.
Delivery: last Christmas orders by 2nd week of December. Hand-made so limited supplies.
Refunds: yes, if faulty and informed in 7 days.

Fox's Spices This firm can mail you eight separate peppers from Brazilian black to Indian green, and it has ready-mixed hot cajun and piri-piri mixes to sprinkle on food or incorporate in recipes. It has specials from Indonesia, India, China and runs a subscription scheme sending regular gifts of carefully chosen peppers, herbs and mustards to friends or yourself.

Fox's Spices Ltd, Masons Road, Stratford upon Avon, Warwickshire CV37 9NF.
Tel: 01789 266420.
Price range: £1 to £30. Catalogue free.
Payment: cheque.
Postage & packing: postal rate by weight.
Delivery: by return if possible.
Refunds: by arrangement.

Gourmet Dips The last thing the harried cook needs is to mess about with mixtures of spices and herbs when the turkey is underdone and the pudding on fire. Good cooks believe that you should reduce the work by judicious ready-made help and these blends, which can be added to mayonnaise or yoghurt to make delicious dips, are most useful. They can also be added to pasta sauces, casseroles and baked potatoes. Flavours include hot cajun, caesar, tikka and chilli.

Gourmet Dips, Church Hill, Olveston, Bristol BS12 3BZ.
Tel/Fax: 01454 201729.
Price range: £2.50 for 50g. Catalogue free (plus recipes).

Payment: cheque, Eurocheque with order.

Postage & packing: 75p for up to 3 dips, £1.25 for 4 to 6, £1.75 for 7 to 10, £2.25 for 11 to 15, free thereafter.

Delivery: normally despatched in 48 hours but allow up to 14 days. Phone to check on Christmas rush.

Refunds: replaced or refunded if substandard.

Hambleden Herbs The firm specialises in organically grown herbs and spices certified by the Soil Association as being free from additives and preservatives. The selection covers all those herbs and spices used in a good kitchen – lemon grass, caraway seed, poppy seed – and there's helpful advice on their uses and storage. They recommend old Marmite bottles to keep the herbs in the dark. There is also a good collection of herbal teas and tea bags.

Hambleden Herbs, Court Farm, Milverton, Somerset TA4 1NF.
Tel: 01823 401205. **Fax:** 01823 400276.
Price range: 75p to £14. Catalogue free.
Payment: currently cheque with order.
Postage & packing: £3 per UK order.
Delivery: allow 10 days before Christmas.
Refunds: yes.

Kari Mix Micky Bausola is the daughter of a Sri Lankan diplomat father and Chinese film-star mother born in Malaysia, so she's in a fine position to understand various oriental spice mixtures. Her list includes dry spice mixes for Indian Madras or Korma curry, Malaysian Beef Rendang and Sri Lankan yellow rice along with pickles, relishes and chutneys of tamarind, shrimp, aubergine and chilli. A delicious way to make a change from turkey and all the trimmings over the holiday. Her leaflet also includes recipes.

Kari Mix Ltd, Limuru, Cowgate Lane, Hawkinge, Folkestone, Kent CT18 7AR.
Tel/Fax: 01303 892134.
Price range: £1 to £2.90. Send SAE for catalogue.
Payment: cheque.

Postage & packing: £2.90; orders over £30 free.

Delivery: last Christmas order 1st week December.

Refunds: no.

Steamboat Exotic Foods The chunky catalogue offers over 175 different herbs and spices from seven countries in the Far East, including Japan, China, Thailand and Indonesia, not to mention cajun spices, Hungarian goulash mixes, Caribbean salt cod, Mexican chillis and Christmas pudding mixed spice. Then there are aromatherapy oils, fresh ginger and kaffir limes, cookery books to help out and pans to cook everything in. Chinese and Japanese wines and beers from around the world including Kenyan Tusker beer and Merryman's Old Fart (UK) are also available. Just get the catalogue, it's a revelation.

Steamboat Exotic Foods, PO Box 452, Bradford, West Yorkshire BD4 7TF.

Tel/Fax: 01274 742936.

Price range: 49p to £53. Catalogue free.

Payment: cheque, Access, Visa, Mastercard, Eurocard.

Postage & packing: £2.95 for orders to £39.99, free thereafter to one address.

Delivery: last Christmas orders by 18 December.

Refunds: telephone to discuss.

Specials: search service. Closed for annual holiday 5-19 February.

See also: Culpeper for herbs and spices (Luxuries), Morel Bros, Cobbett & Sons for good range of salts, peppers, mustards and spices (General Food Catalogues), Wendy Brandon for chutneys and preserves (Food for Presents).

FRUIT AND VEGETABLES

This is a very disappointing area for the fanatic mail orderer. When you can get bread and wild boar delivered to the door, I don't see why you can't get good vegetables. Yet I have failed to discover a good nationwide selection.

With a bit of ingenuity, however, you can solve the problem. First, pick your favourite farm shop or small but classy vegetable store and write out an order. Most will weigh and pack it neatly in your absence when there's a quiet moment. Many will deliver it at the end of the day (if the order is large enough or you are a regular customer). If not, get a local taxi firm to do it for you. Once you've made the arrangements for Christmas, you'll find it will work all year round.

The problem over the holiday is keeping fruit and vegetables fresh. I discovered how over a bitterly cold Christmas – store everything in an unheated room at just above freezing. Even lettuces and spinach will keep for an extraordinarily long time. Root vegetables should also be kept in the dark.

FRUIT AND VEGETABLES – LISTINGS

Charlton Orchards This company can provide you with boxes of the best English apples from Somerset. You can have a box of Cox's Orange Pippin (which will keep for several months after Christmas) or a mixture of old varieties. Another box will include apples and apple juice from the same trees. Apples are excellent over Christmas – fry them in sugar and butter, serve them with cheese, mix with celery and walnuts for salad or just plunge your teeth straight in.

Charlton Orchards, Charlton Road, Creech St Michael, Taunton, Somerset TA3 5PF.
Tel: 01823 412959/412979. **Fax:** 01823 412959.
Price range: £12 to £25. Leaflet free.
Payment: cheque.
Postage & packing: included.
Delivery: last Christmas orders 12 December.
Refunds: yes, without returning goods.

The Fresh Food Co I almost despaired of finding any mail-order vegetables until I came upon Thoby Young's great enterprise. The firm will organise boxes of fresh organic fruit and veg grown by a thirty-plus group of organic farmers in East Anglia. You sign up for a three-month subscription and the company delivers a box either once a week or once a fortnight, average weight 14lb. For Christmas, Thoby plans an unprecedented service – a special box for a minimum of four people including organic geese, turkey, bacon, sausages, organic flour and herbs and, of course, his fruit and vegetables. The firm also delivers boxes of fish from Cornwall on the same subscription basis.

The Fresh Food Co, Freepost Fresh Food, 326 Portobello Road, London W10 5RU.
Tel: 0181 969 0351. **Fax:** 0181 964 8050. **E-mail:** 100600.3527@compuserve.com
Price range: £22.95 to over £400. Information on request.
Postage & packing: included.
Delivery: overnight from growers.
Refunds: by arrangement.
Specials: grand Christmas box.

Tropical Wholefoods This company helps over 100 farmers in sub-Saharan Africa to sun-dry their produce and sells the results, ensuring that the farmers get a fair price. The dried fruits are banana, pineapple and mango; dried vegetables are oyster and shiitake mushrooms, sun-dried tomatoes and root vegetable crisps. Other products include chillis, honey, mueslis and fruitjacks. Because this is designed to help the farmers, packaging is minimal and the fruits look careworn. However, they taste delicious, reconstitute in water and cook well in soups and pasta dishes.

Tropical Wholefoods, Unit 15-17, 62 Tritton Road, London SE21 8DE.
Tel: 0181 670 1114. **Fax:** 0181 670 1117.
Price range: 61p to £32. Send large SAE for price lists and recipe sheets.

Payment: cheque with order.
Postage & packing: £3.50.
Delivery: last orders for Christmas 15 December.
Refunds: no.

BREAD, PUDDINGS AND CAKES

If everyone is to enjoy Christmas, including the put-upon cook, it's important to make life easy. There is no point in baking your own cakes and making Christmas puddings unless you positively relish the prospect. Mail-order suppliers can probably do it cheaper and you won't have to worry about a thing.

Rich Christmas recipes, dating from medieval times, were intended to preserve food. Most fruit cakes and puddings therefore improve with age so are ideal to mail order. Phone early because these foods are often made by single farmhouse cooks.

You can also stock up, nearer the holiday, with other delicious breads and puddings which will ensure a series of delicious meals – cooked by someone else.

BREAD, PUDDINGS AND CAKES – LISTINGS

Crosse Farm Bakery Suppliers of amazing puddings and of rich Christmas cakes – decorated or plain. There are usually chocolate puddings with chestnut, truffle or mocha sauce; fresh lemon and apple tarts (good to cut the richness of poultry); sticky toffee pudding; Bakewell

tart; walnut and pecan pie (which you can pretend you made yourself) on offer. Also super cakes for special occasions and brownies, flapjacks, florentines and olive-oily focaccia bread.

Crosse Farm Bakery, Cheriton Bishop, Exeter, Devon EX6 6JD.
Tel: 01647 24442. **Fax:** 01647 24884.
Price range: £6.50 to £35. Catalogue free.
Payment: cheque with order.
Postage & packing: separately quoted.
Delivery: by arrangement.
Refunds: no.
Specials: gift service.

Doves Farm Organic This farm has been producing organic foods since 1978, specialising in different grains. Some of these make interesting breads and cakes; others are for those with allergies to gluten. The ordinary wheat flour includes wholemeal, white, bleached and unbleached, and self-raising. Stoneground rye flour makes North European speciality breads while 'spelt' was a discovery of early man. There is gram flour for Indian dishes and brown rice flour for baby food and gluten-free bread. There are also organic cornflakes and digestive biscuits.

Doves Farm Foods Ltd, Salisbury Road, Hungerford, Berkshire RG17 0RF.
Tel: 01488 684880. **Fax:** 01488 685235.
Price range: £6.60 to £19.58. Send A4 SAE for catalogue.
Payment: cheque, postal order.
Postage & packing: £6 to 25 kg, thereafter £8.
Delivery: allow 21 days but it's usually 7.
Refunds: by arrangement.

Squires Kitchen If you enjoy making elaborate cakes, this is the firm to talk to. Their catalogue is renowned among cake-makers everywhere. They sell equipment for baking cakes and for displaying them, as well as ingredients such as flavouring essences and icing colours. There are tools for complex icing and modelling, stencils (including a Christmas range) plus videos and books on the subject.

Squires Kitchen, Squires House, 3 Waverley Lane, Farnham, Surrey GU9 8BB.
Tel: 01252 711749/734309. **Fax:** 01252 714714. Send A4 envelope, 43p in stamps, for catalogue.
Payment: cheque, Access, Visa, Mastercard, Eurocard.
Postage & packing: from £1.50 on £5 order, free over £100 order.
Delivery: within 2 weeks.
Refunds: will replace within 10 days.
Specials: gift vouchers.

Truffles Barbara Bayfield's grandmother was a genuine country-house cook and she inspired this range of Victorian puddings made single-handedly by her granddaughter. The traditional plum or Christmas pudding is quite different from mass-produced ones, being light in texture and fruity without the usual bitterness. The fruit is soaked in ale and sherry and the liqueur added after cooking so the spirit doesn't evaporate. More recently, Truffles introduced a fig and ginger pudding with cider brandy and an apricot and pineapple pudding with rum.

Truffles, 72 Belle Vue Road, Salisbury, Wiltshire SP1 3YD.
Tel: 01722 331978.
Price range: £2.95 for 8 oz pudding to £11.50 for 4lb. Larger on request. No catalogue.
Payment: cheque, postal order.
Postage & packing: £1 for smallest to £3.50 for largest.
Delivery: last Christmas orders by 15 December.
Refunds: yes, if faulty – but it's never happened.

Village Bakery Andrew Whitley has been making organic bread, puddings and cakes using traditional wood-fired ovens for twenty years. His range is small but good. Bread includes French and Russian rye and the smart breads with olives, tomato and wild mushroom mixed into the dough. There are gingerbreads and tea breads as well as Christmas cakes and mince pies, shortbread, parkin and flapjacks. Brandy butter, Cumberland rum butter and organic Christmas hampers are also available.

The Village Bakery, Melmerby, Penrith, Cumbria CA10 1HE.
Tel: 01768 881515. **Fax:** 01768 881848.
Price range: £3.25 to £25. Catalogue free.
Payment: cheque, Access, Mastercard, Visa, Diners.
Postage & packing: included.
Delivery: within 14 days.
Refunds: yes.
Specials: gift orders.

See also: Cakes and Biscuits entries in Food for Presents.

DRINK

In pagan times, midwinter was the time to misbehave – to enliven dark days with a pleasant orgy or two. Early Christians ensured that Christmas was a great feast with plenty of booze on the side. And so it remains.

The secret of enjoying the holiday is to make it special, and one way of doing that is to choose drinks which are different. This might be the time to buy the best wine you can afford, to have port or a vin santo with the nuts and raisins or to welcome guests with a heady mulled wine.

It is also a good time to jettison the instant coffee and teabags and produce the real thing. Flavoured tea and coffees such as teas with orange peel and spices and coffees blended with rum and almond flavours specially formulated for winter are becoming increasingly popular. Or you can experiment with your own blend by basing spices on a good China tea or Colombian coffee.

DRINKS – LISTINGS

Adnams Wine Merchants Simon Loftus regularly wins the Wine Merchant of the Year award largely by offering such a varied list and by collaborating with the growers, whose photographs appear in the bustling catalogue. The wines come from all the expected places – Spain, Portugal, California, New Zealand as well as France and Italy – and from the unexpected, such as Lebanon and England. There's an amazing Indian sparkling wine called Omar Khayyam, which is better than its name. Adnams also sell spirits, oils, pickles and corkscrews and are based in a lovely hotel, where you can stay and sample.

> **Adnams**, The Crown, High Street, Southwold, Suffolk IP18 6DP.
> **Tel:** 01502 727220 (general); 01502 727222 (mail order). **Fax:** 01502 727223.
> **Price range:** £3.20 to £78.50. Catalogue £2.50.
> **Payment:** cheque, Access, Visa.
> **Postage & packing:** included.
> **Delivery:** despatched within 2 days by carrier.
> **Refunds:** notify within 24 hours.

Beer Cellar A collection of over 170 classic beers from more than forty countries which can be ordered in single cases, mixed cases and special selection cases of twelve or twenty-four bottles. The British selection, slightly smaller than that from Belgium, starts with Adnams (qv) and ends with Woodforde's. There's a raspberry beer from France and one called Sans Culottes; from Germany there's Schloss Hell and there are also beers from Thailand and Tahiti, Israel and Peru,

Sri Lanka and Cyprus. Special collections include five beers brewed by Belgian monks and a case of American beer. Nothing, however, from Ireland.

The Beer Cellar Co Ltd, 31 Norwich Road, Strumpshaw, Norwich NR13 4AG.

Tel: 01603 714884. **Fax:** 01603 714624. **E-mail:** cellar@paston.co.uk

Price range: £1.70 to £46. Catalogue free.

Payment: cheque, postal order, Visa, Access, Amex, Diners, Connect.

Postage & packing: £3.60 per case up to £8 for 4 cases.

Delivery: last orders 3 days before Christmas.

Refunds: yes, if damaged or not delivered.

Boaters Flavoured teas have been with us since ancient China but Boaters are pioneering flavoured coffees. Unlike teas, which are best with sharp or scented flavours added, coffee needs something warm and nutty. This list has pecan pie, amaretto and cinnamon hazelnut flavours along with liqueurs like southern and highland whisky, Irish cream and Grand Marnier. Another good mix is coffee and chocolate. There is a seasonal Christmas pud mix and gift sets are supplied. The base is Arabica beans and the flavoured coffees should be treated in the same way as unflavoured. No sugar is added.

Boaters Coffee Co Ltd, The Coffee Factory, Ampthill Business Park, Station Road, Ampthill, Bedfordshire MK45 2QP.

Tel: 01525 404781. **Fax:** 01525 404981.

Price range: £2.50 to £7.95. Catalogue free.

Payment: cheque, Access, Visa, Amex.

Postage & packing: £1.50 on orders under £7.50, £2.50 between £7.50 and £15, free thereafter.

Delivery: last Christmas orders by 16 December.

Refunds: no

Enotria Winecellars If you enjoy Italian wines, as I do, this is the place to go. The list includes four Vin Santos, Sicilian Marsala and Vino Liquoroso, all ideal with heavy Christmas pudding and fruit cake, plus three sparkling Proseccos, which are hard to find – strange, because two are less than £10 a bottle. There are also olive oils and flours from Italy. Enotria is now trying to build up wines from Australia and Europe, including Spain, Hungary and Austria. It's a good and exciting list.

Enotria Winecellars Ltd, 153-155 Wandsworth High Street, London SW18 4JB.

Tel: 0181 871 2668. **Fax:** 0181 874 8380.

Price range: £2.75 to £69.95. Catalogue free.

Payment: cheque, Visa, Access, Switch.

Postage & packing: free inside M25, free outside for more than 2 cases. Otherwise £5.

Delivery: where possible in 72 hours. Some items limited.

Refunds: if notified within 3 days.

Halves Tim Jackson believes we underrate the half bottle of wine. Smaller bottles help people on their own, those who want more than one wine per meal or people who can't agree on what they want. His range covers champagne, brandy and port and includes a good selection of wines from France and the fashionable new world. There's a good cooking sherry, a few grander foods like truffles and saffron and a selection of Christmas halves – again a good present for singles.

Halves, Wood Yard, off Corve Street, Ludlow, Shropshire SY8 2PX.

Tel: 01584 877866. **Fax:** 01584 877677.

Price range: £3 upwards. Catalogue free.

Payment: cheque, Mastercard, Visa, Delta, Switch, Amex.

Postage & packing: £4.70 for small orders. Included for a case upwards.

Delivery: 10 working days, but last Christmas orders 11 December.

Refunds: yes, for wine, if returned within a month undamaged. Otherwise by arrangement.

H.R. Higgins This family firm, which has been mailing a fine selection of coffees and teas for decades, has a faultless list and never lets you down. I know, I've been a customer for years. There are Guatemala Huehuetenanga and Ethiopian Harar

Longberry coffees, Lapsang Souchong and gunpowder tea along with teas flavoured for summer and winter and with mango and lemon. There are the firm's own blends, a choice of dark and light roastings and decaff coffee.

H.R. Higgins (Coffee Man) Ltd, 10 Lea Road Industrial Park, Waltham Abbey, Essex EN9 1AS.

Tel: 01992 768254. **Fax:** 01992 787523.

Price range: £9.44 to £28 per kg. Catalogue free.

Payment: cheque, Visa, Access, Switch.

Postage & packing: from £2.66 per kg, orders over 3 kg free.

Delivery: last Christmas orders by 1st week December.

Refunds: yes.

Specials: Christmas gift packs.

Justerini & Brooks The Queen's wine merchants, who have been going for 200 years, thus also serving George III, IV and VI, Victoria and Edward VII, who knew something about wines. Their house wines, from £3.95 a bottle, are excellent value, especially the house claret. These are safe to buy and serve even wine buffs. You can also buy a 1924 first growth Haut Brion for £280 if you feel less secure. This is very much a traditional list, heavy on good port but with little from the new world. The house London Dry Gin stays at 40% proof while others have gone down to 37.5%. There is also a sloe gin.

Justerini & Brooks Ltd, 61 St James's Street, London SW1A 1LZ.

Tel: 0171 493 8721. **Fax:** 0171 499 4653.

Price range: £3.95 to £2,290. Catalogue free.

Payment: cheque, Visa, Amex, Mastercard.

Postage & packing: £9 for under than 2 cases, free thereafter.

Delivery: last orders 10 days before Christmas.

Refunds: yes, but please return offending bottle.

Specials: Christmas gift cases.

Lay & Wheeler This wine merchant's catalogue is a book in itself, 136 pages long. The wines come from all over the world with strong presences from Australia, New Zealand, South

Africa and California, a good selection of ports and sherries plus some new world sparkling wines. The firm is neither pompous nor over-priced though some of its descriptions of wines are beguiling – how about 'imminently drinkable'?

Lay & Wheeler, 6 Culver Street West, Colchester, Essex CO1 1JA.

Tel: 01206 764446. **Fax:** 01206 560002.

Price range: £2.74 to £109.50. Catalogue free.

Payment: cheque, Access, Visa, Amex.

Postage & packing: £5.50 for a dozen bottles; 2 dozen upwards free.

Delivery: by carrier, 2-day service at extra charge.

Refunds: if returned in a month.

Master of Malt The firm specialises, as you might guess, in single malt whiskies, the aristocrats of the spirit world. They regularly have over 200 brands from Askaig to Tullibardine, including my favourite Glenmorangie. Other whiskies include bourbons from America, whiskies from Ireland, North and South, and even Wales. You can also send a bottle with a personalised label – a neat change from champagne.

The Master of Malt Ltd, The Corn Exchange, The Pantiles, Royal Tunbridge Wells, Kent TN2 5TE.

Tel/Fax: 01892 513295. **Fax:** 01892 750487.

Price range: £3 to £200. Catalogue free.

Payment: cheque, Amex, Diners, Visa, Eurocard, Mastercard, JCB.

Postage & packing: £4.95, free over £60.

Delivery: last Christmas orders 15 December. Some whiskies rare and in short supply.

Refunds: yes, only if damaged or incorrect.

The Somerset Cider Brandy Company The cider and apple brandy are made from traditional cider apples such as Sweet Alford, Brown Snout and Somerset Red Streak grown in 120 acres of orchards surrounding the farm where this cider is made (the brandy has to be distilled under lock and key by law). The art of distilling cider was lost in Tudor times but the owners researched the skill in Normandy, home of calvados, and in the whisky distilleries of Scotland. It is created in two French stills, called Josephine and Fifi, and is deliciously spicy and rather more appley than calvados. A perfect way to round off a traditional Christmas meal, especially if you favour duck or goose over turkey.

The Somerset Cider Brandy Company Ltd, Burrow Hill, Kingsbury Episcopi, Martock, Somerset TA12 5BU.
Tel/Fax: 01460 240782.
Price range: £11 to £24. Send SAE for catalogue.
Payment: cheque, major credit cards.
Postage & packing: 1 bottle £3.94 by post, 4 bottles £1.50 each.
Delivery: last Christmas orders 18 December.
Refunds: no.

The Sussex Tea Company Sounds unlikely, but the company's special Sussex tea is blended in Uckfield and is a mix of Kenyan leaves which make a good strong cuppa described as 'brisk' by the firm. Other blends include my favourite, Lapsang Souchong, with its tarry flavour, and Earl Grey perfumed with bergamot and jasmine. I have also just learned to enjoy their Winter and Summer tea: for winter, China tea is mixed with cloves, orange peel and almonds and, for summer (which can be iced), with cornflower, mallow, marigold and thistle. The catalogue also includes fruit teas like autumn berries, peach and apple and there is a single coffee blend. The teas, by the way, can make the base for hot toddies or julep-type drinks.

The Sussex Tea Company Ltd, PO Box 66, Uckfield, East Sussex TN22 3ZR.
Tel: 01825 732601. **Fax:** 01825 732730.
Price range: £1.19 to £8.95. Send A4 SAE for catalogue.
Payment: cheque with cheque card number.
Postage & packing: £1 for 375gms, £2 for 750gms, £3 for 1,250 gms, £4.50 more than 1,250gms.
Delivery: orders by 1st week of December, next day delivery at extra cost.
Refunds: never had a dissatisfied customer.

Tanners A family-run wine merchant which prides itself on its mail-order business, with some 12,000 customers including top hotels and restaurants. Their list is interesting and sensibly priced. There is a red sparkling Burgundy and fizzies from Australia, India, South Africa and New Zealand, plus two pink sparklers from Australia. They sell my favourite Chianti by Antinori and the hefty Tignanello, also by Antinori and ideal for Christmas lunch. There's an excellent selection of single malt whiskies and even a Welsh whisky, Swn y mor.

Tanners Wines Ltd, 26 Wyle Cop, Shrewsbury SY1 1XD.
Tel: 01743 232400/232007. **Fax:** 01743 344401.
Price range: from £3.50. Catalogue free.
Payment: cheque, Access, Visa, Amex.
Postage & packing: £6 per address, orders over £75 free.
Delivery: last orders by 14 December.
Refunds: yes, including opened bottles.

Vintage Roots Organic wine is produced without synthetic fertilisers, pesticides and natural preservatives like sulphur dioxide. This company specialises in pure wine made like it used to be from all the usual countries, including Sedlescombe in Sussex. There are also organic liqueurs like Cassis and Crème de Mûr, Cognac and calvados. There is a small selection of organic beers from Germany and Scotland, cider and perry and fruit juices.

Vintage Roots, Sheeplands Farm, Wargrave, Berkshire
RG10 8DT.
Tel: 01734 401222. **Fax:** 01734 404814.
Price range: £1.35 to £29.95. Catalogue free.
Payment: cheque, Visa, Access.
Postage & packing: £3.95 for 1 case; £5 for 2, £6 for 3 to 5 cases, free thereafter.
Delivery: within 7 days, overnight at extra cost.
Refunds: within 3 days for breakage.
Specials: hampers for vegans.

World Coffees Top quality coffees from some of the world's best estates are supplied as beans or coarse or fine ground. All varieties – full-bodied Costa Rica Tres Rios, slightly sharper Kenya Estate AA and full-flavoured Sumatra Lintong, for instance – come in the latest vacuum packs which allow the beans to breathe without losing flavour. It's worth trying out a few to see which suits your tap water. The firm also sells gift packs of coffee makers, grinders, airtight jars and espresso cups.

World Coffees, 16 The Old Stables, More House Farm Business Centre, Wivelsfield, West Sussex RH17 7RE.
Tel: 01444 471130. **Fax:** 01444 471131.
Price range: £5.50 to £50. Catalogue free.
Payment: cheque, Visa, Mastercard.
Delivery: last Christmas orders 20 December.
Refunds: yes.
Specials: gift parcels with messages.

See also: Hambleden Herbs for herb teas, Steamboat Exotic Foods for interesting beers (Herbs and Spices), Jeroboams (Food for Presents).

CHEESE

A good bit of cheese is an integral part of Christmas. Stilton is the established favourite but I like a strong, farmhouse Cheddar which can be eaten with Cox's apples. I think, too, you should have a good mixture on the cheese board – a brie or camembert, a fresh parmesan (also useful for grating or shaving over salads etc) and perhaps something unusual like Northumberland cheese with nettles.

Cheese on its own with water biscuits or bread, fresh celery and pickle makes an excellent quick meal when the cook has had enough. A stock of cheaper Cheddar to grate allows for last-minute gratins.

CHEESE – LISTINGS

The Northumberland Cheese Co If you want something really unusual, this company sells rare Northumberland cheeses. A few are made from goats' milk but most from cows'. The baby cheeses come either plain or with added garlic, chives, pepper or even nettles. Another is smoked. The firm also sells Coquetdale, Wensleydale and Elsdon goat cheeses. Specials are small wedges of each in a basket or cuts off larger cheeses.

> **The Northumberland Cheese Company Ltd**, Make me Rich Farm, Blagdon, Seaton Burn, Northumberland NE13 6BZ.
> **Tel:** 01670 789798. **Fax:** 01670 789644.
> **Price range:** £7 to £11. Catalogue free.
> **Payment:** cheque with order.
> **Postage & packing:** included.
> **Delivery:** last Christmas orders 6 December.
> **Refunds:** by arrangement.
> **Specials:** will enclose your own gift cards.

Paxton & Whitfield The most famous cheese shop in London, visited by all the crusty clubmen who like their Stilton. It has an excellent selection of the best Cheddars in the world chosen from farms around Cheddar Gorge and also sells 4lb truckles which make good presents. Other hard cheeses include Caerphilly, Wensleydale, double and single Gloucester from small farms and Wellington, from Guernsey cows on the Duke of Wellington's estate. Stilton is traditional at Christmas and the firm has been picking the best since 1797. They come as whole cheeses, baby cheeses or in jars. The firm provides a good product guide to the varieties but some are seasonal.

> **Paxton & Whitfield Ltd**, 93 Jermyn Street, London SW1Y 6JE.
> **Tel:** 0171 930 0259. **Fax:** 0171 321 0621.
> **Price range:** £25 upwards. Catalogue free.
> **Payment:** cheque, Access, Visa, Mastercard, Amex, Diners.

Postage & packing: under review but from £7.50.
Delivery: last orders for Christmas 15 December.
Refunds: yes, if poor quality.

See also: Cheese entries in Food for Presents section, General Food Catalogues and many other firms in Christmas food section.

Chapter Three

KITCHENWARE

If you are entertaining a large group of family or friends over Christmas, you'll probably need to review your cooking arrangements – and chances are you'll find them wanting. One of the great annoyances about cooking in big quantities is that the pans are never large enough, the potato peeler has gone blunt and there isn't an oven large enough for the giant turkey.

It is costly to get the right equipment but it's worth it. A top caterer I interviewed has no fewer than three fridges: one for drink, one for vegetables and the third for everything else, plus special wheeled wastebins for the rubbish in her flat. She collects white crockery and beautiful gilded glasses to make meals an occasion. All, however, are dishwasher friendly.

Like her, I think it's important to pick exactly what suits you. Solid pans are expensive but will last decades; a good garlic squeezer or peppermill saves gritted teeth so, if yours is a dud, toss it out. If you want to boil a whole ham or salmon, get the correct pan – it's far easier and tastier than faffing around with foil in the oven.

Finally – and this may be counsel of perfection in the run-up to Christmas – have an oven that works. Many a family has had a gruesome holiday with a smoking oven, an irate cook and an underdone turkey.

KITCHENWARE – LISTINGS

Buyers and Sellers Considering how bothersome it is to buy big kitchen equipment, it's a delight to use this firm which tries to stock everything and make life easy. They have, or will get, almost every current make and model of fridge, freezer, washing machine, cooker and oven, hob, hood, microwave, tumble drier and vacuum cleaner. They will help and advise and often have special offers.

> **Buyers and Sellers Ltd**, 120-122 Ladbroke Grove, London W10 5NE.
> **Tel:** 0171 229 1947/8468. **Fax:** 0171 221 4113.
> **Price range:** £100 to £100,000. Catalogue free.
> **Payment:** cheque, all major cards.
> **Postage & packing:** by arrangement.
> **Delivery:** last Christmas order end November.
> **Refunds:** under the Sale of Goods Act.

Chefs Choice I love kitchen things and don't feel at all offended if I get pots and pans as presents. This catalogue has nearly everything a keen cook could need: lots of knives, classics like Dualit toasters, basters and sieves, cake icing equipment and iron omelette pans. There are also new cookbooks and a chef's hat to make your point.

> **Nisbets Chefs Choice**, 1110b Aztec West, Bristol BS12 4HR.
> **Tel:** 01454 855655. **Fax:** 01454 855565.
> **Price range:** £1 to £250. Catalogue free.
> **Payment:** cheque, Visa, Access, Amex.
> **Postage & packing:** £2.95 on orders to £30, thereafter free.

Delivery: last Christmas orders 23 December.
Refunds: yes, if returned in 30 days.

David Mellor David Mellor is a top designer and silversmith and, even if some of the goods are not designed by him, they all reflect his sense of style and practicality. The knives, pans, chopping boards, even the measuring jugs, sieves and rolling pins, are as beautiful as they are useful. Most are traditional shapes but often in modern stainless steel with non-stick inners. Ranges of kitchen knives and cutlery are designed by him. The catalogue is simple and beautiful too.

David Mellor, 4 Sloane Square, London SW1W 8EE.
Tel: 0171 730 4259 **Fax:** 0171 730 7240.
Price range: 90p to £1,000. Catalogue £1.
Payment: cheques, credit cards except Amex and Diners.
Postage & packing: from £3.50.
Delivery: last Christmas orders by 20 December.
Refunds: yes, if faulty or at manager's discretion.

Divertimenti No one interested in cooking could fail to find necessities and luxuries in this catalogue, a honed-down version of the lovely French-orientated London shop. It ranges from the sensible potato peeler which swivels for left-handers like me to classic American blenders and stylish Irish linen teatowels. Divertimenti was a pioneer in creating butcher's block tables for the ordinary kitchen and importing tough peasant crockery from France. The curvy green Provençal pottery is a classic while a set of plates, each with a pear being eaten from whole to core, is new and jokey.

Divertimenti (Mail Order) Ltd, Freepost (Gl2881), London SW6 6YX.
Tel: 0171 386 9911. **Fax:** 0171 386 9393.
Price range: £3.95 to £399.95. Catalogue free.
Payment: cheque, postal order, Access, Mastercard, Visa.
Postage & packing: £3.95.
Delivery: allow 21 days.
Refunds: if returned in 28 days.

Lakeland Plastics This is a no-nonsense kitchen supply company which started out selling plastic storage boxes. Excellent for all-the-year-round appliances, at Christmas it puts out a special catalogue of presents. These include a heavy red tartan tablecloth, red and green candles and old-fashioned wire-bound soda siphons, foods such as marinated figs, marzipan fruits from France and marrons glacés plus lots of pretty wrapping papers and ribbons. As always, a good standby and the service is notably friendly.

Lakeland Plastics Ltd, Alexandra Buildings, Windermere, Cumbria LA23 1BQ.

Tel: 01539 488100 **Fax:** 01539 488300.

Price range: £3 to £100. Catalogue free.

Payment: cheque, postal order, Access, Visa, Mastercard, Switch.

Postage & packing: £2.50 on orders to £35, free thereafter.

Delivery: mid December for Christmas (see catalogue). Next day for £5 extra.

Refunds: yes

See also: Engraved Greetings for old spice labels (Cards and Wrapping Paper), entries under Home Interest for catalogues including kitchenware.

Chapter Four

CREATING AN ATMOSPHERE

One of the most important but hard-to-define parts of celebrating the Christmas holiday is getting the atmosphere right. And the atmosphere of Christmas falls into two distinct parts.

The first and easiest to create is that leading up to the holiday. The decorations, the tree, the cards arranged just so, the mistletoe strategically positioned – everything that adds to the anticipation of the day itself – are written about ad nauseam. To the reams of paper expended annually in papers and magazines on the subject, I would add that simplicity is as charming as opulence and that attention to the unseen, especially scent, contributes greatly. Firms are now producing perfumed candles, burning oils, pot pourris and room sprays specially formulated for winter. Others are designed specially for Christmas – warm perfumes made up of spices like cinnamon and cloves, orange and lemon oils. Add to this the smells of Christmas itself – cigar smoke, baking bread and pine needles – and you already create a welcome.

The mellow light of candles is important to setting the scene. Use banks of stumpy wax candles inside hurricane lanterns to

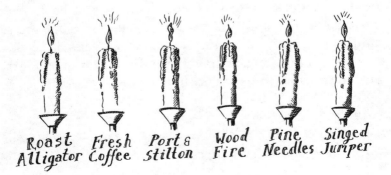

Roast Alligator   Fresh Coffee   Port & Stilton   Wood Fire   Pine Needles   Singed Jumper

protect against fire (be very careful with naked flames with excited children and combustible trees and cards about) or in chandeliers hung at the centre of the dining table. Take a tip from Scandinavia and set candles on deep window sills to reflect in the glass and glow outside or set them, 18th-century style, against mirrors. Choose good quality beeswax or non-drip varieties in creamy white, gold, silver or to match the room.

The second – and much neglected – phase of Christmas atmosphere comes in those replete days from Christmas dinner droning on into Boxing Day. People may need help in perking up their spirits, especially as brisk country walks, outdoor games and sports are often defeated by the weather.

So, deftly but not bossily, try to steer family and friends into games. There are variations of croquet and bowls to play on the carpet; or try jigsaws designed to beguile the whole family (such as the personalised one from Jayem where the picture is compiled of family snaps or the NSPCC's jigsaw map of Britain); there are masks and dressing-up outfits for children and traditional games and jokes which will recall holidays long past to the adults. There are Victorian zoetropes, soldier skittles and kazoos at Hawkin by Post, solitaire, jumbo jacks and bagatelle boards at the Hill Toy Company, even a whoopee cushion from the NSPCC.

For those who cannot survive parlour games, there are cassettes and videos of loved old films, TV and radio programmes – Monty Python, *Carry On Camping*, Laurel and Hardy, 'Round the Horne', *Monsieur Hulot's Holiday* – and talking books. You can organise videos of great family moments and, when you've run them forwards, play them backwards for gales of giggles. Get everyone laughing, reminiscing and larking about and you will have defeated the post-Christmas blues.

Refer to:

Books, Cassettes, CDs and Videos: Listening Post, Tadpole Lane, Video Plus Direct, Talking Tapes Direct.

Charities: Help the Aged, NSPCC, Royal Horticultural Society.

Children: Green Board Game Co, Grove, Hill Toy Co, Infant Isle, Jigroll, Layden Designs, Orchard Toys, Tridias!

Christmas Trees and Decorations: Balloon City, Chatsworth, Cherie Colman, Hector's Candles, Smallwood Christmas Trees Direct.

General Catalogues: Fortnum & Mason, General Trading Co, Harrods, Spotted Duck.

Herbs and Spices: Fox's Spices, Hambleden Herbs, Steamboat Exotic Foods.

Home Interest: Anta, Ciel Decor, Cologne & Cotton, Funky Stuff, Global Village, Jerry's Home Store, Shaker.

Luxuries: Angela Flanders Aromatics, Aromatherapy Associates, Crabtree & Evelyn, Culpeper, Czech & Speake, D.R. Harris, Gifts by Post, Glenelg Candles, Groom Bros, L'Artisan Parfumeur, Norfolk Lavender, Officina Profuma Santa Maria Novella, Penhaligon's, Percivals, Pinks by Post.

Personalised Presents: Arty-Zan, Jayem Jigsaws, Memories on Video, Tetbury Video Workshop.

Stocking Fillers: Frog Hollow, Hawkin by Post.

Sports: John Jaques.

YOUR LEGAL RIGHTS

If you buy goods by mail order, you are automatically protected by the laws and rights that cover retail shopping. The most important of these is the Sale and Supply of Goods Act of 1994 which toughened the earlier Sale of Goods Acts.

The first right you have is that goods must be or do what they say they are or will. A potato peeler must peel potatoes, a cotton sweater must be made out of cotton. The goods must also be of 'satisfactory quality' – that is, durable, safe and free from small faults. The description given in a mail-order catalogue should be accurate. If not, you have the right to reject anything and get your money back as long as you do so in a 'reasonable' time. However, 'reasonable' is not defined.

You can also claim compensation if a tool or toy breaks down after too short a time because, again, it is not 'satisfactory'. You are entitled to a full refund of your money – not a credit note or exchange – if that's what you want. This protection also covers mail-order sale goods, unless they are clearly called seconds. Sale goods also have to be 'satisfactory'.

If you simply don't like what you have bought, you do not have these legal rights. However, many mail-order firms will still help because it is important to them to encourage the use of mail order for shopping. I must add that the public do not always treat firms well. A number of firms insist that returned goods must be clean, unworn or undamaged and that broken bits or faulty parts must be returned. This is because some people order an expensive shirt, wear it to a party and then try to send it back. Or they claim breakages when there are none. If we find some firms wary or even brusque, it may be our own fault.

Clearly, when you order something custom-made or

engraved with initials, it is even harder to send it back. I suggest that mail-order shoppers commissioning an item in this way should sort out an arrangement in advance about this. The same applies to perishable foods which cannot be resold.

A further problem with Christmas presents is that the legal protection covers only the buyer, not the recipient, and firms often insist on seeing a receipt, probably because the public cannot always be trusted. Recipients can't always own up that they are unhappy with their present and are too embarrassed to ask for the receipt. But this is what they will have to do before they can legally claim.

There is a code of mail-order practice (though some of the firms listed here may not belong to it) which suggests that all goods should arrive within thirty days and that, if returned within seven days, money should be refunded. Another key point to watch out for is delivery times. Many of the firms in this guide ask for twenty-eight days for delivery while adding that goods are usually delivered within a week. With timing being so important over Christmas, make it a condition of contract with the seller by writing the vital delivery time onto your order.

If you return an item because it is not 'satisfactory' under law, then your postage costs should be refunded along with the price; if you return because you don't like it, then you will probably have to pay postage.

There is not much protection if companies go out of business and they are not likely to tell you if they are on their last legs. But if you pay a bill of over £100 by credit card (and this is a major reason for doing so) you can be compensated by the card company which is 'jointly and severally liable' with the mail-order company.

In January 1996, *Which?* magazine gave advice on how to complain successfully. Relevant points were these:

- Be clear about the problem.

- Keep your receipt.

- Decide whether you want a refund, exchange or repair.

- Return the goods as soon as possible.

- If the goods are too big to return, write or ring...saying why you are rejecting them.

- Speak to the manager and state your case firmly.

- Follow up your complaint in writing and set a reasonable time limit for a response.

- If you are still dissatisfied, seek advice from a Consumer Advice Centre, Citizen's Advice Bureau or Trading Standards Department.

INDEX OF SUPPLIERS

Readers' Report Form

Future editions of this book will be improved if you write with your comments, letting us know (i) if any mail order suppliers are not included which you think should be and (ii) if you have any comments on a supplier listed in the Guide. Please print your name clearly.

Send your comments to:

Metro Publishing Ltd
19 Gerrard Street
London W1V 7LA

Christmas Made Easy   Report Form

To the Author

From my own experience the following supplier should/should not be included

SUPPLIER NAME ....

Address: ....

....

Telephone: ....

Comments: ....

....

....

....

YOUR NAME: ....

Address: ....

....

....